LETTERS

OF

EMILY DICKINSON

Volume I

LETTERS

OF

EMILY DICKINSON

VOLUME I

U or M

NSON

OMIS TODD

BOSTON
LLIS BROTHERS
18..

LETTERS

OF

EMILY DICKINSON

EDITED BY

MABEL LOOMIS TODD

IN TWO VOLUMES

VOLUME I

BOSTON

ROBERTS BROTHERS

1894

University Press
JOHN WILSON AND SON, CAMBRIDGE, U.S.A.

INTRODUCTORY

—————◆—————

THE lovers of Emily Dickinson's poems have been so eager for some of her prose that her sister has asked me to prepare these volumes of her letters.

Emily Dickinson's verses, often but the reflection of a passing mood, do not always completely represent herself, — rarely, indeed, showing the dainty humor, the frolicsome gayety, which continually bubbled over in her daily life. The sombre and even weird outlook upon this world and the next, characteristic of many of the poems, was by no means a prevailing condition of mind; for, while fully apprehending all the tragic elements in life, enthusiasm and bright joyousness were yet her normal qualities, and stimulating moral heights her native dwelling-place. All this may be glimpsed in her letters, no less full of charm, it is believed, to the general reader, than to Emily Dickinson's personal friends. As she kept no journal, the letters are the more interesting because they contain all the prose which she is known to have written.

257509

It was with something almost like dread that I approached the task of arranging these letters, lest the deep revelations of a peculiarly shy inner life might so pervade them that in true loyalty to their writer none could be publicly used. But with few exceptions they have been read and prepared with entire relief from that feeling, and with unshrinking pleasure ; the sanctities were not invaded. Emily kept her little reserves, and bared her soul but seldom, even in intimate correspondence. It was not so much that she was always on spiritual guard, as that she sported with her varying moods, and tested them upon her friends with apparent delight in the effect, as airy and playful as it was half unconscious.

So large is the number of letters to each of several correspondents, that it has seemed best to place these sets in separate chapters. The continuity is perhaps more perfectly preserved in this way than by the usual method of mere chronological succession ; especially as, in a life singularly uneventful, no marked periods of travel or achievement serve otherwise to classify them. On this plan a certain order has been possible, too ; the opening letters in each chapter are always later than the first of the preceding, although the last letters of one reach a date beyond the beginning of the next. The less remarkable writing, of course, fills the first chapters ; but even this shows her love of study, of Nature, and a devotion to home almost as intense as in strange Emily Brontë.

Nothing is perhaps more marked than the change of style between the diffuseness of girlhood and the brilliant sententiousness of late middle life, often startlingly unexpected. And yet suggestions of future picturesque and epigrammatic power occasionally flash through the long, youthful correspondence. Lowell once wrote of the first letters of Carlyle, 'The man . . . is all there in the earliest of his writing that we have (potentially there, in character wholly there).' It is chiefly for these 'potential' promises that Emily Dickinson's girlish letters are included, all the variations in the evolution of a style having hardly less interest for the student of human nature than of literature. Village life, even in a college town, was very democratic in the early days when the first of these letters were written, and they suggest a refreshing atmosphere of homely simplicity.

Unusual difficulties have been encountered in arranging the letters with definite reference to years, as none but the very earliest were dated. The change in handwriting, of which specimens are given in facsimile, was no less noticeable than Emily Dickinson's development in literary style; and this alone has been a general guide. The thoughtfulness of a few correspondents in recording the time of the letters' reception has been a farther and most welcome assistance; while occasionally the kind of postage-stamp and the postmark helped to indicate when they were written, although generally the envelopes had not been preserved. But the larger part have been placed by searching out the dates of contemporaneous incidents mentioned, — for instance, numerous births, marriages, and deaths; any epoch in the life of a friend was an event to Emily Dickinson, always noticed by a bit of flashing verse, or a graceful, if mystically expressed, note of comfort or congratulation. If errors are found in assignment to the proper time, it will not be from lack of having interrogated all available sources of information.

In more recent years, dashes instead of punctuation, and capitals for all important words, together with the quaint handwriting, give to the actual manuscript an individual fascination quite irresistible. But the coldness of print destroys that elusive charm, so that dashes and capitals have been restored to their conventional use.

In her later years, Emily Dickinson rarely addressed the envelopes: it seemed as if her sensitive nature shrank from the publicity which even her handwriting would undergo, in the observation of indifferent eyes. Various expedients were resorted to, — obliging friends frequently performed this office for her; sometimes a printed newspaper label was pasted upon the envelope; but the actual strokes of her own pencil were, so far as possible, reserved exclusively for friendly eyes.

Emily Dickinson's great disinclination for an exposition of the theology current during her girlhood is matter for small wonder. While her fathers were men of recognized originality and force, they did not question the religious teaching of the time; they were leaders in town and church, even strict and uncompromising in their piety. Reverence for accepted ways and forms, merely as such, seems entirely to have been left out of Emily's constitution. To her, God was not a far-away and dreary Power to be daily addressed, — the great 'Eclipse' of which she wrote, — but He was near and familiar and pervasive. Her garden was full of His brightness and glory; the birds sang and the sky glowed because of Him. To shut herself out of the sunshine in a church, dark, chilly, restricted, was rather to shut herself away from Him; almost pathetically she wrote, 'I believe the love of God may be taught not to seem like bears.'

In essence, no real irreverence mars her poems or her letters. Of malice aforethought, — an intentional irreverence, — she is never once guilty. The old interpretation of the biblical estimate of life was cause to her for gentle, wide-eyed astonishment. No one knew better the phrases which had become cant, and which seemed always to misrepresent the Father Whom she knew with personal directness and without necessity for human intervention. It was a theologically misconceived idea of a 'jealous God,' for which she had a profound contempt; and the fact that those ideas were still held by the stricter New England people of her day made not the slightest difference in her expression of disapproval. Fearless and daring, she had biblical quotation at her finger-tips; and even if she sometimes used it in a way which might shock a conventionalist, she had in her heart too profound an adoration for the great, ever-living, and present Father to hold a shadow of real irreverence toward Him, so peculiarly near. No soul in which dwelt not a very noble and actual love and respect for the essentials could have written as she did of real triumph, of truth, of aspiration.

> 'We never know how high we are,
>   Till we are called to rise;
> And then, if we are true to plan,
>   Our statures touch the skies.
>
> 'The heroism we recite
>   Would be a daily thing
> Did not ourselves the cubits warp,
>   For fear to be a king.'

Must not one who wrote that have had her ever-open shrine, her reverenced tribunal?

The whims and pretences of society, its forms and unrealities, seemed to her thin and unworthy. Conventionalities, while they amused, exasperated her also; and the little poem beginning,

> 'The show is not the show,
>   But they that go,'

expresses in large measure her attitude toward society, when she lived in the midst of it. Real life, on the other hand, seemed vast and inexpressibly

solemn. Petty trivialities had no part in her constitution, and she came to despise them more and
more, — so much, indeed, that with her increasing
shyness, she gradually gave up all journeys, and
finally retired completely from even the simple life
of a New England college town.

As has been said of Emily Brontë, ' To this natural
isolation of spirit we are in a great measure indebted for that passionate love of Nature which
gives such a vivid reality and exquisite simplicity to
her descriptions.' Emily Dickinson's letters, almost
as much as the poems, exhibit her elf-like intimacy
with Nature. She sees and apprehends the great
mother's processes, and shares the rapture of all
created things under the wide sky. The letters
speak of flowers, of pines and autumnal colors ; but
no natural sight or sound or incident seems to have
escaped her delicate apprehension.

Bird songs, crickets, frost, and winter winds, even
the toad and snake, mushrooms and bats, have an in-
describable charm for her, which she in turn brings
to us. March, 'that month of proclamation,' was
especially dear ; and among her still unpublished
verses is a characteristic greeting to the windy
month. In all its aspects ' Nature became the
unique charm and consolation of her life, and as
such she has written of it.'

Warm thanks are due the friends who have gen-
erously lent letters for reproduction. That they
were friends of Emily Dickinson, and willing to

share her words with the larger outside circle, waiting and appreciative, entitles them to the gratitude,
not merely of the Editor, but of all who make up
the world that Emily 'never saw,' but to which,
nevertheless, she sent a 'message.'

MABEL LOOMIS TODD

AMHERST, MASSACHUSETTS
  October 1894

TABLE OF CONTENTS

VOLUME I

———◆———

LIST OF ILLUSTRATIONS

LETTERS OF EMILY DICKINSON

———•———

CHAPTER I

To Mrs A. P. Strong

THE letters in this chapter were written to a schoolmate and early friend. The first is one of the oldest yet found, dated when Emily Dickinson had but recently passed her fourteenth birthday.

Before the era of outer envelopes, it is quaintly written on a large square sheet, and so folded that the fourth page forms a cover bearing the address. Most of the remaining letters to Mrs Strong are thus folded, and sealed either with wax or wafers, — occasionally with little rectangular or diamond papers bearing mottoes stamped in gold. The handwriting is almost microscopic, the pages entirely filled. Merely personal items have been generally omitted.

It will be seen that the name 'Emilie E. Dickinson' is sometimes used. The *ie* was a youthful vagary, and the second initial, E., stood for Elizabeth, a ' middle name ' entirely discarded in later years.

AMHERST, Feb. 23, 1845.

DEAR A., — After receiving the smitings of conscience for a long time, I have at length succeeded in stifling the voice of that faithful monitor by a promise of a long letter to you ; so leave everything and sit down prepared for a long siege in the shape of a bundle of nonsense from friend E.

. . . I keep your lock of hair as precious as gold and a great deal more so. I often look at it when I go to my little lot of treasures, and wish the owner of that glossy lock were here. Old Time wags on pretty much as usual at Amherst, and I know of nothing that has occurred to break the silence ; however, the reduction of the postage has excited my risibles somewhat. Only think ! We can send a letter before long for five little coppers only, filled with the thoughts and advice of dear friends. But I will not get into a philosophizing strain just yet. There is time enough for that upon another page of this mammoth sheet. . . . Your *beau idéal* D. I have not seen lately. I presume he was changed into a star some night while gazing at them, and placed in the constellation Orion between Bellatrix and Betelgeux. I doubt not if he was here he would wish to be kindly remembered to you. What delightful weather we have had for a week !

It seems more like smiling May crowned with flowers than cold, arctic February wading through snowdrifts. I have heard some sweet little birds sing, but I fear we shall have more cold weather and their little bills will be frozen up before their songs are finished. My plants look beautifully. Old King Frost has not had the pleasure of snatching any of them in his cold embrace as yet, and I hope will not. Our little pussy has made out to live. I believe you know what a fatality attends our little kitties, all of them, having had six die one right after the other. Do you love your little niece J. as well as ever? Your soliloquy on the year that is past and gone was not unheeded by me. Would that we might spend the year which is now fleeting so swiftly by to better advantage than the one which we have not the power to recall! Now I know you will laugh, and say I wonder what makes Emily so sentimental. But I don't care if you do, for I sha'n't hear you. What are you doing this winter? I am about everything. I am now working a pair of slippers to adorn my father's feet. I wish you would come and help me finish them. . . . Although it is late in the day, I am going to wish you a happy New Year, — not but what I think your New Year will pass just as happily without it, but to make a little return for your kind wish, which so far in a good many respects has been granted, probably because you wished that it might be so. . . . I go to singing-school Sabbath evenings to improve my voice. Don't you envy me? . . .

I wish you would come and make me a long visit. If you will, I will entertain you to the best of my abilities, which you know are neither few nor small. Why can't you persuade your father and mother to let you come here to school next term, and keep me company, as I am going? Miss ——, I presume you can guess who I mean, is going to finish her education next summer. The finishing stroke is to be put on at Newton. She will then have learned all that we poor foot-travellers are toiling up the hill of knowledge to acquire. Wonderful thought! Her horse has carried her along so swiftly that she has nearly gained the summit, and we are plodding along on foot after her. Well said and sufficient this. We'll finish an education sometime, won't we? You may then be Plato, and I will be Socrates, provided you won't be wiser than I am. Lavinia just now interrupted my flow of thought by saying give my love to A. I presume you will be glad to have some one break off this epistle. All the girls send much love to you. And please accept a large share for yourself.   From your beloved
          EMILY E. DICKINSON.

Please send me a copy of that Romance you were writing at Amherst. I am in a fever to read it. I expect it will be against my Whig feelings.

After this postscript many others follow, across the top, down the edges, tucked in

wherever space will allow.   There are also a
few lines from each of three girl friends to
'dear A.'

DEAR A., — It seems almost an age since I have
seen you, and it is indeed an age for friends to be
separated.   I was delighted to receive a paper from
you, and I also was much pleased with the news it
contained, especially that you are taking lessons on
the 'piny,' as you always call it.   But remember not to
get on ahead of me.   Father intends to have a piano
very soon.   How happy I shall be when I have one
of my own !   Old Father Time has wrought many
changes here since your last short visit.   Miss S. T.
and Miss N. M. have both taken the marriage vows
upon themselves.   Dr Hitchcock has moved into
his new house, and Mr Tyler across the way from
our house has moved into President Hitchcock's old
house.   Mr C. is going to move into Mr T.'s former
house, but the worst thing old Time has done here is
he has walked so fast as to overtake H. M. and carry
her to Hartford on last week Saturday.   I was so
vexed with him for it that I ran after him and made
out to get near enough to him to put some salt on
his tail, when he fled and left me to run home alone.
. . . Viny went to Boston this morning with father,
to be gone a fortnight, and I am left alone in all my
glory.   I suppose she has got there before this time,
and is probably staring with mouth and eyes wide

open at the wonders of the city. I have been to walk to-night, and got some very choice wild flowers. I wish you had some of them. Viny and I both go to school this term. We have a very fine school. There are 63 scholars. I have four studies. They are Mental Philosophy, Geology, Latin, and Botany. How large they sound, don't they? I don't believe you have such big studies. . . . My plants look finely now. I am going to send you a little geranium leaf in this letter, which you must press for me. Have you made you an herbarium yet? I hope you will if you have not, it would be such a treasure to you ; 'most all the girls are making one. If you do, perhaps I can make some additions to it from flowers growing around here. How do you enjoy your school this term? Are the teachers as pleasant as our old school-teachers? I expect you have a great many prim, starched up young ladies there, who, I doubt not, are perfect models of propriety and good behavior. If they are, don't let your free spirit be chained by them. I don't know as there [are] any in school of this stamp. But there 'most always are a few, whom the teachers look up to and regard as their satellites. I am growing handsome very fast indeed ! I expect I shall be the belle of Amherst when I reach my 17th year. I don't doubt that I shall have perfect crowds of admirers at that age. Then how I shall delight to make them await my bidding, and with what delight shall I witness their suspense while I make my final decision. But away with my nonsense. I have written one composition this term, and I need not assure you it was exceedingly edifying to myself as well as everybody else. Don't you want to see it? I really wish you could have a chance. We are obliged to write compositions once in a fortnight, and select a piece to read from some interesting book the week that we don't write compositions.

We really have some most charming young women in school this term. I sha'n't call them anything but women, for women they are in every sense of the word. I must, however, describe one, and while I describe her I wish Imagination, who is ever present with you, to make a little picture of this self-same young lady in your mind, and by her aid see if you cannot conceive how she looks. Well, to begin. . . . Then just imagine her as she is, and a huge string of gold beads encircling her neck, and don't she present a lively picture ; and then she is so bustling, she is always whizzing about, and whenever I come in contact with her I really think I am in a hornet's nest. I can't help thinking every time I see this singular piece of humanity of Shakespeare's description of a tempest in a teapot. But I must not laugh about her, for I verily believe she has a good heart, and that is the principal thing now-a-days. Don't you hope I shall become wiser in the company of such virtuosos? It would certainly be desirable. Have you noticed how beautifully the trees look now? They seem to be completely covered with fragrant blossoms. . . . I had so many things to do for Viny, as she was going away, that very much against my wishes I deferred writing you until now, but forgive and forget, dear A., and I will promise to do better in future. Do write me soon, and let it be a long, long letter; and when you can't get time to write, send a paper, so as to let me know you think of me still, though we are separated by hill and stream. All the girls send much love to you. Don't forget to let me receive a letter from you soon. I can say no more now as my paper is all filled up.

Your affectionate friend,

EMILY E. DICKINSON.

[Written in 1845; postmarked Amherst, August 4.]

Sabbath Eve.

DEAR A., — I have now sat down to write you a long, long letter. My writing apparatus is upon a stand before me, and all things are ready. I have no flowers before me as you had to inspire you. But then you know I can imagine myself inspired by them, and perhaps that will do as well. You cannot imagine how delighted I was to receive your letter. It was so full, and everything in it was interesting to me because it came from you. I presume you did not doubt my gratitude for it, on account of my delaying so long to answer it, for you know I have had no leisure for anything. When I tell you that our term has been eleven weeks long, and that I have had four studies and taken music lessons, you

can imagine a little how my time has been taken up
lately.   I will try to be more punctual in such matters for the future.   How are you now?   I am very
sorry to hear that you are unable to remain in your
school on account of your health, it must be such
a disappointment to you.   But I presume you are
enjoying yourself much to be at home again.   You
asked me in your last letter if old Father Time
wagged on in Amherst pretty much as ever.   For
my part, I see no particular change in his move-
ments unless it be that he goes on a swifter pace
than formerly, and that he wields his sickle more
sternly than ever.   How do you like taking music
lessons?   I presume you are delighted with it.   I
am taking lessons this term of Aunt S——, who is
spending the summer with us.   I never enjoyed
myself more than I have this summer; for we
have had such a delightful school and such pleasant
teachers, and besides I have had a piano of my
own.   Our examination is to come off next week
on Monday.   I wish you could be here at that time.
Why can't you come?   If you will, you can come
and practise on my piano as much as you wish to.
I am already gasping in view of our examination;
and although I am determined not to dread it I
know it is so foolish, yet in spite of my heroic resolutions, I cannot avoid a few misgivings when I
think of those tall, stern trustees, and when I know
that I shall lose my character if I don't recite as
precisely as the laws of the Medes and Persians.

But what matter will that be a hundred years hence? I will distress you no longer with my fears, for you know well enough what they are without my entering into any explanations. Are you practising now you are at home? I hope you are, for if you are not you would be likely to forget what you have learnt. I want very much to hear you play. I have the same instruction book that you have, Bertini, and I am getting along in it very well. Aunt S—— says she sha'n't let me have many tunes now, for she wants I should get over in the book a good ways first. Oh, A., if Sarah G——, H——, and yourself were only here this summer, what times we should have! I wish if we can't be together all the time that we could meet once in a while at least. I wish you would all come to our house, and such times as we would have would be a caution. I want to see you all so much that it seems as if I could not wait. Have you heard anything from Miss Adams, our dear teacher? How much I would give to see her once more, but I am afraid I never shall. She is so far away. You asked me in your letter to tell you all the news worth telling, and although there is not much, yet I will endeavor to think of everything that will be new to you. In the first place, Mrs J. and Mrs S. M. have both of them a little daughter. Very promising children, I understand. I don't doubt if they live they will be ornaments to society. I think they are both to be considered as embryos of future usefulness. Mrs W. M. has

now two grand-daughters. Is n't she to be envied?
. . . I am sorry that you are laying up H.'s sins
against her. I think you had better heap coals of
fire upon her head by writing to her constantly until
you get an answer. I have some patience with
these 'school marms.' They have so many trials.
I hope you will decide to blot out her iniquities
against her. I don't know about this Mr E. giving you concert tickets. I think for my part it
looks rather suspicious. He is a young man, I suppose. These music teachers are always such high-
souled beings that I think they would exactly suit
your fancy. My garden looks beautifully now. I
wish you could see it. I would send you a bouquet
if I could get a good opportunity. My house plants
look very finely, too. You wished me to give you
some account of S. P. ˙ She is attending school this
term and studying Latin and Algebra. She is very
well and happy and sends much love to you. All
the girls send much love to you, and wish you to
write to them. I have been working a beautiful
book-mark to give to one of our school-girls. Perhaps you have seen it. It is an arrow with a beautiful wreath around it. Have you altered any since
I have seen you? Is n't it a funny question for one
friend to ask another? I have n't altered any, I
think, except that I have my hair done up, and that
makes me look different. I can imagine just how
you look now. I wonder what you are doing this
moment. I have got an idea that you are knitting

edging. Are you? Won't you tell me when you answer my letter whether I guessed right or not? . . . You gave me a compliment in your letter in regard to my being a faithful correspondent. I must say I think I deserve it. I have been learning several beautiful pieces lately. The 'Grave of Bonaparte' is one, 'Lancers Quickstep,' and 'Maiden, weep no more,' which is a sweet little song. I wish much to see you and hear you play. I hope you will come to A. before long. Why can't you pass commencement here? I do wish you would. . . . I have looked my letter over, and find I have written nothing worth reading. . . . Accept much love from your affectionate friend,

EMILY E. D.

Thursday, Sept. 26, 1845.

DEAREST A., — As I just glanced at the clock and saw how smoothly the little hands glide over the surface, I could scarcely believe that those self-same little hands had eloped with so many of my precious moments since I received your affectionate letter, and it was still harder for me to believe that I, who am always boasting of being so faithful a correspondent, should have been guilty of negligence in so long delaying to answer it. . . . I am very glad to hear that you are better than you have been, and I hope in future disease will not be as neighborly as he has been heretofore to either of us. I long to see you, dear A., and speak with you face

to face; but so long as a bodily interview is denied
us, we must make letters answer, though it is hard
for friends to be separated. I really believe you
would have been frightened to have heard me scold
when Sabra informed me that you had decided not
to visit Amherst this fall. But as I could find no
one upon whom to vent my spleen for your decision,
I thought it best to be calm, and therefore have at
length resigned myself to my cruel fate, though with
not a very good grace. I think you do well to
inquire whether anything has been heard from H.
I really don't know what has become of her, unless
procrastination has carried her off. I think that
must be the case. I think you have given quite a
novel description of the wedding. Are you quite
sure Mr F., the minister, told them to stand up and
he would tie them in a great bow-knot? But I beg
pardon for speaking so lightly of so solemn a cere-
mony. You asked me in your letter if I did not
think you partial in your admiration of Miss Helen
H., ditto Mrs P. I answer, Not in the least. She
was universally beloved in Amherst. She made us
quite a visit in June, and we regretted more than
ever that she was going where we could not see her
as often as we had been accustomed. She seemed
very happy in her prospects, and seemed to think
distance nothing in comparison to a home with the
one of her choice. I hope she will be happy,
and of course she will. I wished much to see her
once more, but was denied the privilege. . . . You

asked me if I was attending school now. I am not. Mother thinks me not able to confine myself to school this term. She had rather I would exercise, and I can assure you I get plenty of that article by staying at home. I am going to learn to make bread to-morrow. So you may imagine me with my sleeves rolled up, mixing flour, milk, saleratus, etc., with a deal of grace. I advise you if you don't know how to make the staff of life to learn with dispatch. I think I could keep house very comfortably if I knew how to cook. But as long as I don't, my knowledge of housekeeping is about of as much use as faith without works, which you know we are told is dead. Excuse my quoting from Scripture, dear A., for it was so handy in this case I could n't get along very well without it. Since I wrote you last, the summer is past and gone, and autumn with the sere and yellow leaf is already upon us. I never knew the time to pass so swiftly, it seems to me, as the past summer. I really think some one must have oiled his chariot wheels, for I don't recollect of hearing him pass, and I am sure I should if something had not prevented his chariot wheels from creaking as usual. But I will not expatiate upon him any longer, for I know it is wicked to trifle with so revered a personage, and I fear he will make me a call in person to inquire as to the remarks which I have made concerning him. Therefore I will let him alone for the present. . . . How are you getting on with your music? Well, I

hope and trust. I am taking lessons and am getting along very well, and now I have a piano, I am
very happy. I feel much honored at having even a
doll named for me. I believe I shall have to give
it a silver cup, as that is the custom among old
ladies when a child is named for them. . . . Have
you any flowers now? I have had a beautiful flower-
garden this summer; but they are nearly gone now.
It is very cold to-night, and I mean to pick the prettiest ones before I go to bed, and cheat Jack Frost
of so many of *the treasures* he calculates to rob
to-night. Won't it be a capital idea to put him at
defiance, for once at least, if no more? I would
love to send you a bouquet if I had an opportunity,
and you could press it and write under it, The last
flowers of summer. Would n't it be poetical, and
you know that is what young ladies aim to be now-
a-days. . . . I expect I have altered a good deal
since I have seen you, dear A. I have grown tall a
good deal, and wear my golden tresses done up in
a net-cap. Modesty, you know, forbids me to mention whether my personal appearance has altered.
I leave that for others to judge. But my [word
omitted] has not changed, nor will it in time to
come. I shall always remain the same old six-
pence. . . . I can say no more now, as it is after
ten, and everybody has gone to bed but me. Don't
forget your affectionate friend,

EMILY E. D.

AMHERST, Jan. 12, 1846.

A., MY DEAR, — Since I received your precious letter another year has commenced its course, and the old year has gone never to return. How sad it makes one feel to sit down quietly and think of the flight of the old year, and the unceremonious obtrusion of the new year upon our notice ! How many things we have omitted to do which might have cheered a human heart, or whispered hope in the ear of the sorrowful, and how many things have we done over which the dark mantle of regret will ever fall ! How many good resolutions did I make at the commencement of the year now flown, merely to break them and to feel more than ever convinced of the weakness of my own resolutions ! The New Year's day was unusually gloomy to me, I know not why, and perhaps for that reason a host of unpleasant reflections forced themselves upon me which I found not easy to throw off. But I will no longer sentimentalize upon the past, for I cannot recall it. I will, after inquiring for the health of my dear A., relapse into a more lively strain. I can hardly have patience to write, for I have not seen you for so long that I have worlds of things to tell you, and my pen is not swift enough to answer my purpose at all. However, I will try to make it communicate as much information as possible and wait to see your own dear self once more before I relate all my thoughts which have come and gone since I last saw you. I suppose from your letter that you are enjoying yourself finely this winter at Miss C.'s school. I would give a great deal if I was there with you. I don't go to school this winter except to a recitation in German. Mr C. has a very large class, and father thought I might never have another opportunity to study it. It takes about an hour and a half to recite. Then I take music lessons and practise two hours in a day, and besides these two I have a large stand of plants to cultivate. This is the principal round of my occupation this winter. . . . I have just seen a funeral procession go by of a negro baby, so if my ideas are rather dark you need not marvel. . . . Old Santa Claus was very polite to me the last Christmas. I hung up my stocking on the bed-post as usual. I had a perfume bag and a bottle of otto of rose to go with it, a sheet of music, a china mug with *Forget me not* upon it, from S. S., — who, by the way, is as handsome, enter-taining, and as fine a piano player as in former times, — a toilet cushion, a watch case, a fortune-teller, and an amaranthine stock of pin-cushions and needlebooks, which in ingenuity and art would rival the works of Scripture Dorcas. I found abundance of candy in my stocking, which I do not think has had the anticipated effect upon my disposition, in case it was to sweeten it, also two hearts at the bottom of all, which I thought looked rather omi-nous ; but I will not enter into any more details, for they take up more room than I can spare.

Have n't we had delightful weather for a week or two? It seems as if Old Winter had forgotten himself. Don't you believe he is absent-minded? It has been bad weather for colds, however. I have had a severe cold for a few days, and can sympathize with you, though I have been delivered from a stiff neck. I think you must belong to the tribe of Israel, for you know in the Bible the prophet calls them a stiff-necked generation. I have lately come to the conclusion that I am Eve, alias Mrs Adam. You know there is no account of her death in the Bible, and why am not I Eve? If you find any statements which you think likely to prove the truth of the case, I wish you would send them to me without delay.

Have you heard a word from H. M. or S. T.? I consider them lost sheep. I send them a paper every week on Monday, but I never get one in return. I am almost a mind to take a hand-car and go around to hunt them up. I can't think that they have forgotten us, and I know of no reason unless they are sick why they should delay so long to show any signs of remembrance. Do write me soon a very long letter, and tell me all about your school and yourself too.

Your affectionate friend,

EMILY E. DICKINSON.

Friday Eve [summer], 1846.

MY DEAR A., — Though it is a long time since I received your affectionate epistle, yet when I give you my reasons for my long delay, I know you will freely forgive and forget all past offences.

It seems to me that time has never flown so swiftly with me as it has the last spring. I have been busy every minute, and not only so, but hurried all the time. So you may imagine that I have not had a spare moment, much though my heart has longed for it, to commune with an absent friend. . . . I presume you will be wondering by this time what I am doing to be in so much haste as I have declared myself to be. Well, I will tell you. I am fitting to go to South Hadley Seminary, and expect if my health is good to enter that institution a year from next fall. Are you not astonished to hear such news? You cannot imagine how much I am anticipating in entering there. It has been in my thought by day, and my dreams by night, ever since I heard of South Hadley Seminary. I fear I am anticipating too much, and that some freak of fortune may overturn all my airy schemes for future happiness. But it is my nature always to anticipate more than I realize. . . . Have you not heard that Miss Adams — dear Miss Adams — is here this term? Oh, you cannot imagine how natural it seems to see her happy face in school once more. But it needs Harriet, Sarah, and your own dear self to complete the ancient picture. I hope we shall get you all back before Miss Adams goes away again. Have you yet heard a word from that prodigal, — H.? . . .

Your affectionate friend,

EMILY E. D.

I send you a memento in the form of a pressed flower, which you must keep.

A converted Jew has been lecturing here for the last week. His lectures were free, and they were on the present condition of the Jews. Dr Scudder, a returned missionary, is here now, and he is lecturing also. Have you seen a beautiful piece of poetry which has been going through the papers lately? *Are we almost there ?* is the title of it. . . . I have two hours to practise daily now I am in school. I have been learning a beautiful thing, which I long to have you hear. . . .

BOSTON, Sept. 8, 1846.

MY DEAR FRIEND A., — It is a long, long time since I received your welcome letter, and it becomes me to sue for forgiveness, which I am sure your affectionate heart will not refuse to grant. But many and unforeseen circumstances have caused my long delay. . . . Father and mother thought a journey would be of service to me, and accordingly I left home for Boston week before last. I had a delightful ride in the cars, and am now getting settled down, if there can be such a state in the city. I am visiting in my aunt's family, and am happy. Happy! did I say? No; not happy, but contented. I have been here a fortnight to-day, and in that time I have both seen and heard a great many wonderful things. Perhaps you might like to know how I have spent the time here. I have

been to Mount Auburn, to the Chinese Museum, to
Bunker Hill; I have attended two concerts and one
Horticultural Exhibition. I have been upon the
top of the State House, and almost everywhere that
you can imagine. Have you ever been to Mount
Auburn? If not, you can form but slight con-
ception of this ' City of the Dead.' It seems as if
nature had formed this spot with a distinct idea in
view of its being a resting-place for her children,
where, wearied and disappointed, they might stretch
themselves beneath the spreading cypress, and close
their eyes ' calmly as to a night's repose, or flowers
at set of sun.'

The Chinese Museum is a great curiosity. There
are an endless variety of wax figures made to resemble the Chinese, and dressed in their costume.
Also articles of Chinese manufacture of an innu-
merable variety deck the rooms. Two of the
Chinese go with this exhibition. One of them is a
professor of music in China, and the other is teacher
of a writing-school at home. They were both
wealthy, and not obliged to labor, but they were
also opium-eaters; and fearing to continue the practice lest it destroyed their lives, yet unable to
break the ' rigid chain of habit ' in their own land,
they left their families, and came to this country.
They have now entirely overcome the practice.
There is something peculiarly interesting to me in
their self-denial. The musician played upon two of
his instruments, and accompanied them with his

voice. It needed great command over my risible faculties to enable me to keep sober as this amateur was performing; yet he was so very polite to give us some of his native music that we could not do otherwise than to express ourselves highly edified with his performances. The writing-master is constantly occupied in writing the names of visitors who request it, upon cards in the Chinese language, for which he charges $12\frac{1}{2}$ cents apiece. He never fails to give his card besides to the persons who wish it. I obtained one of his cards for Viny and myself, and I consider them very precious. Are you still in Norwich, and attending to music? I am not now taking lessons, but I expect to when I return home.

Does it seem as though September had come? How swiftly summer has fled, and what report has it borne to heaven of misspent time and wasted hours? Eternity only will answer. The ceaseless flight of the seasons is to me a very solemn thought; and yet why do we not strive to make a better improvement of them? With how much emphasis the poet has said, ' We take no note of time but from its loss. 'T were wise in man to give it then a tongue. Pay no moment but in just purchase of its worth, and what its worth ask death-beds. They can tell. Part with it as with life reluctantly.' Then we have higher authority than that of man for the improvement of our time. For God has said, ' Work while the day lasts, for the night is coming in the which no man can work.' Let us strive together to part with time more reluctantly, to watch the pinions of the fleeting moment until they are dim in the distance, and the new-coming moment claims our attention. I have perfect confidence in God and His promises, and yet I know not why I feel that the world holds a predominant place in my affections. . . . Your affectionate friend,

EMILY E. D.

Numerous postscripts are appended, as usually : —

I have really suffered from the heat the last week. I think it remarkable that we should have such weather in September. There were over one hundred deaths in Boston last week, a great many of them owing to the heat. Mr Taylor, our old teacher, was in Amherst at Commencement time, Oh, I do love Mr Taylor. It seems so like old times to meet Miss Adams and Mr Taylor together again. I could hardly refrain from singing, 'Auld Lang Syne.' It seemed so very *à propos*. Have you forgotten the memorable ride we all took with Mr Taylor, 'Long, long ago'? . . . Austin entered college last Commencement. Only think! I have a brother who has the honor to be a Freshman! Will you not promise me that you will come to Commencement when he graduates? Do! Please! I have altered very much since you were here. I am now very tall, and wear long dresses nearly. Do you believe we shall know each other when we meet? Don't forget to write soon.   E.

Sabbath Eve, 1846.

MY DEAR A., — When I last wrote you I was in Boston, where I spent a delightful visit of four weeks. I returned home about the middle of September in very good health and spirits, for which it seems to me I cannot be sufficiently grateful to the Giver of all mercies. I expected to go into the Academy upon my return home, but as I stayed longer than I expected to, and as the school had already commenced, I made up my mind to remain at home during the fall term and pursue my studies the winter term, which commences a week after Thanksgiving. I kept my good resolution for once in my life, and have been sewing, practising upon the piano, and assisting mother in household affairs. I am anticipating the commencement of the next term with a great deal of pleasure, for I have been an exile from school two terms on account of my health, and you know what it is to ' love school.' Miss Adams is with us now, and will remain through the winter, and we have an excellent Principal in the person of Mr Leonard Humphrey, who was the last valedictorian. We now have a fine school. I thank you a thousand times for your long and affectionate letter. . . . I found a quantity of sewing waiting with open arms to embrace me, or rather for me to embrace it, and I could hardly give myself up to ' Nature's sweet restorer,' for the ghosts of out-of-order garments crying for vengeance upon my defenceless head.   However, I am happy to inform you, my dear friend, that I have nearly finished my sewing for winter, and will answer all the letters which you shall deem worthy to send so naughty a girl as myself, at short notice. . . .

Write soon.   Your affectionate

EMILY E. D.

[March 15, 1847.]

Sabbath Eve, 1847.

EVER DEAR A., — . . . We have spent our vacation of a fortnight, and school has commenced again since you wrote me.   I go this term, and am studying Algebra, Euclid, Ecclesiastical History, and reviewing Arithmetic again to be upon the safe side of things next autumn.   We have a delightful school this term under the instruction of our former principals, and Miss R. Woodbridge, daughter of Rev. Dr W. of Hadley, for preceptress.   We all love her very much.   Perhaps a slight description of her might be interesting to my dear A.   She is tall and rather slender, but finely proportioned, has a most witching pair of blue eyes, rich brown hair, delicate complexion, cheeks which vie with the opening rose-bud, teeth like pearls, dimples which come and go like the ripples in yonder little merry brook, and then she is so affectionate and lovely. Forgive my glowing description, for you know I am always in love with my teachers.   Yet, much as we love her, it seems lonely and strange without 'our dear Miss Adams.' I suppose you know that she has left Amherst, not again to return as a teacher. It is indeed true that she is to be married. Are you not astonished? Nothing was known but that she was to return to the school, until a few days before she left for Syracuse, where she has gone to make her 'wedding gear.' She is to be married the first of next April, to a very respectable lawyer in Conway, Massachusetts. She seemed to be very happy in anticipation of her future prospects, and I hope she will realize all her fond hopes. I cannot bear to think that she will never more wield the sceptre and sit upon the throne in our venerable schoolhouse, and yet I am glad she is going to have a home of her own, and a kind companion to take life's journey with her. I am delighted that she is to live so near us, for we can ride up and see her often. You cannot imagine how much I enjoyed your description of your Christmas fête at Miss Campbell's. How magnificent the 'Christmas tree' must have been, and what a grand time you must have had, so many of you! Oh!!

I had a great many presents, Christmas and New Year's holidays, both, but we had no such celebration of the former which you describe. . . . Do write me soon — a long letter — and tell me how soon you are coming, and how long we can keep you when you come. Your affectionate

EMILY E. DICKINSON.

MT HOLYOKE SEMINARY, NOV. 6, 1847.

MY DEAR A., — I am really at Mount Holyoke
Seminary, and this is to be my home for a long year.
Your affectionate letter was joyfully received and I
wish that this might make you as happy as yours did
me. It has been nearly six weeks since I left home,
and that is a longer time than I was ever away from
home before now. I was very homesick for a few
days, and it seemed to me I could not live here.
But I am now contented and quite happy, if I can
be happy when absent from my dear home and
friends. You may laugh at the idea that I cannot
be happy when away from home, but you must
remember that I have a very dear home and that
-this is my first trial in the way of absence for any
length of time in my life. As you desire it, I will
give you a full account of myself since I first left the
paternal roof. I came to South Hadley six weeks ago
next Thursday. I was much fatigued with the ride,
and had a severe cold besides, which prevented me
from commencing my examinations until the next
day, when I began. I finished them in three days,
and found them about what I had anticipated, though
the old scholars say they are more strict than they
ever have been before. As you can easily imagine,
I was much delighted to finish without failures, and
I came to the conclusion then, that I should not be
at all homesick, but the reaction left me as homesick
a girl as it is not usual to see. I am now quite con-

tented and am very much occupied in reviewing the Junior studies, as I wish to enter the middle class. The school is very large, and though quite a number have left, on account of finding the examinations more difficult than they anticipated, yet there are nearly 300 now. Perhaps you know that Miss Lyon is raising her standard of scholarship a good deal, on account of the number of applicants this year, and she makes the examinations more severe than usual.

You cannot imagine how trying they are, because if we cannot go through them all in a specified time, we are sent home. I cannot be too thankful that I got through as soon as I did, and I am sure that I never would endure the suspense which I endured during those three days again for all the treasures of the world.

I room with my cousin Emily, who is a Senior. She is an excellent room-mate, and does all in her power to make me happy. You can imagine how pleasant a good room-mate is, for you have been away to school so much. Everything is pleasant and happy here, and I think I could be no happier at any other school away from home. Things seem much more like home than I anticipated, and the teachers are all very kind and affectionate to us. They call on us frequently and urge us to return their calls, and when we do, we always receive a cordial welcome from them. I will tell you my order of time for the day, as you were so kind as to give

me yours. At 6 o'clock we all rise. We breakfast
at 7. Our study hours begin at 8. At 9 we all meet
in Seminary Hall for devotions. At 10¼ I recite a
review of Ancient History, in connection with which
we read Goldsmith and Grimshaw. At 11, I recite
a lesson in Pope's *Essay on Man*, which is merely
transposition. At 12 I practise calisthenics, and at
12¼ read until dinner, which is at 12½, and after
dinner, from 1½ until 2, I sing in Seminary Hall.
From 2¾ until 3¾ I practise upon the piano. At 3¾
I go to Sections, where we give in all our accounts
for the day, including absence, tardiness, communi-
cations, breaking silent study hours, receiving company in our rooms, and ten thousand other things
which I will not take time or place to mention. At
4½ we go into Seminary Hall and receive advice from
Miss Lyon in the form of a lecture. We have supper
at 6, and silent study hours from then until the retiring bell, which rings at 8¾, but the tardy bell does
not ring until 9¾, so that we don't often obey the
first warning to retire. Unless we have a good and
reasonable excuse for failure upon any of the items
that I mentioned above, they are recorded and a
black mark stands against our names. As you can
easily imagine, we do not like very well to get 'exceptions,' as they are called scientifically here.

My domestic work is not difficult and consists
in carrying the knives from the first tier of tables
at morning and noon, and at night washing and
wiping the same quantity of knives. I am quite

well and hope to be able to spend the year here, free from sickness. You have probably heard many reports of the food here; and if so, I can tell you that I have yet seen nothing corresponding to my ideas on that point from what I have heard. Everything is wholesome and abundant and much nicer than I should imagine could be provided for almost 300 girls. We have also a great variety upon our tables and frequent changes. One thing is certain, and that is, that Miss Lyon and all the teachers seem to consult our comfort and happiness in everything they do, and you know that is pleasant. When I left home I did not think I should find a companion or a dear friend in all the multitude. I expected to find rough and uncultivated manners, and, to be sure, I have found some of that stamp, but on the whole, there is an ease and grace, a desire to make one another happy, which delights and at the same time surprises me very much. I find no Abby nor Abiah nor Mary, but I love many of the girls. Austin came to see me when I had been here about two weeks, and brought Viny and A. I need not tell you how delighted I was to see them all, nor how happy it made me to hear them say that 'they were *so lonely.*' It is a sweet feeling to know that you are missed and that your memory is precious at home. This week, on Wednesday, I was at my window, when I happened to look towards the hotel and saw father and mother, walking over here as dignified as you please. I need not tell you that I danced and clapped my hands, and flew to meet them, for you can imagine how I felt. I will only ask you, do you lovè your parents? They wanted to surprise me, and for that reason did not let me know they were coming. I could not bear to have them go, but go they must, and so I submitted in sadness. Only to think that in 2½ weeks I shall be at my *own dear home* again. You will probably go home at Thanksgiving time, and we can rejoice with each other.

You don't [know] how I laughed at your description of your introduction to Daniel Webster, and I read that part of your letter to cousin Emily. You must feel quite proud of the acquaintance, and will not, I hope, be vain in consequence. However, you don't know Governor Briggs, and I do, so you are no better off than I. . . . A., you must write me often, and I shall write you as often as I have time. . . .

From your affectionate
EMILY E. D.

MT HOLYOKE FEMALE SEMINARY, Jan. 17, 1848.

MY DEAR A., — Your welcome epistle found me upon the eve of going home, and it is needless to say very happy. We all went home on Wednesday before Thanksgiving, and a stormy day it was, but the storm must not be in our way, so we tried to make the best of it and look as cheerful as we could. Many of the girls went very early in the morning in order to reach home the same day, and when we all sat down to the breakfast table, it seemed lonely enough to see so many places vacant. After breakfast, as we were not required to keep all the family rules, a number of us met together at one of the windows in the Hall to watch for our friends, whom we were constantly expecting. No morning of my life ever passed so slowly to me, and it really seemed to me they never were coming, so impatiently did I wait their arrival. At last, almost tired out, I spied a carriage in the distance, and surely Austin was in it. You, who have been away so much, can easily imagine my delight and will not laugh, when I tell you how I dashed downstairs and almost frightened my dignified brother out of his senses. All was ready in a moment or less than a moment, and cousin Emily and myself, not forgetting the driver, were far on our way towards home. The rain fell in torrents and the wind howled around the sides of the mountain over our heads, and the brooks below, filled by the rain, rushed along their pebbly beds almost frightfully, yet nothing daunted, we rode swiftly along, and soon the colleges and the spire of our venerable meeting-house rose to my delighted vision.

Never did Amherst look more lovely to me, and gratitude rose in my heart to God, for granting me such a safe return to my *own dear home.* Soon the carriage stopped in front of our own house, and all were at the door to welcome the returned one, from mother, with tears in her eyes, down to pussy, who tried to look as gracious as was becoming her dignity. Oh, A., it was the first meeting, as it had been the first separation, and it was a joyful one to all of us. The storm did not at all subside that night, but in the morning I was waked by the glorious sunshine [it]-self, staring full in my face. We went to church in the morning and listened to an excellent sermon from our own minister, Mr Colton. At noon we returned and had a nice dinner, which, you well know, cannot be dispensed with on Thanksgiving day. We had several calls in the afternoon, and had four invitations out for the evening. Of course we could not accept them all, much to my sorrow, but decided to make two visits. At about 7 o'clock father, mother, Austin, Viny, cousin Emily, and myself to bring up the rear, went down to Professor Warner's, where we spent an hour delightfully with a few friends, and then bidding them good eve, we young folks went down to Mrs S. M.'s, accompanied by *sister Mary*. There was quite a company of young people assembled when we arrived, and after we had played many games we had, in familiar terms, a 'candy scrape.' We enjoyed the evening much, and returned not until the clock pealed out, 'Remember ten o'clock, my dear, remember ten o'clock.' After our return, father wishing to hear the piano, I, like an obedient daughter, played and sang a few tunes, much to his apparent gratification. We then retired, and the next day and the next were as happily spent as the eventful Thanksgiving day itself.

You will probably think me foolish thus to give you an inventory of my time while at home, but I did enjoy so much in those short four days that I wanted you to know and enjoy it too. Monday came so soon, and with it came a carriage to our door, and amidst tears falling thick and fast away I went again. Slowly and sadly dragged a few of the days after my return to the Seminary, and I was very homesick, but 'after a storm there comes a calm,' and so it was in my case. My sorrows were soon lost in study, and I again felt happy, if happiness there can be away from 'home, sweet home.'

Our term closes this week on Thursday, and Friday I hope to see home and friends once more. I have studied hard this term, and aside from my delight at going home, there is a sweetness in approaching rest to me. This term is the longest in the year, and I would not wish to live it over again, I can assure you. I love this Seminary, and all the teachers are bound strongly to my heart by ties of affection. There are many sweet girls here, and dearly do I love some new faces, but I have not yet found the place of a *few* dear ones filled, nor would I wish it to be here. I am now studying Silliman's Chemistry and Cutter's Physiology, in both of which I am much interested. We finish Physiology before this term closes, and are to be examined in it at the spring examinations, about five weeks after the commencement of the next term. I already begin to dread that time, for an examination

in Mount Holyoke Seminary is rather more public
than in our old academy, and a failure would be
more disgraceful then, I opine ; but I hope, to use
my father's own words, 'that I shall not disgrace
myself.' What are you studying now? You did not
mention that item in your last letters to me, and
consequently I am quite in the dark as regards your
progress in those affairs. All I can say is, that I
hope you will not leave poor me far behind. . . .

Your affectionate *sister*,

EMILY E. DICKINSON.

P. S.   Our Section have commenced reading compositions, and we read once in a month, during
which time we write two.

Intellectual brilliancy of an individual type
was already at seventeen her distinguishing
characteristic, and nothing of the recluse was
yet apparent. Traditions of extraordinary
compositions still remain ; and it is certain
that each was an epoch for those who heard,
whether teachers or pupils. An old friend
and schoolmate of Emily tells me that she
was always surrounded by a group of girls at
recess, to hear her strange and intensely funny
stories, invented upon the spot.

MT HOLYOKE FEMALE SEMINARY, May 16, 1848.

MY DEAR A., — You must forgive me, indeed you must, that I have so long delayed to write you, and I doubt not you will when I give you all my reasons for so doing. You know it is customary for the first page to be occupied with apologies, and I must not depart from the beaten track for one of my own imagining. . . . I had not been very well all winter, but had not written home about it, lest the folks should take me home. During the week following examinations, a friend from Amherst came over and spent a week with me, and when that friend returned home, father and mother were duly notified of the state of my health. Have you so treacherous a friend?

Not knowing that I was to be reported at home, you can imagine my amazement and consternation when Saturday of the same week Austin arrived in full sail, with orders from head-quarters to bring me home at all events. At first I had recourse to words, and a desperate battle with those weapons was waged for a few moments, between my *Sophomore* brother and myself. Finding words of no avail, I next resorted to tears. But woman's tears are of little avail, and I am sure mine flowed in vain. As you can imagine, Austin was victorious, and poor, defeated I was led off in triumph. You must not imbibe the idea from what I have said that I do not love home — far from it. But I could not bear to leave teachers and companions before the close of the term and go home to be dosed and receive the physician daily, and take warm drinks and be condoled with on the state of health in general by all the old ladies in town.

Have n't I given a ludicrous account of going home sick from a boarding-school? Father is quite a hand to give medicine, especially if it is not desirable to the patient, and I was dosed for about a month after my return home, without any mercy, till at last out of mere pity my cough went away, and I had quite a season of peace. Thus I remained at home until the close of the term, comforting my parents by my presence, and instilling many a lesson of wisdom into the budding intellect of my only sister. I had almost forgotten to tell you that I went on with my studies at home, and kept up with my class. Last Thursday our vacation closed, and on Friday morn, midst the weeping of friends, crowing of roosters, and singing of birds, I again took my departure from home. Five days have now passed since we returned to Holyoke, and they have passed very slowly. Thoughts of home and friends 'come crowding thick and fast, like lightnings from the mountain cloud,' and it seems very desolate.

Father has decided not to send me to Holyoke another year, so this is my *last term*. Can it be possible that I have been here almost a year? It startles me when I really think of the advantages I

have had, and I fear I have not improved them as
I ought. But many an hour has fled with its report
to heaven, and what has been the tale of me? . . .
How glad I am that spring has come, and how it
calms my mind when wearied with study to walk out
in the green fields and beside the pleasant streams
in which South Hadley is rich! There are not many
wild flowers near, for the girls have driven them to
a distance, and we are obliged to walk quite a distance to find them, but they repay us by their sweet
smiles and fragrance.

The older I grow, the more do I love spring and
spring flowers. Is it so with you? While at home
there were several pleasure parties of which I was
a member, and in our rambles we found many and
beautiful children of spring, which I will mention
and see if you have found them, — the trailing arbutus, adder's tongue, yellow violets, liver-leaf, blood-
root, and many other smaller flowers.

What are you reading now? I have little time to
read when I am here, but while at home I had a feast
in the reading line, I can assure you. Two or three
of them I will mention: *Evangeline, The Princess,
The Maiden Aunt, The Epicurean,* and *The Twins
and Heart* by Tupper, complete the list. Am not
I a pedant for telling you what I have been reading? Have you forgotten your visit at Amherst last
summer, and what delightful times we had? I have
not, and I hope you will come and make another
and a longer, when I get home from Holyoke.

Father wishes to have me at home a year, and then he will probably send me away again, where I know not. . . .

Ever your own affectionate

EMILIE E. DICKINSON.

P. S. My studies for this series are Astronomy and Rhetoric, which take me through to the Senior studies. What are you studying now, if you are in school, and do you attend to music? I practise only one hour a day this term.

Although nearly two years elapse between the last letter and the following, the handwriting is quite unaltered, being still exceedingly small and clear, and averaging twenty words to a line.

AMHERST, Jan. 29, 1850.

VERY DEAR A., — The folks have all gone away; they thought that they left me alone, and contrived things to amuse me should they stay long, and *I* be lonely. Lonely, indeed, — they did n't look, and they could n't have seen if they had, who should bear me company. *Three* here, instead of *one*, would n't it scare them? A curious trio, part earthly and part spiritual two of us, the other, all heaven, and no earth. *God* is sitting here, looking into my very soul to see if I think right thoughts. Yet I am not afraid, for I try to be right and

good ; and He knows every one of my struggles. He
looks very gloriously, and everything bright seems dull
beside Him ; and I don't dare to look directly at
Him for fear I shall die.   Then *you* are here,
dressed in that quiet black gown and cap, — that
funny little cap I used to laugh at you about, — and
you don't appear to be thinking about anything
in particular, — not in one of your *breaking-dish*
moods, I take it.   You seem aware that I 'm
writing you, and are amused, I should think, at
any such friendly manifestation when you are already present.   *Success*, however, even in making
a fool of myself, is n't to be despised ; so I shall
persist in writing, and you may in laughing at me, —
if you are fully aware of the value of time as regards
your immortal spirit.   I can't say that I advise you
to laugh ; but if you are punished, and I warned
you, that can be no business of mine.   So I fold
up my arms, and leave you to fate — may it deal
very kindly with you !   The trinity winds up with
me, as you may have surmised, and I certainly
would n't be at the fag-end but for civility to you.
This self-sacrificing spirit will be the ruin of me !

· I am occupied principally with a cold just now,
and the dear creature *will* have so much attention
that my time slips away amazingly.   It has heard
so much of New Englanders, of their kind atten-
tions to strangers, that it 's come all the way from
the Alps to determine the truth of the tale.   It says
the half was n't told it, and I begin to be afraid it

was n't.   Only think — came all the way from that
distant Switzerland to find what was the truth ! Neither
husband, protector, nor friend accompanied it, and
so utter a state of loneliness gives friends if nothing
else.   You are dying of curiosity ; let me arrange that
pillow to make your exit easier.   I stayed at home
all Saturday afternoon, and treated some disagree-
able people who insisted upon calling here as toler-
ably as I could ; when evening shades began to fall, I
turned upon my heel, and walked.   Attracted by
the gayety visible in the street, I still kept walking
till a little creature pounced upon a thin shawl I
wore, and commenced riding.   I stopped, and
begged the creature to alight, as I was fatigued
already, and quite unable to assist others.   It
would n't get down, and commenced talking to
itself : 'Can't be New England — must have made
some mistake — disappointed in my reception — don't
agree with accounts.   Oh, what a world of decep-
tion and fraud !   Marm, will you tell me the name
of this country — it 's Asia Minor, is n't it?   I
intended to stop in New England.'   By this time
I was so completely exhausted that I made no further effort to rid me of my load, and travelled home
at a moderate jog, paying no attention whatever to
it, got into the house, threw off both bonnet and
shawl, and out flew my tormentor, and putting both
arms around my neck, began to kiss me immoder-
ately, and express so much love it completely
bewildered me.   Since then it has slept in my bed,

eaten from my plate, lived with me everywhere, and will tag me through life for all I know. I think I 'll wake first, and get out of bed, and leave it ; but early or late, it is dressed before me, and sits on the side of the bed looking right into my face with such a comical expression it almost makes me laugh in spite of myself. I can't call it interesting, but it certainly *is* curious, has two peculiarities which would quite win your heart, — a huge pocket-handkerchief and a very red nose. The first seems so very *abundant*, it gives you the idea of independence and prosperity in business. The last brings up the 'jovial bowl, my boys,' and such an association 's worth the having. If it *ever* gets tired of *me*, I will forward it to *you* — you would love it for *my* sake, if not for its own ; it will tell you some queer stories about me, — how I sneezed so loud one night that the family thought the last trump was sounding, and climbed into the currant-bushes to get out of the way ; how the rest of the people, arrayed in long night-gowns, folded their arms, and were waiting ; but this is a wicked story, — it can tell some better ones. Now, my dear friend, let me tell you that these last thoughts are fictions, — vain imaginations to lead astray foolish young women. They are flowers of speech ; they both make and tell deliberate falsehoods ; avoid them as the snake, and turn aside as from the rattle-snake, and I don't *think* you will be harmed. Honestly, though, a snake-bite is a serious matter,

and there can't be too much said or done about
it. The big serpent bites the deepest; and we get
so accustomed to its bites that we don't mind
about them. 'Verily I say unto you, fear *him*.'
Won't you read some work upon snakes?—I have
a real anxiety for you. *I* love those little green
ones that slide around by your shoes in the grass,
and make it rustle with their elbows; they are
rather my favorites on the whole; but I would n't
influence *you* for the world. There is an air of
misanthropy about the striped snake that will commend itself at once to your taste, — there is no
monotony about it — but we will more of this again.
Something besides severe colds and serpents, and
we will try to find *that* something. It can't be
a garden, can it? or a strawberry-bed, which rather
belongs to a garden; nor it can't be a schoolhouse, nor an attorney-at-law. Oh, dear! I don't
know what it is. Love for the absent don't *sound*
like it; but try it, and see how it goes.

I miss you very much indeed; think of you at
night when the world's nodding, nid, nid, nodding
— think of you in the daytime when the cares of the
world, and its toils, and its continual vexations
choke up the love for friends in some of our
hearts; remember your warnings sometimes — try
to do as you told me sometimes — and sometimes
conclude it's no use to try; then my heart says it
is, and new trial is followed by disappointment
again. I wondered, when you had gone, why we

did n't talk more, — it was n't for want of a subject;
it never *could be* for *that.* Too many, perhaps, —
such a crowd of people that nobody heard the
speaker, and all went away discontented. You
astonished me in the outset, perplexed me in the
continuance, and wound up in a grand snarl I
shall be all my pilgrimage unravelling. Rather a
dismal prospect certainly; but 'it's always the
darkest the hour before day,' and this earlier
sunset promises an earlier rise — a sun in splen-
dor — and glory, flying out of its purple nest.
Would n't you love to see God's bird, when it first
tries its wings? If you were here I would tell you
something — several somethings — which have happened since you went away; but time and space,
as usual, oppose themselves, and I put my treasures away till 'we two meet again.' The hope
that I shall continue in love towards you, and *vice
versa,* will sustain me till then. If you are thinking soon to go away, and to show your face no
more, just inform me, will you? I would have the
'long, lingering look,' which you cast behind, — it
would be an invaluable addition to my treasures,
and 'keep your memory green.' 'Lord, keep
all our memories green,' and help on our affection,
and tie the 'link that doth us bind' in a tight
bow-knot that will keep it from separation, and stop
us from growing old; if that is impossible, make
old age pleasant to us, put its arms around us

kindly, and when we go home, let that home be called heaven.

Your very sincere and *wicked* friend,

EMILY E. DICKINSON.

I have n't thanked you for your letter yet, but not for want of gratitude. I will do so *now* most sincerely, most heartily — gladly and gratefully. You will write me another soon, that I may have *four right* feelings again! They don't come for the asking. I have been introducing you to me in this letter so far; we will traffic in 'joys' and 'sorrows' some other day. Colds make one very carnal, and the spirit is always afraid of them. You will excuse all mistakes in view of ignorance; all sin, in view of 'the fall;' all want of friendly affection, in the sight of the verse, 'The deepest stream the stillest runs;' and other general deficiencies, on the ground of universal incapacity! Here is surely room for charity, and the heavenly visitor would n't have come but for these faults. 'No loss without a gain.' I called to see your cousins an evening since; they were well, and evidently delighted to see one another — and us.

When your letter came, I had two Western cousins — now at South Hadley Seminary — staying their vacation with me. They took an unbounded delight in a sentence I read them; and to pay for it, send you their love.

In the following letter appear farther traces of the later and almost invariable custom of using dashes, instead of conventional punctuation. These, however, will not be given generally. In printing her poems it was found necessary to employ usual punctuation, in order that the meaning should be more easily apprehended; and in the letters the same system, often for the same reason, has been adopted.

AMHERST, May 7, 1850.

DEAR REMEMBERED, — The circumstances under which I write you this morning are at once glorious, afflicting, and beneficial, — glorious in *ends*, afflicting in *means*, and beneficial, I trust, in *both*. Twin loaves of bread have just been born into the world under my auspices, — fine children, the image of their mother; and here, my dear friend, is the *glory*.

On the lounge, asleep, lies my sick mother, suffering intensely from acute neuralgia, except at a moment like this, when kind sleep draws near, and beguiles her, — here is the *affliction*.

I need not draw the beneficial inference, — the good I myself derive, the winning the spirit of patience, the genial housekeeping influence stealing over my mind and soul, — you know all these things I would say, and will seem to suppose they are written, when indeed they are only thought.

On Sunday my mother was taken, had been perfectly well before, and could remember no possible imprudence which should have induced the disease. Everything has been done, and though we think her gradually throwing it off, she still has much suffering. I have always neglected the culinary arts, but attend to them now from necessity, and from a desire to make everything pleasant for father and Austin. Sickness makes desolation, and the day is dark and dreary; but health will come back, I hope, and light hearts and smiling faces. We are sick hardly ever at home, and don't know what to do when it comes, — wrinkle our little brows, and stamp with our little feet, and our tiny souls get angry, and command it to go away. Mrs Brown will be glad to see it, — old ladies expect to die; 'as for *us*, the young and active, with all longings "for the strife," *we* to perish by the roadside, weary with the "march of life " — no, no, my dear " Father Mortality," get out of the way if you please; we will call if we ever want you. Good-morning, sir! ah, good-morning ! '

When I am not at work, I sit by the side of mother, provide for her little wants, and try to cheer and encourage her. I ought to be glad and grateful that I *can* do anything now, but I do feel so very lonely, and so anxious to have her cured. I have n't repined but once, and you shall know all the why. At noon . . . I heard a well-known rap, and a friend I love *so* dearly came and asked me to ride in the woods, the sweet, still woods, — and I wanted to exceedingly.   I told him I could not go, and he said he was disappointed, he wanted me very much.   Then the tears came into my eyes, though I tried to choke them back, and he said I *could* and *should* go, and it seemed to me unjust.   Oh, I struggled with great temptation, and it cost me much of denial; but I think in the end I conquered, — not a glorious victory, where you hear the rolling drum, but a kind of a helpless victory, where triumph would come of itself, faintest music, weary soldiers, nor a waving flag, nor a long, loud shout.   I had read of Christ's temptations, and how they were like our own, only he did n't sin; I wondered if *one* was like mine, and whether it made him angry.   I could n't make up my mind; do you think he ever did?

I went cheerfully round my work, humming a little air till mother had gone to sleep, then cried with all my might — seemed to think I was much abused — that this wicked world was unworthy such devoted and terrible suffering — and came to my various senses in great dudgeon at life, and time, and love for affliction and anguish.

What shall we do, my darling, when trial grows more and more, when the dim, lone light expires, and it 's dark, so very dark, and we wander, and know not where, and cannot get out of the forest — whose is the hand to help us, and to lead, and forever guide us; they talk of a 'Jesus of Nazareth' — will you tell me if it be he? . . .

It's Friday, my dear A., and that in another week, yet my mission is unfulfilled — and you so sadly neglected, and don't know the reason why. Where do you think I've strayed, and from what new errand returned? I have come from 'to and fro, and walking up and down' the same place that Satan hailed from, when God asked him where he'd been; but not to illustrate further, I tell you I have been dreaming, dreaming a *golden* dream, with eyes all the while wide open, and I guess it's almost morning; and besides, I have been at work, providing the 'food that perisheth,' scaring the timorous dust, and being obedient and kind. I am yet the Queen of the Court, if regalia be dust and dirt, have three loyal subjects, whom I'd rather relieve from service. Mother is still an invalid, though a partially restored one; father and Austin still clamor for food; and I, like a martyr, am feeding them. Wouldn't you love to see me in these bonds of great despair, looking around my kitchen, and praying for kind deliverance, and declaring by 'Omai's beard' I never was in such plight? *My* kitchen, I think I called it — God forbid that it was, or shall be, my own — God keep me from what they call *households*, except that bright one of 'faith'!

Don't be afraid of my imprecations — they never did any one harm, and they make me feel so cool, and so very much more comfortable ! . . . I presume you are loving your mother, and loving the stranger and wanderer — visiting the poor and afflicted, and reaping whole fields of blessings — save me a little sheaf, only a very little one ! Remember and care for me sometimes, and scatter a fragrant flower in this wilderness life of mine by writing me, and by not forgetting, and by lingering longer in prayer, that the Father may bless one more !

Your affectionate friend,

EMILY.

Mr Humphrey, spoken of in the following letter, is the same friend of whom Emily had already written (page 24); he graduated from Amherst as valedictorian in 1846, being subsequently Principal of the well-known Amherst Academy, and still later a theological student at Andover, and tutor in Amherst College. His sudden death, November 30, 1850, caused much grief to his many friends, who admired his polished scholarship and lovable personality.

[Amherst, January 2, 1851.]

Tuesday Evening.

I write A. to-night, because it is cool and quiet, and I can forget the toil and care of the feverish day, and then I am *selfish* too, because I am feeling lonely ; some of my friends are gone, and some of my friends are sleeping — sleeping the churchyard

sleep—the hour of evening is sad—it was once my
study hour—my master has gone to rest, and the
open leaf of the book, and the scholar at school
alone, make the tears come, and I cannot brush
them away; I would not if I could, for they are
the only tribute I can pay the departed Humphrey.

You have stood by the grave before; I have walked
there sweet summer evenings and read the names
on the stones, and wondered who would come and
give me the same memorial; but I never have laid
my friends there, and forgot that they too must die;
this is my first affliction, and indeed 't is hard to
bear it.   To those bereaved so often that home is
no more here, and whose communion with friends
is had only in prayers, there must be much to hope
for, but when the unreconciled spirit has nothing left
but God, that spirit is lone indeed.   I don't think
there will be any sunshine, or any singing-birds in
the spring that 's coming. . . . I will try not to say
any more—my rebellious thoughts are many, and
the friend I love and trust in has much *now* to forgive.   I wish I were somebody else—I would pray
the prayer of the 'Pharisee,' but I am a poor little
'Publican.' 'Son of David,' look down on me !

'T was a great while ago when you wrote me, I
remember the leaves were falling—and *now* there
are falling snows; who maketh the two to differ—
are not leaves the brethren of snows?

Then it *can't* be a great while since then, though
I verily thought it *was;* we are not so young as we

once were, and time seems to be growing long. I
dream of being a grandame, and banding my silver
hairs, and I seem to be quite submissive to the
thought of growing old ; no doubt you ride rocking-
horses in your present as in young sleeps — quite
a pretty contrast indeed, of me braiding my own
gray hairs, and my friend at play with her childhood,
a pair of decayed old ladies ! Where *are* you, my
antique friend, or my very dear and young one —
just as you please to please — it *may* seem quite
a presumption that I address you at all, knowing
not if you habit here, or if my 'bird has flown' in
which world her wing is folded. When I think of
the friends I love, and the little while we may
dwell here, and then 'we go away,' I have a yearning feeling, a desire eager and anxious lest any
be stolen away, so that I cannot behold them. I
would have you here, all here, where I can *see* you,
and *hear* you, and where I can say 'Oh, no,' if the
'Son of Man' ever 'cometh' !

It is not enough, now and then, at long and uncertain intervals to hear you're alive and well. I do not
care for the body, I love the timid soul, the blush-
ing, shrinking soul ; it hides, for it is afraid, and the
bold, obtrusive body — Pray, marm, did you call
me ? We are very small, A. — I think we grow still
smaller — this tiny, insect life the portal to another ;
it seems strange — strange indeed. I'm afraid we
are all unworthy, yet we shall 'enter in.'

I can think of no other way than for you, my dear

girl, to come here — we are growing away from each
other, and talk even now like strangers.   To forget
the 'meum and teum,' *dearest* friends must meet
sometimes, and then comes the 'bond of the spirit'
which, if I am correct, is 'unity.'

. . . You are growing wiser than I am, and nip-
ping in the bud fancies which I let blossom — per-
chance to bear no fruit, or if plucked, I may find it
bitter.   The shore is safer, A., but I love to buffet
the sea — I can count the bitter wrecks here in these
pleasant waters, and hear the murmuring winds, but
oh, I love the danger!   You are learning control and
firmness.   Christ Jesus will love you more.   I'm
afraid he don't love me *any!* . . . Write when you
will, my friend, and forget all amiss herein, for as
these few imperfect words to the full communion
of spirits, so this small giddy life to the *better*, the
life eternal, and that *we* may live this life, and be
filled with this true communion, I shall not cease to
pray.   E.

[August, 1851.]

Tuesday Evening.

'Yet a little while I am with you, and again a little while and I am *not* with you,' because you go to
your mother! . . . But the virtue of the text consists in this, my dear, that 'if I *go*, I come again,
and ye shall be with me where I am;' that is to say,
that if you come in November, you shall be mine,
and I shall be thine, and so on, *vice versa*, until *ad*

infinitum, which is n't a great way off. While I
think of it, my dear friend, and we are upon these
subjects, allow me to remark that you have the funniest manner of popping into town, and the most
lamentable manner of popping out again, of any
one I know. It really becomes to me a matter of
serious moment, this propensity of yours concerning
your female friends — the 'morning cloud and the
early dew' are not more evanescent.

I think it was Tuesday evening that we were so
amused by the oratorical feats of three or four young
gentlemen. I remember I sat by you and took
great satisfaction in such seat and society — I remember further our mutual good-nights, our promises to meet again, to tell each other tales of our
own heart and life, to seek and find each other after
so long a time of distant separation. I can hardly
realize that these are recollections, that our happy
to-day joins the great band of yesterdays and marches
on to the dead — too quickly flown, my bird, for
me to satisfy me that you *did* sit and sing beneath
my chamber window! I only went out once after
the time I saw you — the morning of Mr Beecher I
looked for you in vain. I discovered your Palmer
cousins, but if you indeed were there, it must have
been in a form to my gross sense impalpable. I
was disappointed. I had been hoping much a little
visit from you; when will the hour be that we
shall sit together and talk of what we were and what
we are and may be — with the shutters closed, dear

A., and the balmiest little breeze stealing in at the
window? I love those little fancies, yet I would
love them more were they not quite so fanciful as
they have seemed to be. I have fancied so many
times, and so many times gone home to find it was
only fancy, that I am half afraid to hope for what I
long for. It would seem, my dear A., that out of
all the moments crowding this little world, a *few*
might be vouchsafed to spend with those we love —
a separated hour, an hour more pure and true than
ordinary hours, when we could pause a moment,
before we journey on. We had a pleasant time talking the other morning — had I known it was all
my portion, mayhap I'd improved it more, but it
never'll come back again to try, whether or no.
Don't you think sometimes these brief, imperfect
meetings have a tale to tell — perhaps but for the
sorrow which accompanies them we should not be
reminded of brevity and change, and should build
the dwelling earthward whose site is in the skies —
perhaps the treasure here would be too dear a treasure couldn't 'the moth corrupt, and the thief break
through and steal;' and this makes me think how
I found a little moth in my stores the other day,
a very subtle moth that had, in ways and manners to me and mine unknown, contrived to hide
itself in a favorite worsted basket — how long my
little treasure-house had furnished an arena for its
destroying labors it is not mine to tell; it had an
errand there — I trust it fulfilled its mission; it

taught me, dear A., to have no treasure here, or rather it tried to tell me in its little mothy way of another enduring treasure the robber cannot steal, nor time waste away. How many a lesson learned from lips of such tiny teachers — don't it make you think of the Bible, 'not many mighty, nor wise'?

You met our dear Sarah T. after I saw you here. Her sweet face is the same as in those happy school-days — and in vain I search for wrinkles brought on by many cares; we all love Sarah dearly, and shall try to do all in our power to make her visit happy. Isn't it very remarkable that in so many years Sarah has changed so little — not that she has stood still, but has made such *peaceful* progress — her thoughts, though they are older, have all the charm of youth — have not yet lost their freshness, their innocence and peace; she seems so pure in heart, so sunny and serene, like some sweet lark or robin, ever soaring and singing. I have not seen her much — I want to see her more — she speaks often of *you*, and with a warm affection. I hope no change or time shall blight those loves of ours, I would bear them all in my arms to my home in the glorious heaven and say, 'Here am I, my Father, and those whom thou hast given me.' If the life which is to come is better than dwelling *here*, and angels are there and our friends are glorified and are singing there and praising there, need we fear to go when spirits beyond wait for us? I was meaning to see you more and talk about such things with you — I

want to know your views and your eternal feelings
—how things beyond are to you—oh, there is much
to speak of in meeting one you love, and it always
seems to me that I might have spoken more, and I
almost always think that what we found to say might
have been left unspoken.

Shall it *always* be so, A.? Is there no longer day
given for our communion with the spirits of our
love? Writing is brief and fleeting—conversation
will come again, yet if it *will*, it hastes and must
be on its way. Earth is short, but Paradise is long
— there must be many moments in an eternal day;
then sometime we shall tarry while time and tide roll
on, and till then *vale*.

Your own dear

EMILIE.

[Written from Amherst between January 1, and the middle of
June, 1852.]

Sunday Evening.

MY VERY DEAR A.,—I love to sit here alone,
writing a letter to you, and whether your joy in
reading will amount to as much or more, or even
less than mine in penning it to you, becomes to me
just now a very important problem—and I will
tax each power to solve the same for me; if as
happy, indeed, I have every occasion for gratitude
—more so, my absent friend, I may not hope to
make you, but I do hope most earnestly it may not
give you *less*. Oh, I do know it will not, if school-

day hearts are warm and school-day memories precious ! As I told you, it is Sunday to-day, so I find
myself quite curtailed in the selection of subjects,
being myself quite vain, and naturally adverting to
many worldly things which would doubtless grieve
and distress you : much more will I be restrained by
the fact that such stormy Sundays I always remain
at home, and have not those opportunities for hoard-
ing up great truths which I would have otherwise.
In view of these things, A., your kind heart will be
lenient, forgiving all empty words and unsatisfying
feelings on the Sabbath-day ground which we have
just alluded to. I rejoice in one theme appropriate
to every place and time — indeed it cannot intrude
in the hour most unseemly for every other thought
and every other feeling; and sure I am to-day, how-
e'er it may be holy, I shall not break or reproach
by speaking of the links which bind us to each
other, and make the very thought of you, and time
when I last saw you, a sacred thing to me. And
I have many memories, and many thoughts beside,
which by some strange entwining, circle you round
and round ; if you please, a vine of fancies, towards
which dear A. sustains the part of oak, and as up
each sturdy branch there climbs a little tendril so
full of faith and confidence and the most holy trust,
so let the hearts do also, of the dear 'estray;' then
the farther we may be from home and from each
other, the nearer by that faith which 'overcometh
all things' and bringeth us to itself.

Amherst and Philadelphia, separate indeed, and yet how near, bridged by a thousand trusts and a 'thousand times ten thousand' the travellers who cross, whom you and I may not see, nor hear the trip of their feet, yet faith tells us they are there, ever crossing and re-crossing. Very likely, A., you fancy me at home in my own little chamber, writing you a letter, but you are greatly mistaken. I am on the blue Susquehanna paddling down to you; I am not much of a sailor, so I get along rather slowly, and I am not much of a mermaid, though I verily think I shall be, if the tide overtakes me at my present jog. Hard-hearted girl! I don't believe you care, if you did you would come quickly and help me out of this sea; but if I drown, A., and go down to dwell in the seaweed forever and forever, I will not forget your name, nor all the wrong you did me!

Why did you go away and not come to see me? I felt so sure you would come, because you promised me, that I watched and waited for you, and bestowed a tear or two upon my absentee. How very sad it is to have a confiding nature, one's hopes and feelings are quite at the mercy of all who come along; and how very desirable to be a stolid individual, whose hopes and aspirations are safe in one's waistcoat pocket, and *that* a pocket indeed, and one not to be picked!

Notwithstanding your faithlessness I should have come to see you, but for that furious snow-storm;

I did attempt in spite of it, but it conquered in spite of me, and I doffed my hood and shawl, and felt very crestfallen the remainder of the day.   I did want one more kiss, one sweet and sad good-by, before you had flown away; perhaps, my dear A., it is well that I go without it; it might have added anguish to our long separation, or made the miles still longer which keep a friend away.   I always try to think in any disappointment that had I been gratified, it had been sadder still, and I weave from such supposition, *at times*, considerable consolation; consolation upside down as I am pleased to call it.

. . . Shall I have a letter soon — oh, may I very soon, for 'some days are dark and dreary, and the wind is never weary.'

EMILY E.

[Also written before the middle of June, 1852.]

Sabbath Day.

I love to link you, A. and E., I love to put you together and look at you side by side — the picture pleases me, and I should love to watch it until the sun goes down, did I not call to mind a very precious letter for which I have not as yet rendered a single farthing, so let me thank you that midst your many friends and cares and influenzas, you yet found time for me, and loved me.   You remarked that I had written you more affectionately than wont — I have thought that word over and over, and it puzzles me now; whether our few last years have been cooler than our first ones, or whether I write

indifferently when I truly know it not, the query
troubles me.   I do believe sincerely, that the friendship formed at school was no warmer than now, nay
more, that *this* is warmest — they differ indeed to
me as morning differs from noon — one may be
fresher, cheerier, but the other fails not.

You and I have grown older since school-days,
and our years have made us soberer — I mean have
made *me* so, for you were always dignified, e'en
when a little girl, and *I* used, now and then, to
cut a timid caper.   That makes me think of you
the very first time I saw you, and I can't repress
a smile, not to say a hearty laugh, at your little
girl expense.   I have roused your curiosity, so I
will e'en tell you that one Wednesday afternoon,
in the days of that dear old Academy, I went in
to be entertained by the rhetoric of the gentlemen
and the milder form of the girls — I had hardly
recovered myself from the dismay attendant upon
entering august assemblies, when with the utmost
equanimity you ascended the stairs, bedecked with
dandelions, arranged, it seemed, for curls.   I shall
never forget that scene, if I live to have gray hairs,
nor the very remarkable fancies it gave me then of
you, and it comes over me now with the strangest
bygone funniness, and I laugh merrily.   Oh, A.,
you and the early flower are forever linked to me;
as soon as the first green grass comes, up from a
chink in the stones peeps the little flower, precious
'leontodon,' and my heart fills toward you with a

warm and childlike fulness! Nor do I laugh now;
far from it, I rather bless the flower which sweetly,
slyly too, makes me come nearer you.

But, my dear, I can't give the dandelion the privilege due to you, so good-by, little one!

I would love to see you, A., I would rather than
write to you, might I with equal ease, for the
weather is very warm, and my head aches a little,
and my heart a little more, so taking me *collectively*,
I seem quite miserable, but I'll give you the sunny
corners, and you must n't look at the shade. You
were happy when you wrote me; I hope so now,
though I would you were in the country, and could
reach the hills and fields. I can reach them, carry
them home, which I do in my arms daily, and when
they drop and fade, I have only to gather fresh
ones. Your joy would indeed be full, could you
sit as I, at my window, and hear the boundless birds,
and every little while feel the breath of some new
flower! Oh, do you love the spring, and is n't it
brothers and sisters, and blessed, ministering spirits
unto you and me, and us all?

I often see A. — oftener than at sometimes when
friendship drooped a little. Did you ever know
that a flower, once withered and freshened again,
became an immortal flower, — that is, that it rises
again? I think resurrections here are sweeter, it
may be, than the longer and lasting one — for you
expect the one, and only hope for the other. . . .
I will show you the *sunset* if you will sit by me, but

I cannot bring it there, for so much gold is heavy.
Can you see it in Philadelphia?

A rather long interval seems to have elapsed
between the preceding letter and the next,
which was written about July 26, probably
of 1853. The hand-writing is quite different
from the earlier letters, more resembling that
middle period of which an illustration is given
(page 218), yet still somewhat smaller.

The delicate and sunshiny sarcasm in this
note may be the more fully appreciated by
recalling that Emily Dickinson was not yet
twenty-two years old.

Tuesday Evening.

MY DEAR CHILD, — Thank you for that sweet note
which came so long ago, and thank you for asking
me to come and visit you, and thank you for loving
me, long ago, and to-day, and too for all the sweetness, and all the gentleness, and all the tenderness
with which you remember me, — your quaint, old-
fashioned friend.

I wanted very much to write you sooner, and I
tried frequently, but till now in vain, and as I write
to-night, it is with haste, and fear lest something still
detain me. You know, my dear A., that the summer has been warm, that at this pleasant season
we have much company, that this irresolute body
refuses to serve sometimes, and the indignant tenant
can only hold its peace, — all this you know, for I

have often told you, and yet I say it again, if may-hap it persuades you that I do love you indeed, and have not done neglectfully. . . . I think it was in June that your note reached here, and I did snatch a moment to call upon your friend. Yet I went in the dusk, and it was Saturday evening, so even then, A., you see how cares pursued me. I found her very lovely in what she said to me, and I fancied in her face so, although the gentle dusk would draw her curtain close, and I did n't see her clearly. We talked the most of you, — a theme we surely loved, or we had not discussed it in preference to all. I would love to meet her again, and give my love to her, for your sake. You asked me to come and see you — I must speak of that. I thank you, A., but I don't go from home, unless emergency leads me by the hand, and then I do it obstinately, and draw back if I can. Should I ever leave home, which is improbable, I will, with much delight, accept your invitation; till then, my dear A., my warmest thanks are yours, but don't expect me. I'm so old-fash-ioned, darling, that all your friends would stare. I should have to bring my work-bag, and my big spectacles, and I half forgot my grandchildren, and my pincushion, and puss — why, think of it seri-ously, A., — do you think it my *duty* to leave? Will you write me again? Mother and Vinnie send their love, and here's a kiss from me.

Good-night, from

EMILY.

CHAPTER II

To Mr William Austin Dickinson

THE following letters were written to Emily Dickinson's brother between the years 1847 and 1854, the earlier ones being sent from South Hadley, while he was a student in Amherst College. Later ones were written at Amherst, and sent to Boston, where he had charge of a school after graduation, 1851 and 1852; while the latest were addressed to Cambridge during her brother's studies at the Harvard Law School, 1853 and 1854. During these last two years their father, the Hon. Edward Dickinson, was in Congress at Washington.

[South Hadley, Autumn, 1847.]

Thursday Noon.

MY DEAR BROTHER AUSTIN, — I have not really a moment of time in which to write you, and am taking time from 'silent study hours;' but I am determined not to break my promise again, and I generally carry my resolutions into effect. I watched you until you were out of sight Saturday evening, and then went to my room and looked over my treasures; and surely no miser ever counted his heaps of gold with more satisfaction than I gazed upon the presents from home. . . .

I can't tell you now how much good your visit did me.   My spirits have wonderfully lightened since then.   I had a great mind to be homesick after you went home, but I concluded not to, and therefore gave up all homesick feelings.   Was not that a wise determination? . . .

There has been a menagerie here this week. Miss Lyon provided 'Daddy Hawks' as a beau for all the Seminary girls who wished to see the bears and monkeys, and your sister, not caring to go, was obliged to decline the gallantry of said gentleman, — which I fear I may never have another opportunity to avail myself of.   The whole company stopped in front of the Seminary and played for about a quarter of an hour, for the purpose of getting custom in the afternoon, I opine. Almost all the girls went; and I enjoyed the solitude finely.

I want to know when you are coming to see me again, for I want to see you as much as I did before. I went to see Miss F. in her room yesterday. . . . I love her very much, and think I shall love all the teachers when I become better acquainted with them and find out their ways, which, I can assure you, are almost 'past finding out.'

I had almost forgotten to tell you of a dream

which I dreamed last night, and I would like to
have you turn Daniel and interpret it to me ; or if you
don't care about going through all the perils which
he did, I will allow you to interpret it without,
provided you will try to tell no lies about it. Well,
I dreamed a dream, and lo ! father had failed, and
mother said that ' our rye-field, which she and I
planted, was mortgaged to Seth Nims.' I hope it
is not true ; but do write soon and tell me, for you
know I should expire of mortification to have our
rye-field mortgaged, to say nothing of its falling into
the merciless hands of a loco !

Won't you please to tell me when you answer my
letter who the candidate for President is? I have
been trying to find out ever since I came here, and
have not yet succeeded. I don't know anything
more about affairs in the world than if I were in
a trance, and you must imagine with all your
' Sophomoric discernment' that it is but little and
very faint. Has the Mexican War terminated yet,
and how? Are we beaten? Do you know of any
nation about to besiege South Hadley? If so, do
inform me of it, for I would be glad of a chance to
escape, if we are to be stormed. I suppose Miss
Lyon would furnish us all with daggers and order us
to fight for our lives in case such perils should befall
us. . . . Miss F. told me if I was writing to Amherst to send her love. Not specifying to whom,
you may deal it out as your good sense and discretion
prompt. Be a good boy and mind me !

[South Hadley, November 2, 1847.]

Tuesday Noon.

MY DEAR BROTHER AUSTIN, — I have this moment finished my recitation in history, and have a few minutes which I shall occupy in answering your short but welcome letter. You probably heard that I was alive and well yesterday, unless Mr E. Dickinson was robbed of a note whose contents were to that effect. But as robbers are not very plenty now-a-days, I will have no forebodings on that score, for the present. How do you get along without me now, and does ' it seem any more like a funeral ' than it did before your visit to your humble servant in this place? Answer me ! I want much to see you all at home, and expect to three weeks from to-morrow if nothing unusual, like a famine or a pestilence, occurs to prevent my going home. I am anticipating much in seeing you on this week Saturday, and you had better not disappoint me ! for if you do, I will harness the ' furies,' and pursue you with ' a whip of scorpions,' which is even worse, you will find, than the ' long oat ' which you may remember. . . . Tell father I am obliged to him much for his offers of pecuniary assistance, but do not need any. We are furnished with an account-book here, and obliged to put down every mill which we spend, and what we spend it for, and show it to Miss Whitman every Saturday ; so you perceive your sister is learning accounts in addition to the other branches of her education. I am getting along nicely in my studies, and am happy, quite, for me.

Do write a long letter to

Your affectionate sister,

EMILY.

Enclosed with this was a delicately written 'bill of fare' for one of the Seminary dinners.

SOUTH HADLEY SEMINARY

Nov. 2d, 1847

BILL OF FARE

ROAST VEAL
POTATOES
SQUASH
GRAVY
WHEAT AND BROWN BREAD
BUTTER
PEPPER AND SALT

Dessert

APPLE DUMPLING
SAUCE

WATER

Is n't that a dinner fit to set before a king?

[South Hadley, December 11, 1847.]

Saturday, P. M.

MY DEAR BROTHER AUSTIN, — . . . I finished my examination in Euclid last evening, and without a failure at any time. You can easily imagine how glad I am to get through with four books, for you have finished the whole forever. . . . How are you all at home, and what are you doing this vacation? You are reading *Arabian Nights*, according to Viny's statement. I hope you have derived much benefit from their perusal, and presume your powers of imagining will vastly increase thereby. But I must give you a word of advice too. Cultivate your other powers in proportion as you allow imagination to captivate you. Am´ not I a very wise young lady?

I had almost forgotten to tell you what my studies are now — 'better late than never.' They are Chemistry, Physiology, and quarter course in Algebra. I have completed four studies already, and am getting along well. Did you think that it was my birthday yesterday? I don't believe I am *seventeen !* . . .

From your affectionate sister,

EMILY.

[South Hadley, about February 14, 1848.]

Thursday Morn.

MY DEAR AUSTIN, — You will perhaps imagine from my date that I am quite at leisure, and can do

what I please even in the forenoon, but one of our
teachers, who is engaged, received a visit from her
intended quite unexpectedly yesterday afternoon,
and she has gone to her home to show him, I
opine, and will be absent until Saturday.   As I
happen to recite to her in one of my studies, her
absence gives me a little time in which to write.

Your welcome letter found me all engrossed in
the study of sulphuric acid !   I deliberated for a
few moments after its reception on the propriety of
carrying it to Miss Whitman, your friend.   The result of my deliberation was a conclusion to open it
with moderation, peruse its contents with sobriety
becoming my station, and if after a close investigation of its contents I found nothing which savored
of rebellion or an unsubdued will, I would lay it
away in my folio, and forget I had received it.   Are
you not gratified that I am so rapidly gaining correct ideas of female propriety and sedate deport-
ment?   After the proposed examination, finding it
concealed no dangerous sentiments, I with great
gravity deposited it with my other letters, and the
impression that I once had such a letter is entirely
obliterated by the waves of time.

I have been quite lonely since I came back, but
cheered by the thought that I am not to return
another year, I take comfort, and still hope on.
My visit at home was happy, very happy to me ;
and had the idea of in so short a time returning been
constantly in my dreams by night and day, I could

not have been happier. ' There is no rose without a thorn' to me. Home was always dear to me, and dearer still the friends around it; but never did it seem so dear as now. All, all are kind to me, but their tones fall strangely on my ear, and their countenances meet mine not like home-faces, I can assure you most sincerely. Then when tempted to feel sad, I think of the blazing fire and ..ie cheerful meal and the chair empty now I am gone. I can hear the cheerful voices and the merry laugh, and a desolate feeling comes home to my heart, to think I am alone. But my good angel only waits to see the tears coming and then whispers, 'Only this year! only twenty-two weeks more, and then home again you will be to stay.' To you, all busy and excited, I suppose the time flies faster; but to me slowly, very slowly, so that I can see his chariot wheels when they roll along, and himself is often visible. But I will no longer imagine, for your brain is full of *Arabian Nights'* fancies, and it will not do to pour fuel on your already kindled imagination. . . .

I suppose you have written a few and received a quantity of valentines this week. Every night have I looked, and yet in vain, for one of Cupid's messengers. Many of the girls have received very beautiful ones; and I have not quite done hoping for one. Surely my friend *Thomas* has not lost all his former affection for me! I entreat you to tell him I am pining for a valentine. I am sure I

shall not very soon forget last Valentine week, nor
any the sooner the fun I had at that time. . . .
Monday afternoon Mistress Lyon arose in the hall,
and forbade our sending 'any of those foolish notes
called valentines.' But those who were here last
year, knowing her opinions, were sufficiently cunning to write and give them into the care of D.
during the vacation; so that about 150 were de-
spatched on Valentine morn, before orders should
be put down to the contrary effect. Hearing of
this act, Miss Whitman, by and with the advice and
consent of the other teachers, with frowning brow,
sallied over to the Post Office to ascertain, if possible, the number of the valentines, and worse
still, the names of the offenders. Nothing has yet
been heard as to the amount of her information,
but as D. is a good hand to help the girls, and no
one has yet received sentence, we begin to think her
mission unsuccessful. I have not written one, nor
do I intend to.

Your injunction to pile on the wood has not been
unheeded, for we have been obliged to obey it to
keep from freezing up. . . . We cannot have much
more cold weather, I am sure, for spring is near.
. . . Professor Smith preached here last Sabbath,
and such sermons I never heard in my life. We
were all charmed with him, and dreaded to have
him close. . . .

> Your affectionate sister,
>
> EMILY.

[South Hadley, late May, 1848.]

Monday Morn.

MY DEAR AUSTIN,—I received a letter from home
on Saturday by Mr G—— S——, and father wrote
in it that he intended to send for cousin Emily and
myself on Saturday of this week to spend the Sabbath at home. I went to Miss Whitman, after receiving the letter, and asked her if we could go if you
decided to come for us. She seemed stunned by my
request, and could not find utterance to an answer
for some time. At length she said, 'Did you not
know it was contrary to the rules of the Seminary to
ask to be absent on the Sabbath?' I told her I did
not. She then took a Catalogue from her table, and
showed me the law in full at the last part of it. She
closed by saying that we could not go, and I returned
to my room without farther ado. So you see I shall
be deprived of the pleasure of a visit home, and you
that of seeing me, if I may have the presumption to
call it a pleasure! The teachers are not willing to
let the girls go home this term as it is the last one,
and as I have only nine weeks more to spend here,
we had better be contented to obey the commands.
We shall only be the more glad to see one another
after a longer absence, that will be all. I was highly
edified with your imaginative note to me, and think
your flights of fancy indeed wonderful at your age!
When are you coming to see me — it would be very
pleasant to us to receive a visit from your highness

if you can be absent from home long enough for such
a purpose. . . . I can't write longer.

Your affectionate sister,

EMILIE.

The next letter was written three years later,
and sent to Boston.

[Amherst, early in 1851.]

Sunday Evening.

It might not come amiss, dear Austin, to have a tiding or two concerning our state and feelings, particularly when we remember that 'Jamie has gone awa'.'

Our state is pretty comfortable, and our feelings
are somewhat solemn, which we account for satis-
factorily by calling to mind the fact that it is the
Sabbath day. Whether a certain passenger in a certain yesterday's stage has any sombre effect on our
once merry household or the reverse, 'I dinna choose
to tell,' but be the case as it may, we are rather a
crestfallen company, to make the best of us, and
what with the sighing wind, the sobbing rain, and
the whining of Nature generally, we can hardly contain ourselves, and I only hope and trust that your
this-evening's-lot is cast in far more cheery places
than the ones you leave behind.

We are enjoying this evening what is called a
'northeast storm' — a little north of east in case
you are pretty definite.   Father thinks it's 'amazin'
raw,' and I'm half disposed to think that he's in the
right about it, though I keep pretty dark and don't

say much about it! Vinnie is at the instrument, humming a pensive air concerning a young lady who thought she was 'almost there.' Vinnie seems much grieved, and I really suppose *I* ought to betake myself to weeping; I'm pretty sure that I *shall* if she don't abate her singing.

Father's just got home from meeting and Mr Boltwood's, found the last quite comfortable and the first not quite so well. . . . There has been not much stirring since when you went away — I should venture to say prudently that matters had come to a stand — unless something new 'turns up,' I cannot see anything to prevent a quiet season. Father takes care of the doors and mother of the windows, and Vinnie and I are secure against all outward attacks. If we can get our hearts 'under,' I don't have much to fear — I've got all but three feelings down, if I can only keep them! . . .

I shall think of you to-morrow with four and twenty Irish boys all in a row. I miss you very much — I put on my bonnet to-night, opened the gate very desperately, and for a little while the suspense was terrible — I think I was held in check by some invisible agent, for I returned to the house without having done any harm!

If I hadn't been afraid that you would 'poke fun' at my feelings, I had written a sincere letter, but since 'the world is hollow, and dollie's stuffed with sawdust,' I really do not think we had better expose our feelings. . . .

                    Your dear sister,   EMILY.

[Amherst, 1851.]

Sunday Evening.

I received your letter, Austin, permit me to thank you for it and to request some more as soon as it's convenient — permit me to accord with your discreet opinion concerning Swedish Jennie, and to commend the heart brave enough to express it — combating the opinion of two civilized worlds and New York into the bargain must need considerable daring — indeed, it had never occurred to me that amidst the hallelujahs one tongue would dare be dumb, and much less, I assure you, that this dissenting one should be my romantic brother ! For I had looked for delight and a very high style of rapture in such a youth as you. . . .

We have all been rather piqued at Jennie's singing so well, and this first calumnious whisper pleases us so well, we rejoice that we did n't come — our visit is yet before us. . . . You have n't told us yet as you promised about your home — what kind of people they are — whether you find them pleasant — whether those timid gentlemen have yet 'found tongues to say.' Do you find the life and living any more annoying than you at first expected — do you light upon any friends to help the time away — have you whipped any more bad boys — all these are solemn questions, pray give them proper heed !

Two weeks of your time are gone; I can't help wondering sometimes if you would love to see us,

and come to this still home. . . . A Senior levee
was held at Professor and Mrs Haven's on Tuesday
of last week — Vinnie played pretty well. There's
another at the President's this next Friday evening.
Clarum et venerabile Seniors !

[Amherst, March, 1851.]

Sunday Afternoon.

. . . It's a glorious afternoon — the sky is blue
and warm — the wind blows just enough to keep the
clouds sailing, and the sunshine — oh *such* sunshine !
It isn't like gold, for gold is dim beside it ; it isn't
like anything which you or I have seen ! It seems
to me 'Ik Marvel' was born on such a day ; I only
wish you were here. Such days were made on purpose for you and me ; then what in the world are
you gone for? Oh, dear, I do not know, but this I
do know, that if wishing would bring you home, you
were here to-day. Is it pleasant in Boston? *Of
course* it isn't, though. I might have known more
than to make such an inquiry. No doubt the streets
are muddy, and the sky some dingy hue, and I can
think just how everything bangs and rattles, and
goes rumbling along through stones and plank and
clay ! I don't feel as if I could have you there, possibly, another day. I'm afraid you'll turn into a
bank, or a Pearl Street counting-room, if you have
not already assumed some monstrous shape, living
in such a place.

Let me see — April ; three weeks until April —

the very first of April — well, perhaps that will do,
only be sure of the week, the *whole* week, and nothing but the week.   If they make new arrangements,
give my respects to them, and tell them old arrangements are good enough for you, and you will have
them ; then if they raise the wind, why, let it blow
— there 's nothing more excellent than a breeze
now and then !

What a time we shall have Fast day, after we get
home from meeting — why, it makes me dance to
think of it ; and Austin, if I dance so many days
beforehand, what will become of me when the hour
really arrives?   I don't know, I 'm sure ; and I don't
care, much, for that or for anything else but get you
home. . . . Much love from mother and Vinnie ;
we are now pretty well, and our hearts are set on
April, the *very first* of April !

EMILIE.

[Amherst, late March, 1851.]

Thursday Night.

DEAR AUSTIN, — . . . I have read *Ellen Middle-
ton*.   I need n't tell you I like it, nor need I tell
you more, for you know already.

I thank you more and more for all the pleasures
you give me — I can give you nothing, Austin, but
a warm and grateful heart that is yours now and
always.   Love from all.

EMILIE.

Only think, you are coming Saturday !   I don't

know why it is that it 's always *Sunday* immediately you get home. I will arrange it differently. If it was n't twelve o'clock I would stay longer.

[Amherst, June 16, 1851.]

Sunday Evening.

. . . I 'm glad you are so well pleased, I 'm glad you are *not* delighted. I would not that foreign places should wear the smile of home. We are quite alarmed for the *boys* — hope you won't kill or pack away any of 'em — so near Dr Webster's bones 't is not strange you have had temptations ! . . . The country 's still just now, and the severities alluded to will have a salutary influence in waking the people up. Speaking of *getting up*, how early are metropolitans expected to wake up, especially young men — more especially school-masters? I miss my 'department' mornings. I lay it quite to heart that I 've no one to wake up. *Your* room looks lonely enough, I do not love to go in there ; whenever I pass through I find I 'gin to whistle, as we read that little boys are wont to do in the graveyard. I am going to set out crickets as soon as I find time, that they by their shrill singing shall help disperse the gloom ; will they grow if I transplant them?

You importune me for news ; I am very sorry to say 'Vanity of vanities' there 's no such thing as news — it is almost time for the cholera, and then things will take a start ! . . . All of the folks send love.

Your affectionate

EMILY.

[July 5, 1851.]

Sunday Afternoon.

I have just come in from church very hot and faded. . . . Our church grows interesting — Zion lifts her head — I overhear remarks signifying Jerusalem, — I do not feel at liberty to say any more to-day!

. . . I wanted to write you Friday, the night of Jennie Lind, but reaching home past midnight, and my room sometime after, encountering several perils starting and on the way, among which a kicking horse, an inexperienced driver, a number of Jove's thunderbolts, and a very terrible rain, are worthy to have record. All of us went — just four — add an absent individual and that will make full five. The concert commenced at eight, but knowing the world was *hollow* we thought we'd start at six, and come up with everybody that meant to come up with us; we had proceeded some steps when one of the beasts showed symptoms; and just by the blacksmith's shop exercises commenced, consisting of kicking and plunging on the part of the horse, and whips and moral suasion from the gentleman who drove — the horse refused to proceed, and your respected family with much chagrin dismounted, advanced to the hotel, and for a season halted; another horse procured, we were politely invited to take our seats, and proceed, which we refused to do till the animal was warranted. About half through

our journey thunder was said to be heard, and a
suspicious cloud came travelling up the sky. What
words express our horror when rain began to fall,
in drops, sheets, cataracts — what fancy conceive
of drippings and of drenchings which we met on
the way; how the stage and its mourning captives
drew up at Warner's Hotel; how all of us alighted,
and were conducted in, — how the rain did not
abate, — how we walked in silence to the old Ed-
wards church[1] and took our seats in the same —
how Jennie came out like a child and sang and sang
again — how bouquets fell in showers, and the roof
was rent with applause — how it thundered outside,
and inside with the thunder of God and of men —
judge ye which was the loudest; how we all loved
Jennie Lind, but not accustomed oft to her manner
of singing did n't fancy *that* so well as we did *her*.
No doubt it was very fine, but take some notes from
her *Echo*, the bird sounds from the *Bird Song*, and
some of her curious trills, and I 'd rather have a
Yankee.

Herself and not her music was what we seemed
to love — she has an air of exile in her mild blue
eyes, and a something sweet and touching in her
native accent which charms her many friends. *Give
me my thatched cottage* as she sang she grew so
earnest she seemed half lost in song, and for a tran-
sient time I fancied she *had* found it and would be

---

[1] Evidently a slip of the pen, as Jenny Lind sang in the
old First Church at Northampton on that occasion.

seen 'na mair;' and then her foreign accent made
her again a wanderer — we will talk about her sometime when you come. Father sat all the evening
looking *mad*, and yet so much amused you would
have *died* a-laughing. . . . It was n't sarcasm exactly, nor it was n't disdain, it was infinitely funnier
than either of those virtues, as if old Abraham
had come to see the show, and thought it was all
very well, but a little excess of *monkey!* She took
$4,000 for tickets at Northampton aside from all
expenses. . . .

About our coming to Boston — we think we shall
probably come — we want to see our friends, yourself and Aunt L.'s family. We don't care a fig
for the Museum, the stillness, or Jennie Lind. . . .
Love from us all.

Your affectionate sister,

EMILY.

[Late July, 1851.]

Sunday Evening.

. . . Oh how I wish I could see your world and
its little kingdoms, and I wish I could see the king
— Stranger! he was my brother! I fancy little boys
of several little sizes, some of them clothed in blue
cloth, some of them clad in gray — I seat them
round on benches in the school-room of my mind
— then I set them all to shaking — on peril of their
lives that they move their lips or whisper; then
I clothe you with authority and empower you to

punish, and to enforce the law, I call you 'Rabbi, Master,' and the picture is complete ! It would seem very funny, say for Vinnie and me to come round as Committee — we should enjoy the terrors of fifty little boys, and any specimens of discipline in your way would be a rare treat for us. I should love to know how you managed — whether government as a science is laid down and executed, or whether you *cuff* and *thrash* as the occasion dictates; whether you use *pure* law as in the case of commanding, or whether you enforce it by means of sticks and stones as in the case of agents. I suppose you have authority bounded but by their lives. . . . I should think you'd be tired of school and teaching and such hot weather. I really wish you were here, and the Endicott school where you found it. Whenever we go to ride in our beautiful family carriage we think if 'wishes were horses' we four 'beggars would ride.' We shall enjoy brimful everything now but half full, and to have you home once more will be like living again.

We are having a pleasant summer — without one of the five it is yet a lonely one. Vinnie says sometimes — Did n't we have a brother — it seems to me we did, his name was Austin — we call but he answers not again — echo, Where is Austin? laughing, 'Where *is* Austin?' . . . I wish they need not exhibit just for once in the year, and give you up on Saturday instead of the next week Wednesday; but keep your courage up and show forth those

Emerald Isles till school committees and mayors
are blinded with the dazzling !   Would n't I love to
be there ! . . .

Our apples are ripening fast.   I am fully convinced that with your approbation they will not only
pick themselves, but arrange one another in baskets
and present themselves to be eaten.

Love from all.

EMILIE.

[August, 1851.]

Sunday Afternoon.

At my old stand again, dear Austin, and happy
as a queen to know that while I speak those whom
I love are listening, and I am happier still if I shall
make them happy.

I have just finished reading your letter which was
brought in since church.   I like it grandly — very
— because it is so long, and also it 's *so* funny — we
have all been laughing till the old house rung again
at your delineation of men, women, and things.   I
feel quite like retiring in presence of one so grand,
and casting my small lot among small birds and
fishes ; you say you don't comprehend me, you
want a simpler style — gratitude indeed for all my
fine philosophy !   I strove to be exalted, thinking I
might reach *you*, and while I pant and struggle and
climb the nearest cloud, you walk out very leisurely
in your slippers from Empyrean, and without the
slightest notice, request me to get down !   As simple as you please, the simplest sort of simple — I 'll

be a little ninny, a little pussy catty, a little Red Riding Hood; I'll wear a bee in my bonnet, and a rose-bud in my hair, and what remains to do you shall be told hereafter.

Your letters are richest treats, send them always just such warm days — they are worth a score of fans and many refrigerators — the only difficulty they are so *queer*, and laughing such hot weather is anything but amusing. A little more of earnest, and a little less of jest until we are out of August, and then you may joke as freely as the father of rogues himself, and we will banish care, and daily die a-laughing!

It is very hot here now; I don 't believe it 's any hotter in Boston than it is here. . . . Vinnie suggests that she may sometimes occur to mind when you would like more collars made. I told her I would n't tell you — I have n't, however, decided whether I will or not.

I often put on five knives and forks, and another tumbler, forgetting for the moment that 'we are not all here.' It occurs to me, however, and I remove the extra, and brush a tear away in memory of my brother.

We miss you now and always. When God bestows but three, and one of those is withdrawn, the others are left alone. . . . Father is as uneasy when you are gone away as if you catch a trout and put him in Sahara. When you first went away he came home very frequently — walked gravely

towards the barn, and returned looking very stately
— then strode away down street as if the foe was
coming; *now* he is more resigned — contents himself by fancying that 'we shall hear to-day,' and
then when we do not hear, he wags his head profound, and thinks without a doubt there will be
news 'to-morrow.' 'Once one is two,' once one will
be two — ah, I have it here !

I wish you could have some cherries — if there
was any way we would send you a basket of them —
they are very large and delicious, and are just ripening now. Little Austin Grout comes every day to
pick them, and mother takes great comfort in calling him by name, from vague association with her
departed boy. Austin, to tell the truth, it is very
still and lonely — I do wish you were here. . . .
The railroad is 'a-workin'.' My love to all my
friends. I am on my way downstairs to put the
tea-kettle boiling — writing and taking tea cannot
sympathize. If you forget me now, your right hand
shall its cunning.

EMILIE.

[Written after a visit of the sisters in Boston. Amherst,
September 24, 1851.]

Tuesday Evening.

We have got home, dear Austin. It is very lonely
here — I have tried to make up my mind which was
better, home and parents and country, or city and
smoke and dust shared with the only being whom I

can call my brother. The scales *don't* poise very evenly, but so far as I can judge, the balance is in your favor. The folks are much more lonely than while we were away — they say they seemed to feel that we were straying together and together would return, and the unattended sisters seemed very sad to them. . . . They have had a number of friends to call and visit with them. Mother never was busier than while we were away — what with fruit and plants and chickens and sympathizing friends she really was so hurried she hardly knew what to do.

Vinnie and I came safely, and met with no mishap — the bouquet was not withered nor was the bottle cracked. It was fortunate for the freight car that Vinnie and I were there, ours being the only baggage passing along the line. The folks looked very funny who travelled with us that day — they were dim and faded, like folks passed away — the conductor seemed so grand with about half a dozen tickets which he dispersed and demanded in a very small space of time — I judged that the minority were travelling that day, and could n't hardly help smiling at our ticket friend, however sorry I was at the small amount of people passing along his way. He looked as if he wanted to make an apology for not having more travellers to keep him company.

The route and the cars seemed strangely — there were no boys with fruit, there were no boys with pamphlets ; one fearful little fellow ventured into the car with what appeared to be publications and tracts; he offered them to no one, and no one inquired for them, and he seemed greatly relieved that no one wanted to buy them. . . . Mother sends much love, and Vinnie.

Your lonely sister,

EMILY.

[Amherst, Autumn, 1851.]

Saturday Morn.

DEAR AUSTIN, — I've been trying to think this morning how many weeks it was since you went away — I fail in calculations; it seems so long to me since you went back to school that I set down days for years, and weeks for a score of years — not reckoning time by minutes, I don't know what to think of such great discrepancies between the actual hours and those which 'seem to be.' It may seem long to you since you returned to Boston — how I wish you would stay and never go back again. Everything is so still here, and the clouds are cold and gray — I think it will rain soon. Oh, I am so lonely! . . . You had a windy evening going back to Boston, and we thought of you many times and hoped you would not be cold. Our fire burned so cheerfully I couldn't help thinking of how many were here, and how many were away, and I wished so many times during that long evening that the door would open and you come walking in. Home is a holy thing, — nothing of doubt or distrust can enter its blessed portals. I feel it more and more as the great world goes on, and one and another forsake in whom you place your trust, here seems indeed to be a bit of Eden which not the sin of any can utterly destroy, — smaller it is indeed, and it may be less fair, but fairer it is and brighter than all the world beside.

I hope this year in Boston will not impair your health, and I hope you will be as happy as you used to be before. I don't wonder it makes you sober to leave this blessed air — if it were in my power I would on every morning transmit its purest breaths fragrant and cool to you. How I wish you could have it — a thousand little winds waft it to me this morning, fragrant with forest leaves and bright autumnal berries. I would be willing to give you my portion for to-day, and take the salt sea's breath in its bright, bounding stead. . . .

> Your affectionate
>
> EMILY.

. . . Mother sends her love and your waistcoat, thinking you'll like the one, and quite likely need the other.

[Amherst, October 2, 1851.]

Wednesday Noon.

We are just through dinner, Austin, I want to write so much that I omit digestion, and a dyspepsia will probably be the result. . . . I received your letter

yesterday. . . . You say we must n't trouble to send
you any fruit, also your clothes must give us no
uneasiness. I don't ever want to have you say any
more such things. They make me feel like crying.
If you 'd only teased us for it, and declared that you
would have it, I should n't have cared so much that
we could find no way to send you any, but you
resign so cheerfully your birthright of purple grapes,
and do not so much as murmur at the departing
peaches, that I hardly can taste the one or drink the
juice of the other. They are so beautiful, Austin, —
we have such an abundance 'while you perish with
hunger.'

I do hope some one will make up a mind to go
before our peaches are quite gone. The world is
full of people travelling everywhere, until it occurs to
you that you will send an errand, and then by 'hook
or crook' you can't find any traveller who, for money
or love, can be induced to go and carry the oppro-
brious package. It 's a very selfish age, that is all I
can say about it. Mr Storekeeper S—— has been
'almost persuaded' to go, but I believe he has. put
it off 'till a more convenient season,' so to show
my disapprobation I sha'n't buy any more gloves at
Mr S——'s store ! Don't you think it will seem
very cutting to see me pass by his goods and purchase at Mr K——'s? I don't think I shall retract
should he regret his course and decide to go to-
morrow, because it is the principle of disappointing
people which I disapprove ! . . .

The peaches are very large — one side a rosy cheek, and the other a golden, and that peculiar coat of velvet and of down which makes a peach so beautiful. The grapes, too, are fine, juicy, and *such* a purple — I fancy the robes of kings are not a tint more royal. The vine looks like a kingdom, with ripe round grapes for kings, and hungry mouths for subjects — the first instance on record of subjects devouring kings! You *shall* have some grapes, dear Austin, if I have to come on foot in order to bring them to you.

The apples are very fine — it is n't quite time to pick them — the cider is almost done — we shall have some I guess by Saturday, at any rate Sunday noon. The vegetables are not gathered, but will be before very long. The horse is doing nicely; he travels ' like a bird ' to use a favorite phrase of your delighted mother's. You ask about the leaves — shall I say they are falling? They had begun to fall before Vinnie and I came home, and we walked up the steps through little brown ones rustling. . . .

Vinnie tells me she has detailed the news — she reserved the deaths for me, thinking I might fall short of my usual letter somewhere. In accordance with her wishes I acquaint you with the decease of your aged friend Deacon ———. He had no disease that we know of, but gradually went out. . . . Monday evening we were all startled by a violent church-bell ringing, and thinking of nothing but fire, rushed out in the street to see. The sky was a beautiful

red, bordering on a crimson, and rays of a gold pink
color were constantly shooting off from a kind of sun
in the centre.   People were alarmed at this beautiful
phenomenon, supposing that fires somewhere were
coloring the sky.   The exhibition lasted for nearly
fifteen minutes, and the streets were full of people
wondering and admiring.   Father happened to see
it among the very first, and rang the bell himself to
call attention to it.   You will have a full account
from the pen of Mr Trumbull, who, I have not a
doubt, was seen with a long lead pencil a-noting
down the sky at the time of its highest glory. . . .
You will be here now so soon — we are impatient
for it — we want to see you, Austin, how much I
cannot say here.
Your affectionate

EMILY.

[Amherst, early October, 1851.]

Friday Morning.

DEAR AUSTIN, — . . . I would not spend much
strength upon those little school-boys — you will
need it all for something better and braver after you
get away.   It would rejoice my heart if on some
pleasant morning you 'd turn the school-room key
on Irish boys, nurse and all, and walk away to free-
dom and the sunshine here at home.   Father says
all Boston would n't be a temptation to you another
year — I wish it would not tempt you to stay another
day.   Oh, Austin, it is wrong to tantalize you so while

you are braving all things in trying to fulfil duty.
Duty is black and brown — home is bright and shining, 'and the spirit and the bride say com , and let
him that' wandereth come, fo·   .. old ..i things
are ready.' We are having such lovely weather —
the air is as sweet and still — now and then a gay
leaf falling — the crickets sing all day long — high
in a crimson tree a belated bird is singing — a
thousand little painters are tingeing hill and dale. I
admit now, Austin, that autumn is *most* beautiful,
and spring is but the least, yet they ' differ as
stars' in their distinctive glories. How happy if you
were here to share these pleasures with us — the
fruit should be more sweet, and the dying day more
golden — merrier the falling nut if with you we
gathered it and hid it down deep in the abyss of
basket ; but you complain not, wherefore do we?

Tuesday evening we had a beautiful time reading
and talking of the good times of last summer, and
we anticipated — boasted ourselves of to-morrow —
of the future we created, and all of us went to ride
in an air-bubble for a carriage. We cherish all the
past, we glide a-down the present, awake yet dreaming ; but the future of ours together — there the bird
sings loudest, and the sun shines always there. . . .

I had a dissertation from E. C. a day or two ago
— don't know which was the author, Plato or Socrates — rather think Jove had a finger in it. . . .
They all send their love. Vinnie sends hers. How
soon you will be here ! Days, flee away — 'lest with

a whip of scorpions 'I overtake your lingering.' I am in a hurry — this pen is too slow for me — 'it hath done what it could.'

Your affectionate

EMILY.

[Amherst, before 'Cattle Show,' 1851.]

Friday Morning.

. . . The breakfast is so warm, and pussy is here a-singing, and the tea-kettle sings too, as if to see which was loudest, and I am so afraid lest kitty should be beaten — yet a shadow falls upon my morning picture — where is the youth so bold, the bravest of our fold — a seat is empty here — spectres sit in your chair, and now and then nudge father with their long, bony elbows. I wish you were here, dear Austin; the dust falls on the bureau in your deserted room, and gay, frivolous spiders spin away in the corners. I don't go there after dark whenever I can help it, for the twilight seems to pause there, and I am half afraid; and if ever I have to go, I hurry with all my might, and never look behind me, for I know who I should see.

Before next Tuesday — oh, before the coming stage, will I not brighten and brush it, and open the long-closed blinds, and with a sweeping broom will I not bring each spider down from its home so high, and tell it it may come back again when master has gone — and oh, I will bid it to be a tardy spider, to tarry on the way; and I will think my eye is fuller than sometimes, though *why* I cannot tell, when it shall rap on the window and come to live again. I am so happy when I know how soon you are coming that I put away my sewing and go out in the yard to think. I have tried to delay the frosts, I have coaxed the fading flowers, I thought I *could* detain a few of the crimson leaves until you had smiled upon them; but their companions call them, and they cannot stay away.

You will find the blue hills, Austin, with the autumnal shadows silently sleeping on them, and there will be a glory lingering round the day, so you'll know autumn has been here; and the setting sun will tell you, if you don't get home till evening. . . . I thank you for such a long letter, and yet if I might choose, the next should be a longer. I think a letter just about three days long would make me happier than any other kind of one, if you please, — dated at Boston, but thanks be to our Father you may conclude it here. Everything has changed since my other letter, — the doors are shut this morning, and all the kitchen wall is covered with chilly flies who are trying to warm themselves, — poor things, they do not understand that there are no summer mornings remaining to them and me, and they have a bewildered air which is really very droll, did n't one feel sorry for them. You would say 't was a gloomy morning if you were sitting here, — the frost has been severe, and the few lingering leaves seem anxious to be going, and wrap their faded cloaks more closely about them as if to shield them from the chilly northeast wind. The earth looks like some poor old lady who by dint of pains has bloomed e'en till now, yet in a forgetful moment a few silver hairs from out her cap come stealing, and she tucks them back so hastily and thinks nobody sees. The cows are going to pasture, and little boys with their hands in their pockets are whistling to try to keep warm. Don't think that the sky will frown so the day when you come home! She will smile and look happy, and be full of sunshine then, and even should she frown upon her child returning, there is another sky, ever serene and fair, and there is another sunshine, though it be darkness there; never mind faded forests, Austin, never mind silent fields — *here* is a little forest, whose leaf is ever green; here is a brighter garden, where not a frost has been; in its unfading flowers I hear the bright bee hum; prithee, my brother, into *my* garden come!

Your very affectionate sister.

[November, 1851.]

Thursday Evening.

DEAR AUSTIN, — Something seems to whisper ' He is thinking of home this evening,' perhaps because it rains, perhaps because it 's evening and the orchestra of winds perform their strange, sad music. I would n't wonder if home were thinking of him; and it seems so natural for one to think of the other, perhaps it is no superstition or omen of this evening, — no omen 'at all, at all,' as Mrs Mack would say.

Father is staying at home this evening it is so inclement — Vinnie diverts his mind with little snatches of music; and mother mends a garment to make it snugger for you — and what do you think *I* do among this family circle? I am thinking of you with all my might, and it just occurs to me to note a few of my thoughts for your own inspection. 'Keeping a diary' is not familiar to me as to your sister Vinnie, but her own bright example is quite a comfort to me, so I'll try.

I waked up this morning thinking for all the world I had had a letter from you — just as the seal was breaking, father rapped at my door. I was sadly disappointed not to go on and read; but when the four black horses came trotting into town, and their load was none the heavier by a tiding for me — I was not disappointed then, it was harder to me than had I been disappointed. . . . I found I had made no provision for any such time as that. . . . The weather has been unpleasant ever since you went away — Monday morning we waked up in the midst of a furious snow-storm — the snow was the depth of an inch; oh, it looked so wintry! By-and-by the sun came out, but the wind blew violently and it grew so cold that we gathered all the quinces, put up the stove in the sitting-room,

and bade the world good-by.   Kind clouds came
over at evening; still the sinking thermometer gave
terrible signs of what would be on the morning.
At last the morning came, laden with mild south
winds, and the winds have brought the rain, so
here we are. . . . Your very hasty letter just at
your return rejoiced us — that you were ' better —
happier — heartier.'   What made you think of such
beautiful words to tell us how you were, and how
cheerful you were feeling?   It did us a world of
good.   How little the scribe thinks of the value of
his line — how many eager eyes will search its every
meaning, how much swifter the strokes of 'the
little mystic clock, no human eye hath seen, which
ticketh on and ticketh on, from morning until e'en.'
If it were not that I could write you, you could not go
away; therefore pen and ink are very excellent things.

We had new brown bread for tea — when it came
smoking on and we sat around the table, how I did
wish a slice could be reserved for you!   You shall
have as many loaves as we have eaten slices if you
will but come home.   This suggests Thanksgiving,
you will soon be here; then I can't help thinking
of how, when we rejoice, so many hearts are breaking next Thanksgiving day.   What will you say,
Austin, if I tell you that Jennie Grout and merry
Martha Kingman will spend the day above?   They
are not here — ' While we delayed to let them
forth, angels beyond stayed for them.' . . .

Your affectionate

EMILY.

[Amherst, November 17, 1851.]

Sunday Afternoon.

DEAR AUSTIN, — We have just got home from meeting — it is very windy and cold — the hills from our kitchen window are just crusted with snow, which with their blue mantillas makes them seem so beautiful. You sat just here last Sunday, where I am sitting now ; and our voices were nimbler than our pens can be, if they try never so hardly. I should be quite sad to-day, thinking about last Sunday, did n't another Sabbath smile at me so pleasantly, promising me on its word to present you here again when ' six days' work is done.'

Father and mother sit in state in the sitting-room perusing such papers, only, as they are well assured, have nothing carnal in them ; Vinnie is eating an apple which makes me think of gold, and accompanying it with her favorite *Observer*, which, if you recollect, deprives us many a time of her sisterly society. Pussy has n't returned from the afternoon assembly, so you have us all just as we are at present. We were very glad indeed to hear from you so soon, glad that a cheerful fire met you at the door. I *do* well remember how chilly the west wind blew, and how everything shook and rattled before I went to sleep, and I often thought of you in the midnight car, and hoped you were not lonely. . . . We are thinking most of Thanksgiving than anything else just now — how

full will be the circle, less then by none — how the
things will smoke — how the board will groan with
the thousand savory viands — how when the day is
done, lo, the evening cometh, laden with merrie
laugh and happy conversation, and then the sleep
and the dream each of a knight or ' Ladie '— how
I love to see them, a beautiful company coming
down the hill which men call the Future, with their
hearts full of joy and their hands of gladness.
Thanksgiving indeed to a family united once more
together before they go away. . . . Don't mind the
days — some of them are long ones, but who cares
for length when breadth is in store for him? Or
who minds the cross who knows he 'll have a
crown? I wish I could imbue you with all the
strength and courage which can be given men — I
wish I could assure you of the constant remembrance of those you leave at home — I wish — but
oh ! how vainly — that I could bring you back
again and never more to stray. You are tired now,
dear Austin, with my incessant din, but I can't help
saying any of these things.

The very warmest love from Vinnie and every one
of us. I am never ready to go.

Reluctant

EMILY.

[December, 1851].

Monday Morning.

DEAR AUSTIN, — . . . I was so glad to get your
letter. I had been making calls all Saturday afternoon, and came home very tired, and a little
disconsolate, so your letter was more than welcome. . . . Oh Austin, you don't know how we all
wished for you yesterday. We had such a splendid
sermon from Professor Park — I never heard anything like it, and don't expect to again, till we stand
at the great white throne, and 'he reads from the
Book, the Lamb's Book.' The students and chapel
people all came to our church, and it was very full,
and still, so still the buzzing of a fly would have
boomed like a cannon. And when it was all over,
and that wonderful man sat down, people stared at
each other, and looked as wan and wild as if they
had seen a spirit, and wondered they had not died.
How I wish you had heard him — I thought of it
all the time. . . .

Affectionately,

EMILIE.

[Amherst, January, 1852.]

Monday Morning.`

Did you think I was tardy, Austin? For two Sunday afternoons it has been so cold and cloudy that
I did n't feel in my very happiest mood, and so I
did not write until next Monday morning, determin-

ing in my heart never to write to you in any but
cheerful spirits.

Even this morning, Austin, I am not in merry
case, for it snows slowly and solemnly, and hardly
an outdoor thing can be seen a-stirring — now and
then a man goes by with a large cloak wrapped
around him, and shivering at that; and now and
then a stray kitten out on some urgent errand creeps
through the flakes and crawls so fast as *may* crawl
half frozen away.   I am glad for the sake of your
body that you are not here this morning, for it is a
trying time for fingers and toes — for the heart's
sake I would verily have you here.   You know there
are winter mornings when the cold without only
adds to the warm within, and the more it snows and
the harder it blows brighter the fires blaze, and
chirps more merrily the 'cricket on the hearth.'
It is hardly cheery enough for such a scene this
morning, and yet methinks it would be if you were
only here.   The future full of sleigh-rides would
chase the gloom from our minds which only deepens
and darkens with every flake that falls.

Black Fanny would 'toe the mark' if you should
be here to-morrow; but as the prospects are, I presume Black Fanny's hoofs will not attempt to fly.
Do you have any snow in Boston?   Enough for a
ride, I hope, for the sake of 'Auld Lang Syne.'
Perhaps the 'ladie' of curls would not object to a
drive. . . . We miss you more and more, we do
not become accustomed to separation from you.

I almost wish sometimes we need n't miss you so much, since duty claims a year of you entirely to herself; and then again I think that it is pleasant to miss you if you must go away, and I would not have it otherwise, even if I could. In every pleasure and pain you come up to our minds so wishfully — we know you 'd enjoy our joy, and if you were with us, Austin, we could bear little trials more cheerfully. . . . When I know of anything funny I am just as apt to cry, far more so than to laugh, for I know who loves jokes best, and who is not here to enjoy them. We don't have many jokes, though, now, it is pretty much all sobriety ; and we do not have much poetry, father having made up his mind that it's pretty much all real life.   Father's real life and mine sometimes come into collision but as yet escape unhurt. . . . I am so glad you are well and in such happy spirits — both happy and well is a great comfort to us when you are far away.

EMILIE.

[February 6, 1852.]

Friday Morning.

. . . Since we have written you the grand railroad decision is made, and there is great rejoicing throughout this town and the neighboring; that is, Sunderland, Montague, and Belchertown. Everybody is wide awake, everything is stirring, the streets are full of people walking cheeringly, and you should really be here to partake of the jubilee.   The event was celebrated by D. Warner and cannon; and the silent satisfaction in the hearts of all is its crowning attestation.

Father is really sober from excessive satisfaction, and bears his honors with a most becoming air. Nobody believes it yet, it seems like a fairy tale, a most miraculous event in the lives of us all. The men begin working next week; only think of it, Austin; why, I verily believe we shall fall down and worship the first 'son of Erin' that comes, and the first sod he turns will be preserved as an emblem of the struggle and victory of our heroic fathers. Such old fellows as Col. S. and his wife fold their arms complacently and say, 'Well, I declare, we have got it after all.' Got it, *you* good-for-nothings! and so we have, in spite of sneers and pities and insults from all around; and we will keep it too, in spite of earth and heaven! How I wish you were here — it is really too bad, Austin, at such a time as now. I miss your big hurrahs, and the famous stir you make upon all such occasions; but it is a comfort to know that you are here — that your whole soul is here, and though apparently absent, yet present in the highest and the truest sense. . . . Take good care of yourself, Austin, and think much of us all, for we do so of you.

Emilie.

Several subsequent letters, all piquant and breezy, but dealing quite entirely with family

matters, experiences with callers, and other
personal subjects, have been omitted.

[March 24, 1852.]

Wednesday Morn.

You would n't think it was spring, Austin, if you
were at home this morning, for we had a great snow-
storm yesterday, and things are all white this morning. It sounds funny enough to hear birds singing
and sleigh-bells at a time. But it won't last long,
so you need n't think 't will be winter at the time
when you come home.

I waited a day or two, thinking I might hear from
you, but you will be looking for me, and wondering
where I am, so I sha'n't wait any longer. We 're
rejoiced that you 're coming home — the first thing
we said to father when he got out of the stage was
to ask if you were coming. I was sure you would
all the while, for father said ' of course you would,'
he should ' consent to no other arrangement,' and
as you say, Austin, ' what father says he means.'
How very soon it will be now — why, when I really
think of it, how near and how happy it is ! My
heart grows light so fast that I could mount a grasshopper and gallop around the world, and not fatigue
him any ! The sugar weather holds on, and I do
believe it will stay until you come. . . . ' Mrs S.' is
very feeble ; ' can't bear allopathic treatment, can't
have homœopathic, don't want hydropathic,' oh,

what a pickle she is in.   Should n't think she would
deign to live, it is so decidedly vulgar !   They have
not yet concluded where to move — Mrs W. will
perhaps obtain board in the celestial city, but I 'm
sure I can't imagine what will become of the rest.
. . . Much love from us all.

EMILIE.

[May 10, 1852.]

Monday Morning, 5 *o'c.*

DEAR AUSTIN, — . . . Vinnie will tell you all the
news, so I will take a little place to describe a thun-
der-shower which occurred yesterday afternoon, —
the very first of the season.   Father and Vinnie
were at meeting, mother asleep in her room, and
I at work by my window on a 'Lyceum lecture.'
The air was really scorching, the sun red and hot,
and you know just how the birds sing before a thun-
der-storm, a sort of hurried and agitated song —
pretty soon it began to thunder, and the great
'cream-colored heads' peeped out of their windows.   Then came the wind and rain, and I hurried
around the house to shut all the doors and windows.   I wish you had seen it come, so cool and
so refreshing — and everything glistening from it as
with a golden dew — I thought of you all the time.
This morning is fair and delightful.   You will awake
in dust, and with it the ceaseless din of the untiring
city.   Would n't you change your dwelling for my
palace in the dew ?   Good-by for now.   I shall see
you so soon.

E.

Mr Edward Dickinson was in Baltimore when the following letter was written, in attendance upon the Whig Convention which sought, unsuccessfully, the nomination of Daniel Webster for the presidency.

[Amherst, June 21, 1852.]

Sunday Morning.

. . . Father has not got home, and we don't know when to expect him. We had a letter from him yesterday, but he did n't say when he should come. He writes that he 'should think the whole world was there, and some from other worlds.' He says he meets a great many old friends and acquaintances, and forms a great many new ones — he writes in very fine spirits, and says he enjoys himself very much. . . . I wish you could have gone with him, you would have enjoyed it so, but I did not much suppose that selfish old school would let you. . . . Last week the Senior levee came off at the President's. I believe Professor Haven is to give one soon — and there is to be a reception at Professor Tyler's next Tuesday evening which I shall attend. You see Amherst is growing lively, and by the time you come everything will be in a buzz. . . . We all send you our love.

EMILIE.

[Amherst, July 23, 1852.]

Sunday Night.

. . . You 'd better not come home ; I say the law will have you, a pupil of the law o'ertaken by the law, and brought to condign punishment, — scene for angels and men, or rather for archangels, who being a little higher would seem to have a 'vantage so far as view 's concerned.   '*Are* you pretty comfortable, though,' — and are you deaf and dumb and gone to the asylum where such afflicted persons learn to hold their tongues?

The next time you are n't going to write me, I 'd thank you to let me know — this kind of *protracted* insult is what no man can bear.   Fight with me like a man — let me have fair shot, and you are *caput mortuum et cap-a-pie*, and that ends the business ! If you really think I so deserve this silence, tell me why — how — I 'll be a thorough scamp or else I won't be any, just which you prefer.

T—— of S——'s class went to Boston yesterday ; it was in my heart to send an apple by him for your private use, but father overheard some of my intentions, and said they were ' rather small ' — whether this remark was intended for the apple, or for my noble self I did not think to ask him ; I rather think he intended to give us both a cut — however, he may not !

You are coming home on Wednesday, as perhaps you know, and I am very happy in prospect of your coming, and hope you want to see us as much as we do you. Mother makes nicer pies with reference to your coming, I arrange my thoughts in a convenient shape, Vinnie grows only perter and more pert day by day.

The horse is looking finely — better than in his life — by which you may think him dead unless I add *before*. The carriage stands in state all covered in the chaise-house — we have one foundling hen into whose young mind I seek to instil the fact that 'Massa is a-comin !'

The garden is amazing — we have beets and beans, have had splendid potatoes for three weeks now. Old Amos weeds and hoes and has an oversight of all thoughtless vegetables. The apples are fine and large in spite of my impression that father called them 'small.'

Yesterday there was a fire. At about three in the afternoon Mr Kimberly's barn was discovered to be on fire; the wind was blowing a gale directly from the west, and having had no rain, the roofs [were] as dry as stubble. Mr Palmer's house was charred — the little house of father's — and Mr Kimberly's also. The engine was broken, and it seemed for a little while as if the whole street must go; the Kimberlys' barn was burnt down, and the house much charred and injured, though not at all destroyed — Mr Palmer's barn took fire, and Deacon Leland's also, but were extinguished with only part burned roofs. We all feel very thankful at such a narrow escape.

Father says there was never such imminent danger, and such miraculous escape.   Father and Mr Frink took charge of the fire — or rather of the *water*, since fire usually takes care of itself.   The men all worked like heroes, and after the fire was out father gave commands to have them march to Howe's where an entertainment was provided for them. After the whole was over they gave 'three cheers for Edward Dickinson,' and three more for the insurance company.   On the whole, it is very wonderful that we did n't all burn up, and we ought to hold our tongues and be very thankful.   If there *must* be a fire, I 'm sorry it could n't wait until you had got home, because you seem to enjoy such things so very much.

There is nothing of moment now which I can find to tell you, except a case of measles in Hartford. . . . Good-by, Sir.   Fare you well.   My benison to your school.

[Amherst, Spring, 1853.]

Tuesday Noon.

DEAR AUSTIN, — . . . How soon now you are coming, and how happy we are in the thought of seeing you !   I can't realize that you will come, it is so still and lonely it does n't seem possible it can be otherwise ; but we shall see, when the nails hang full of coats again, and the chairs hang full of hats, and I can count the slippers under the chair.   Oh, Austin, how we miss them all, and more than them, somebody who used to hang them there, and get many a hint ungentle to carry them away. Those times seem far off now, a great way, as things we did when children. I wish we were children now — I wish we were always children, how to grow up I don't know. . . . Cousin J. has made us an Æolian harp which plays beautifully whenever there is a breeze.

Austin, you must n't care if your letters do not get here just when you think they will — they are always new to us, and delightful always, and the more you send us the happier we shall be. We all send our love to you, and think much and say much of seeing you again — keep well till you come, and if knowing that we all love you makes you happier, then, Austin, you may sing the whole day long !

Affectionately,

EMILIE.

[Amherst, March 18, 1853.]

Friday Morning.

DEAR AUSTIN, — I presume you remember a story that Vinnie tells of a breach of promise case where the correspondence between the parties consisted of a reply from the girl to one she had never received but was daily expecting. Well, *I* am writing an answer to the letter I have n't had, so you will see the force of the accompanying anecdote. I have been looking for you ever since despatching my last, but this is a fickle world, and it 's a great source of complacency that 't will all be burned up by and by. I should be pleased with a line when you 've published your work to father, if it 's perfectly convenient !

Your letters are very funny indeed — about the only jokes we have, now you are gone, and I hope you will send us one as often as you can. Father takes great delight in your remarks to him — puts on his spectacles and reads them o'er and o'er as if it was a blessing to have an only son. He reads all the letters you write, as soon as he gets them, at the post-office, no matter to whom addressed; then he makes me read them aloud at the supper table again, and when he gets home in the evening, he cracks a few walnuts, puts his spectacles on, and with your last in his hand, sits down to enjoy the evening. . . . I believe at this moment, Austin, that there 's nobody living for whom father has such respect as for you. But my paper is getting low, and I must hasten to tell you that we are very happy to hear good news from you, that we hope you 'll have pleasant times and learn a great deal while you 're gone, and come back to us greater and happier for the life lived at Cambridge. We miss you more and more. I wish that we could see you, but letters come the next — write them often, and tell us everything.

Affectionately,

EMILIE.

[June 14, 1853.]

. . . We have been free from company by the 'Amherst and Belchertown Railroad' since J. went home, though we live in constant fear of some other visitation. 'Oh, would some power the giftie gie' folks to see themselves as we see them. — *Burns*.

I have read the poems, Austin, and am going to read them again. They please me very much, but I must read them again before I know just what I think of 'Alexander Smith.' They are not very coherent, but there 's a good deal of exquisite frenzy, and some wonderful figures as ever I met in my life. We will talk about it again. The grove looks nicely, Austin, and we think must certainly grow. We love to go there — it is a charming place. Everything is singing now, and everything is beautiful that *can* be in its life. . . . The time for the New London trip has not been fixed upon. I sincerely wish it may wait until you get home from Cambridge if you would like to go.

The cars continue thriving — a good many passengers seem to arrive from somewhere, though nobody knows from where. Father expects his new buggy to arrive by the cars every day now, and that will help a little. I expect all our grandfathers and all their country cousins will come here to spend Commencement, and don't doubt the stock will rise several per cent that week. If we children could obtain board for the week in some 'vast wilderness,'

I think we should have good times. Our house is crowded daily with the members of this world, the high and the low, the bond and the free, the 'poor in this world's goods,' and the 'almighty dollar;' and what in the world they are after continues to be unknown. But I hope they will pass away as insects or vegetation, and let us reap together in golden harvest time. You and I and our sister Vinnie must have a pleasant time to be unmolested together when your school-days end. You must come home from school, not stopping to play by the way. . . . We all send our love to you, and miss you very much, and think of seeing you again very much. Write me again soon. I have said a good deal to-day.

EMILIE.

The new railroad was opened for the first regular trip from Palmer to Amherst, May 9, 1853. Mr Edward Dickinson wrote on that day, 'We have no railroad jubilee till we see whether all moves right, then we shall glorify becomingly.' Everything was apparently satisfactory, for the celebration occurred early in June, when more than three hundred New London people visited Amherst. In the following letter from Emily are indications of her growing distaste to mingle in a social *mêlée*, despite genuine interest in itself and its cause.

[June 20, 1853.]

Monday Morning.

MY DEAR AUSTIN, — . . . The New London day passed off grandly, so all the people said. It was pretty hot and dusty, but nobody cared for that. Father was, as usual, chief marshal of the day, and went marching around with New London at his heels like some old Roman general upon a triumph day. Mrs H. got a capital dinner, and was very much praised. Carriages flew like sparks, hither and thither and yon, and they all said 't was fine. I 'spose' it was. I sat in Professor Tyler's woods and saw the train move off, and then came home again for fear somebody would see me, or ask me how I did. Dr Holland was here, and called to see us — was very pleasant indeed, inquired for you, and asked mother if Vinnie and I might come and see them in Springfield. . . . We all send you our love.

EMILIE.

[Postmarked, July 2, 1853.]

Friday Afternoon.

DEAR AUSTIN, — . . . Some of the letters you 've sent us we have received, and thank you for affectionately. Some we have not received, but thank you for the memory, of which the emblem perished. Where all those letters go, yours and ours, somebody surely knows, but we do not. There's a new postmaster to-day, but we don't know who's to blame.

You never wrote me a letter, Austin, which I liked half so well as the one father brought me. We think of your coming home with a great deal of happiness, and are glad you want to come.

Father said he never saw you looking in better health or seeming in finer spirits. He did n't say a word about the Hippodrome or the Museum, and he came home so stern that none of us dared to ask him, and besides grandmother was here, and you certainly don't think I 'd allude to a Hippodrome in the presence of that lady! I 'd as soon think of popping fire-crackers in the presence of Peter the Great. But you 'll tell us when you get home — how soon — how soon ! . . . I admire the ' Poems ' very much. We all send our love to you — shall write you again Sunday.

EMILIE.

[Summer, 1853.]

Sunday Afternoon.

. . . It is cold here to-day, Austin, and the west wind blows — the windows are shut at home, and the fire burns in the kitchen. How we should love to see you — how pleasant it would be to walk to the grove together. We will walk there when you get home. We all went down this morning, and the trees look beautifully — every one is growing, and when the west wind blows, the pines lift their light leaves and make sweet music. Pussy goes down there too, and seems to enjoy much in her own observations.

Mr Dwight has not answered yet ; he probably will this week. I do think he will come, Austin, and shall be so glad if he will. . . . We all wish you here always, but I hope 't will seem only dearer for missing it so long. Father says you will come in three weeks — that won't be long now — keep well and happy, Austin, and remember us all you can, and much love from home and

EMILIE.

Thursday Evening.

. . . G. H. has just retired from an evening's visit here, and I gather my spent energies to write a word to you.

'Blessed are they that are persecuted for right-eousness' sake, for they shall have their reward!' Dear Austin, I don't *feel* funny, and I hope you won't laugh at anything I say. I am thinking of you and Vinnie — what nice times you are having, sitting and talking together, while I am lonely here, and I *wanted* to sit and think of you, and fancy what you were saying, all the evening long, but — ordained otherwise. I hope you will have grand times, and don't forget the unit without you, at home.

I have had some things from you to which I per-ceive no meaning. They either were very vast, or they did n't mean anything, I don't know certainly which. What did you mean by a note you sent me day before yesterday? Father asked me what you

wrote, and I gave it to him to read. He looked very
much confused, and finally put on his spectacles,
which did n't seem to help him much — I don't
think a telescope would have assisted him.   I hope
you will write to me — I love to hear from you, and
now Vinnie is gone I shall feel very lonely. . . .
Love for them all if there are those to love and
think of me, and more and most for you, from

EMILY.

Tuesday Evening.

Well, Austin, dear Austin, you have got back
again, codfish and pork and all — all but the slippers, so nicely wrapped to take, yet found when
you were gone under the kitchen chair.   I hope you
won't want them. Perhaps you have some more
there — I will send them by opportunity, should
there be such a thing. Vinnie proposed franking
them, but I fear they are rather large !   What should
you think of it ?   It is n't every day that we have a
chance to sponge Congress, . . . but Cæsar is such
'an honorable man' that we may all go to the poor-
house for all the American Congress will lift a finger
to help us. . . .

The usual rush of callers, and this beleaguered
family as yet in want of time.   I do hope immortality will last a little while, but if the A——s
should happen to get there first, we shall be driven
there. . . .

EMILIE.

[March 17, 1854.]

. . . Since you went back to Cambridge the weather has been wonderful, — the thermometer every noon between 60 and 70 above zero, and the air full of birds.

To-day has not seemed like a day. It has been most unearthly, — so mild, so bright, so still, the windows open, and fires uncomfortable.

Since supper it lightens frequently. In the south you can see the lightning — in the north the northern lights. Now a furious wind blows just from the north and west, and winter comes back again. . . .

There is to be a party at Professor Haven's to-morrow night, for married people merely. Celibacy excludes me and my sister. Father and mother are invited. Mother will go. . . . Mother and Vinnie send love. They are both getting ready for Washington. Take care of yourself.

EMILIE.

Already Emily seems to have exhibited disinclination for journeys, as, in a letter to his son in Cambridge, dated at Washington, March 13, 1854, Mr Edward Dickinson said, 'I have written home to have Lavinia come with your mother and you, and Emily, too, if she will, but that I will not insist upon her coming.' Emily, however, did go to Washington with her family, later in the spring, as a subsequent letter to Mrs Holland will show.

[Amherst, March 27, 1854.]

Sunday Evening.

Well, Austin, — it's Sunday evening. Vinnie is
sick with the ague — mother taking a tour of the
second story as she is wont, Sabbath evening — the
wind is blowing high, the weather very cold, and I
am rather cast down in view of all these circumstances. . . . I went to meeting alone all day. I
assure you I felt very solemn. I went to meeting
five minutes before the bell rang, morning and afternoon, so not to have to go in after all the people
had got there. I wish you had heard Mr Dwight's
sermons to-day. He has preached wonderfully, and
I thought all the afternoon how I wished you were
there. . . . I will tell you something funny. You
know Vinnie sent father [at Washington] a box of
maple sugar — she got the box at the store, and it
said on the outside of it, '1 doz. genuine Quaker
Soap.' We did n't hear from the box, and so many
days passed we began to feel anxious lest it had never
reached him ; and mother, writing soon, alluded in
her letter to the 'sugar sent by the girls,' and the
funniest letter from father came in answer to hers.
It seems the box went straightway, but father not
knowing the hand, merely took off the papers in
which the box was wrapped, and the label 'Quaker
Soap' so far imposed upon him that he put the box
in a drawer with his shaving materials, and supposed
himself well stocked with an excellent Quaker Soap.

. . . We all send our love to you, and want you should write us often.   Good-night, from

EMILIE.

. . . The Germanians gave a concert here the evening of exhibition day.   Vinnie and I went with J.   I never heard sounds before.   They seemed like brazen robins, all wearing broadcloth wings, and I think they were, for they all flew away as soon as the concert was over.

[Late Spring, 1854.]

Saturday Noon.

DEAR AUSTIN, — I rather thought from your letter to me that my essays, together with the lectures at Cambridge, were too much for you, so I thought I would let you have a little vacation; but you must have got rested now, so I shall renew the series.   Father was very severe to me; he thought I'd been trifling with you, so he gave me quite a trimming about 'Uncle Tom' and 'Charles Dickens' and these 'modern literati' who, he says, are nothing, compared to past generations who flourished when he was a boy.   Then he said there were 'somebody's rev-e-ries,' he did n't know whose they were, that he thought were very ridiculous — so I'm quite in disgrace at present, but I think of that 'pinnacle' on which you always mount when anybody insults you, and that's quite a comfort to me. . . .

After a page or two of information about friends in the village, the letter continues:

This is all the news I can think of, but there is one old story, Austin, which you may like to hear — it is that we think about you the whole of the live-long day, and talk of you when we 're together. And you can recollect when you are busy studying that those of us at home not so hard at work as you are, get much time to be with you. We all send our love to you.

EMILIE.

[Amherst, May, 1854.]

Saturday Morn.

DEAR AUSTIN, — A week ago we were all here — to-day we are not all here — yet the bee hums just as merrily, and all the busy things work on as if the same. They do not miss you, child, but there is a humming-bee whose song is not so merry, and there are busy ones who pause to drop a tear. Let us thank God, to-day, Austin, that we can love our friends, our brothers and our sisters, and weep when they are gone, and smile at their return. It is indeed a joy which we are blest to know.

To-day is very beautiful — just as bright, just as blue, just as green and as white and as crimson as the cherry-trees full in bloom, and the half-opening peach-blossoms, and the grass just waving, and sky and hill and cloud can make it, if they try. How I wish you were here, Austin; you thought last Saturday beautiful, yet to this golden day 't was but one single gem to whole handfuls of jewels. You will ride to-day, I hope, or take a long walk somewhere, and recollect us all, — Vinnie and me and father and mother and home. Yes, Austin, every one of us, for we all think of you, and bring you to recollection many times each day — not bring you to recollection, for we never put you away, but keep recollecting on. . . .

You must think of us to-night while Mr Dwight takes tea here, and we will think of you far away down in Cambridge.

Don't mind the can, Austin, if it is rather dry, don't mind the daily road though it is rather dusty, but remember the brooks and the hills, and remember while you 're but one, we are but four at home !

EMILIE.

CHAPTER III

To Mrs Gordon L. Ford, Mr Bowdoin, Mrs Anthon, and Miss Lavinia Dickinson

WITH a number of early letters to herself, Mrs Ford of Brooklyn sent me also a short sketch of her remembrance of Emily Dickinson's girlhood, which seems to show her in a somewhat different aspect from anything which other friends have given.

Mrs Ford was a daughter of the late Professor Fowler of Amherst College, and her recollections, making a pleasant picture of life in Amherst nearly fifty years ago, have all the charm of early friendship and intercourse in the days when plain living and high thinking were not an exceptional combination.

In speaking of several letters which she could not find, Mrs Ford wrote, 'The other things which I wish I could put my hand on were funny — sparkling with fun, and that is a new phase to the public; but she certainly began as a humorist.' Although sent to me for publication in this volume of *Letters*,

Mrs Ford had hoped to revise and perhaps shorten the sketch in the proof; and her sudden death, within a few days after writing it, lends a saddened interest to these memories of a vanished friendship.

'My remembrances of my friend Emily Dickinson are many and vivid, and delightful to me personally, yet they are all of trifles in themselves, and only interesting to the general public as they cast light on the growth and changes in her soul.

'Our parents were friends, and we knew each other from childhood, but she was several years younger, and how and when we drew together I cannot recall, but I think the friendship was based on certain sympathies and mutual admirations of beauty in nature and ideas. She loved the great aspects of nature, and yet was full of interest and affection for its smaller details. We often walked together over the lovely hills of Amherst, and I remember especially two excursions to Mount Norwottock, five miles away, where we found the climbing fern, and came home laden with pink and white trilliums, and later, yellow lady's-slippers. She knew the wood-lore of the region round about, and could name the haunts and the habits of every wild or garden growth within her reach. Her eyes were wide open to nature's sights, and her ears to nature's voices.

' My chief recollections of her are connected with these woodland walks, or out-door excursions with a merry party, perhaps to Sunderland for the "sugaring off" of the maple sap, or to some wild brook in the deeper forest, where the successful fishermen would afterward cook the chowder. She was a free talker about what interested her, yet I cannot remember one personal opinion expressed of her mates, her home, or her habits.

' Later we met to discuss books. *The Atlantic Monthly* was a youngster then, and our joy over a new poem by Lowell, Longfellow, and Whittier, our puzzles over Emerson's "If the red slayer think he slays," our laughter at Oliver Wendell Holmes, were full and satisfying. Lowell was especially dear to us, and once I saw a passionate fit of crying brought on, when a tutor of the College, who died while contesting the senatorship for Louisiana,[1] told us from his eight years of seniority, that "Byron had a much

[1] The Hon. Henry M. Spofford, Justice of the Supreme Court of Louisiana, a graduate of Amherst College in the Class of 1840, and brother of Mr Ainsworth R. Spofford, the Librarian of Congress.

better style," and advised us "to leave Lowell, Motherwell and Emerson alone." Like other young creatures, we were ardent partisans.

'There was a fine circle of young people in Amherst, and we influenced each other strongly. We were in the adoring mood, and I am glad to say that many of those idols of our girlhood have proved themselves golden. The eight girls who composed this group had talent enough for twice their number, and in their respective spheres of mothers, authors or women, have been noteworthy and admirable. Three of them have passed from earth, but the others live in activity and usefulness.

'This group started a little paper in the Academy, now the village High School, which was kept up for two years. Emily Dickinson was one of the wits of the school, and a humorist of the "comic column." Fanny Montague often made the head title of the paper — *Forest Leaves* — in leaves copied from nature, and fantasies of her own pen-work. She is now a wise member of art circles in Baltimore, a manager of the Museum of Art, and the appointed and intelligent critic of the Japanese exhibit at the Exposition in Chicago. Helen Fiske (the "H. H." of later days) did no special work on the paper for various reasons.

'This paper was all in script, and was passed around the school, where the contributions were easily recognized from the handwriting, which in Emily's case was very beautiful — small, clear, and finished. Later, though her writing retained its elegance, it became diffi-cult to read. I wish very much I could find a copy of *Forest Leaves*, but we recklessly gave the numbers away, and the last one I ever saw turned up at the Maplewood Insti-tute in Pittsfield, Massachusetts, where they started a similar paper. Emily's contributions were irresistible, but I cannot recall them. One bit was stolen by a roguish editor for the College paper, where her touch was instantly recognized; and there were two paragraphs in *The Springfield Republican.*

'We had a Shakespeare Club — a rare thing in those days, — and one of the tutors pro-posed to take all the copies of all the members and mark out the questionable passages. This plan was negatived at the first meeting, as far as "the girls" spoke, who said they did not want the strange things emphasized, nor their books spoiled with marks. Finally we told the men to do as they liked — "we shall read everything." I remember the lofty air with which Emily took her departure, saying, "There 's nothing wicked in Shakespeare, and if there is I don't want to know it." The men read for perhaps three meetings from their expurgated editions, and then gave up their plan, and the whole text was read out boldly.

'There were many little dances, with cake and lemonade at the end, and one year there was a valentine party, where the lines of various authors were arranged to make apparent sense, but absolute nonsense, the play being to guess the names and places of the misappropriated lines.

'Emily was part and parcel of all these gatherings, and there were no signs, in her life and character, of the future recluse. As a prophetic hint, she once asked me if it did not make me shiver to hear a great many people talk — they took "all the clothes off their souls" — and we discussed this matter. She mingled freely in all the companies and excursions of the moment, and the evening frolics.

'Several of this group had beauty, all had intelligence and character, and others had charm. Emily was not beautiful, yet she had great beauties. Her eyes were lovely auburn, soft and warm, her hair lay in rings of the same color all over her head, and her skin and teeth were fine. At this time she had a demure manner which brightened easily into fun where she felt at home, but among strangers

she was rather shy, silent, and even depreca-
ting. She was exquisitely neat and careful in
her dress, and always had flowers about her,
another pleasant habit of modernity.

'I have so many times seen her in the
morning at work in her garden where everything throve under her hand, and wandering
there at eventide, that she is perpetually asso-
ciated in my mind with flowers — a flower
herself, — especially as for years it was her
habit to send me the first buds of the arbutus
which we had often hung over together in the
woods, joying in its fresh fragrance as the very
breath of coming spring.

'My busy married life separated me from
these friends of my youth, and intercourse
with them has not been frequent; but I rejoice
that my early years were passed in scenes of
beautiful nature, and with these mates of
simple life, high cultivation and noble ideals.
In Emily as in others, there was a rare combination of fervor and simplicity, with good
practical living, great conscience and directness of purpose. She loved with all her
might, there was never a touch of the world-
ling about her, and we all knew and trusted
her love.

'Dr Holland once said to me, "Her poems
are too ethereal for publication." I replied,

"They are beautiful — so concentrated — but they remind me of air-plants that have no roots in earth." "That is true," he said, "a perfect description;" and I think these lyrical ejaculations, these breathed-out projectiles, sharp as lances, would at that time have fallen into idle ears. But gathered in a volume where many could be read at once as her philosophy of life, they explain each other, and so become intelligible and delightful to the public.

'The first poem I ever read was the robin chorister[1] (published in the first volume) which she gave my husband years ago. I think in spite of her seclusion, she was longing for poetic sympathy, and that some of her later habits of life originated in this suppressed and ungratified desire.

'I only wish the interest and delight her poems have aroused could have come early enough in her career to have kept her social and communicative, and at one with her friends. Still, these late tributes to her memory are most welcome to the circle that loved her, even though they are but laurels to lay on her grave.

                                        'E. E. F. F.'

---

[1] 'Some keep the Sabbath going to church, etc.'— *Poems*, First Series, page 74.

The first letter was written in 1848; the others at intervals until 1853. Though placed in order, they were not dated by Mrs Ford.

[1848.]

DEAR EMILY, — I said when the barber came I would save you a little lock, and fulfilling my promise, I send you one to-day. I shall never give you anything again that will be half so full of sunshine as this wee lock of hair, but I wish no hue more sombre might ever fall to you.

All your gifts should be rainbows if I owned half the shine, and but a bit of sea to furnish raindrops for one. Dear Emily, this is all — it will serve to make you remember me when locks are crisp and gray, and the quiet cap, and the spectacles, and ' John Anderson my Jo ' are all that is left of you.

I must have one of yours. Please spare me a little lock sometime when you have your scissors and there is one to spare.

Your very affectionate

EMILIE.

The buds are small, dear Emily, but will you please accept one for your cousin and yourself? I quite forgot the rosebugs when I spoke of the buds, last evening, and I found a family of them taking an early breakfast on my most precious bud, with a smart little worm for landlady, so the sweetest are gone, but accept my love with the smallest, and I 'm

Your affectionate

EMILIE.

Tuesday Morn.

DEAR EMILY, — I come and see you a great many times every day, though I don't bring my body with me, so perhaps you don't know I'm there. But I love to come just as dearly, for nobody sees me then, and I sit and chat away, and look up in your face, and no matter who calls if 'my Lord the King,' he does n't interrupt me. Let me say, dear Emily, both mean to come at a time, so you shall be very sure I am sitting by your side, and not have to trust the fancy. . . .

Affectionately,

E.

[1849 ?]

Thursday Morning.

DEAR EMILY, — I fear you will be lonely this dark and stormy day, and I send this little messenger to say you must not be.

The day is long to me. I have wanted to come and see you. I have tried earnestly to come, but always have been detained by some ungenerous care, and now this falling snow sternly and silently lifts up its hand between.

How glad I am affection can always leave and go. How glad that the drifts of snow pause at the outer door and go no farther, and it is as warm within as if no winter came. . . . Let us think of the pleasant summer whose gardens are far away, and whose robins are singing always. If it were not for blossoms . . . and for that brighter sunshine above, beyond, away, these days were dark indeed; but I try to keep recollecting that we are away from home, and have many brothers and sisters who are expecting us. Dear Emilie, don't weep, for you will both be so happy where 'sorrow cannot come.'

Vinnie left her Testament on a little stand in our room, and it made me think of her, so I thought I would open it, and the first words I read were in those sweetest verses, 'Blessed are the poor — Blessed are they that mourn — Blessed are they that weep, for they shall be comforted.' Dear Emily, I thought of you, and I hastened away to send this message to you.

EMILIE.

Thursday Morn.

DEAR EMILY, — I can't come in this morning, because I am so cold, but you will know I am here ringing the big front door-bell, and leaving a note for you.

Oh, I want to come in, I have a great mind now to follow little Jane into your warm sitting-room; are you there, dear Emily?

No, I resist temptation and run away from the door just as fast as my feet will carry me, lest if I once come in I shall grow so happy that I shall stay there always and never go home at all. You will have read this note by the time I reach the office, and you can't think how fast I run.

Affectionately,

EMILY.

P. S. I have just shot past the corner, and now all the wayside houses, and the little gate flies open to see me coming home.

Saturday Morn.

It has been a long week, dear Emily, for I have not seen your face, but I have contrived to think of you very much instead, which has half reconciled me to not seeing you for so long. I was coming several times, but the snow would start the first, and then the paths were damp, and then a friend would drop in to chat, and the short afternoon was gone before I was aware.

Did Mr D—— give you a message from me? He promised to be faithful, but I don't suppose divines think earthly loves of much consequence. My flowers come in my stead to-day, dear Emily. I hope you will love to see them, and whatever word of love or welcome kindly you would extend to me, 'do even so to them.' They are small, but so full of meaning if they only mean the half of what I bid them.

Very affectionately,

EMILY.

Thursday Morning.

. . . When I am as old as you, and have had so many friends, perhaps they won't seem so precious, and then I sha'n't write any more little *billets-doux* like these, but you will forgive me now, because I can't find many so dear to me as you. Then I know I can't have you always; some day a 'brave dragoon' will be stealing you away, and I will have farther to go to discover you at all, so I shall recollect all these sweet opportunities, and feel so sorry if I did n't improve them. . . .

About this time (December, 1849), the following little note was sent to Mr Bowdoin, a law student in Mr Dickinson's office, 'on returning *Jane Eyre*. The leaves mentioned were box leaves.'

[December, 1849.]

MR BOWDOIN, — If all these leaves were altars, and on every one a prayer that Currer Bell might be saved, and you were God — would you answer it?

Mr Bowdoin, who was considered by the young girls at that time 'a confirmed bachelor,' also received the accompanying valentine from Emily.

VALENTINE WEEK [1850].

Awake, ye muses nine, sing me a strain divine,
Unwind the solemn twine, and tie my Valentine.

. . . .

Oh the earth was *made* for lovers, for damsel, and
    hopeless swain,
For sighing, and gentle whispering, and *unity* made
    of *twain*.
All things do go a courting, in earth or sea, or air,
God hath made nothing single but *thee* in His world
    so fair !

The *bride* and then the *bridegroom*, the *two*, and
  then the *one*,
Adam, and Eve, his consort, the moon and then the
  sun;
The life doth prove the precept, who obey shall
  happy be,
Who will not serve the sovereign, be hanged on fatal
  tree.
The high do seek the lowly, the great do seek the
  small,
None cannot find who seeketh, on this terrestrial
  ball;
The bee doth court the flower, the flower his suit
  receives,
And they make a merry wedding, whose guests are
  hundred leaves;
The wind doth woo the branches, the branches they
  are won,
And the father fond demandeth the maiden for his
  son.
The storm doth walk the seashore humming a mournful tune,
The wave with eye so pensive, looketh to see the
  moon,
Their spirits meet together, they make them solemn
  vows,
No more he singeth mournful, her sadness she doth
  lose.
The worm doth woo the mortal, death claims a living
  bride,

Night unto day is married, morn unto eventide;
Earth is a merry damsel, and heaven a knight so
    true,
And Earth is quite coquettish, and beseemeth in vain
    to sue.
Now to the application, to the reading of the roll,
To bringing thee to justice, and marshalling thy soul:
Thou art a *human* solo, a being cold, and lone,
Wilt have no kind companion, thou reapest what
    thou hast sown.
Hast never silent hours, and minutes all too long,
And a deal of sad reflection, and wailing instead of
    song?
There 's *Sarah*, and *Eliza*, and *Emeline* so fair,
And *Harriet* and *Sabra*, and she with curling hair.
Thine eyes are sadly blinded, but yet thou mayest
    see
Six true and comely maidens sitting upon the tree;
Approach that tree with caution, then up it boldly
    climb,
And seize the one thou lovest, nor care for space, or
    time.
Then bear her to the greenwood, and build for her
    a bower,
And give her what she asketh, jewel, or bird, or
    flower —
And bring the fife, and trumpet, and beat upon the
    drum —
And bid the world Goodmorrow, and go to glory
    home !

Valentines seemed ever near the thoughts of the young people of this generation, and another clever one, written by Emily in 1852, somehow found its way into *The Republican*, probably through some friend. It was originally sent to Mr William Howland.

[1852.]

Sic transit gloria mundi,
How doth the busy bee —
Dum vivimus vivamus,
I stay mine enemy.

Oh, *veni, vidi, vici,*
Oh, *caput, cap-a-pie,*
And oh, *memento mori*
When I am far from thee.

Hurrah for Peter Parley,
Hurrah for Daniel Boone,
Three cheers, sir, for the gentlemen
Who first observed the moon.

Peter put up the sunshine,
Pattie arrange the stars,
Tell Luna tea is waiting,
And call your brother Mars.

Put down the apple, Adam,
And come away with me ;
So shall thou have a pippin
From off my father's tree.

I climb the hill of science
I ' view the landscape o'er,'
Such transcendental prospect
I ne'er beheld before.

Unto the Legislature
My country bids me go.
I 'll take my india-rubbers,
In case the wind should blow.

During my education,
It was announced to me
That gravitation, stumbling,
Fell from an apple-tree.

The earth upon its axis
Was once supposed to turn,
By way of a gymnastic
In honor to the sun.

It was the brave Columbus,
A-sailing on the tide,
Who notified the nations
Of where I would reside.

Mortality is fatal,
Gentility is fine,
Rascality heroic,
Insolvency sublime.

Our fathers being weary
Lay down on Bunker Hill,
And though full many a morning,
Yet they are sleeping still.

The trumpet, sir, shall wake them,
In dream I see them rise,
Each with a solemn musket
A-marching to the skies.

A coward will remain, sir,
Until the fight is done,
But an immortal hero
Will take his hat and run.

Good-by, sir, I am going —
My country calleth me.
Allow me, sir, at parting
To wipe my weeping e'e.

In token of our friendship
Accept this *Bonnie Doon*,
And when the hand that plucked it
Has passed beyond the moon,

The memory of my ashes
Will consolation be.
Then farewell, Tuscarora,
And farewell, sir, to thee.

To Mrs Ford

Sunday Afternoon [1852].

I have just come home from meeting, where I
have been all day, and it makes me so happy to
think of writing you that I forget the sermon and

minister and all, and think of none but you. . . .
I miss you always, dear Emily, and I think now and
then that I can't stay without you, and half make
up my mind to make a little bundle of all my earthly
things, bid my blossoms and home good-by, and set
out on foot to find you. But we have so much
matter of fact here that I don't dare to go, so I keep
on sighing, and wishing you were here.

I know you would be happier amid this darling
spring than in ever so kind a city, and you would get
well much faster drinking our morning dew — and
the world here is so beautiful, and things so sweet
and fair, that your heart would be soothed and
comforted.

I would tell you about the spring if I thought it
might persuade you even now to return, but every
bud and bird would only afflict you and make you
sad where you are, so not one word of the robins,
and not one word of the bloom, lest it make the
city darker, and your own home more dear.

But nothing forgets you, Emily, not a blossom, not
a bee ; for in the merriest flower there is a pensive
air, and in the bonniest bee a sorrow — they know
that you are gone, they know how well you loved
them, and in their little faces is sadness, and in their
mild eyes, tears. But another spring, dear friend,
you must and shall be here, and nobody can take
you away, for I will hide you and keep you — and
who would think of taking you if I hold you tight in
my arms?

Your home looks very silent — I try to think of things funny, and turn the other way when I am passing near, for sure I am that looking would make my heart too heavy, and make my eyes so dim. How I do long once more t~ ꞓ⌐ai the household voices, and see you there at twilight sitting in the door — and I shall when the leaves fall, sha'n't I, and the crickets begin to sing?

You must not think sad thoughts, dear Emily. I fear you are doing so, from your sweet note to me, and it almost breaks my heart to have you so far away, where I cannot comfort you.

All will be well, I know, and I know all will be happy, and I so wish I was near to convince my dear friend so. I want very much to hear how Mr Ford is now. I hope you will tell me, for it's a good many weeks since I have known anything of him. You and he may come this way any summer; and how I hope he may — and I shall pray for him, and for you, and for your home on earth, which will be next the one in heaven.

Your very affectionate,

EMILIE.

I thank you for writing me, one precious little 'forget-me-not' to bloom along my way. But one little one is lonely — pray send it a blue-eyed mate, that it be not alone. Here is love from mother and father and Vinnie and me. . . .

[1853.]

Wednesday Eve.

DEAR EMILY, — Are you there, and shall you always stay there, and is it not dear Emily any more, but Mrs Ford of Connecticut, and must we stay alone, and will you not come back with the birds and the butterflies, when the days grow long and warm?

Dear Emily, we are lonely here. I know Col. S—— is left, and Mr and Mrs K——, but pussy has run away, and you do not come back again, and the world has grown so long! I knew you would go away, for I know the roses are gathered, but I guessed not yet, not till by expectation we had become resigned. Dear Emily, when it came, and hidden by your veil you stood before us all and made those promises, and when we kissed you, all, and went back to our homes, it seemed to me translation, not any earthly thing, and if a little after you'd ridden on the wind, it would not have surprised me.

And now five days have gone, Emily, and long and silent, and I begin to know that you will not come back again. There's a verse in the Bible, Emily, I don't know where it is, nor just how it goes can I remember, but it's a little like this — 'I can go to her, but she cannot come back to me.' I guess that isn't right, but my eyes are full of tears, and I'm sure I do not care if I make mistakes or not. Is it happy there, dear Emily, and is the fireside warm, and have you a little cricket to chirp upon the hearth?

How much we think of you — how dearly love you — how often hope for you that it may all be happy.

Sunday evening your father came in — he stayed a little while. I thought he looked solitary. I thought he had grown old. How lonely he must be — I 'm sorry for him.

Mother and Vinnie send their love, and hope you are so happy. Austin has gone away. Father comes home to-morrow. I know father will miss you. He loved to meet you here.

> ' So fades a summer cloud away,
>   So smiles the gale when storms are o'er,
> So gently shuts the eye of day,
>   So dies a wave along the shore.'

Kiss me, dear Emily, and remember me if you will, with much respect, to your husband. Will you write me sometime?

Affectionately,

EMILY.

To Mrs Anthon

AMHERST [1859].

. . . Sweet at my door this March night another candidate. Go home! We don't like Katies here! Stay! My heart votes for you, and what am I, indeed, to dispute her ballot!

What are your qualifications? Dare you dwell in the East where we dwell? Are you afraid of the

sun? When you hear the new violet sucking her
way among the sods, shall you be resolute? All we
are strangers, dear, the world is not acquainted with
us, because we are not acquainted with her; and
pilgrims. Do you hesitate? And soldiers, oft —
some of us victors, but those I do not see to-night,
owing to the smoke. We are hungry, and thirsty,
sometimes, we are barefoot and cold — will you still
come?

Then, bright I record you — Kate, gathered in
March! It is a small bouquet, dear, but what it
lacks in size it gains in fadelessness. Many can
boast a hollyhock, but few can bear a rose! And
should new flower smile at limited associates, pray
her remember were there many, they were not
worn upon the breast, but tilled in the pasture. So
I rise wearing her — so I sleep holding, — sleep at
last with her fast in my hand, and wake bearing my
flower.   EMILIE.

To the Same

There are two ripenings, one of sight,
Whose forces spheric wind,
Until the velvet product
Drops spicy to the ground.
A homelier maturing,
A process in the burr
That teeth of frosts alone disclose
On far October air.
                                        EMILIE.

To the Same

[1860.]

The prettiest of pleas, dear, but with a lynx like
me quite unavailable. Finding is slow, facilities for
losing so frequent, in a world like this, I hold with
extreme caution. A prudence so astute may seem
unnecessary, but plenty moves those most, dear, who
have been in want, and Saviour tells us, Kate, the
poor are always with us. Were you ever poor? I
have been a beggar, and rich to-night, as by God's
leave I believe I am, the 'lazzaroni's' faces haunt,
pursue me still !

You do not yet 'dislimn,' Kate. Distinctly sweet
your face stands in its phantom niche — I touch
your hand — my cheek your cheek — I stroke your
vanished hair. Why did you enter, sister, since you
must depart? Had not its heart been torn enough
but you must send your shred?

Oh, our condor Kate ! Come from your crags
again ! Oh, dew upon the bloom fall yet again a
summer's night ! Of such have been the frauds
which have vanquished faces, sown plant of flesh the
church-yard plats, and occasioned angels.

There is a subject, dear, on which we never touch.
Ignorance of its pageantries does not deter me. I
too went out to meet the dust early in the morning.
I too in daisy mounds possess hid treasure, therefore
I guard you more. You did not tell me you had

once been a 'millionaire.' Did my sister think that
opulence could be mistaken? Some trinket will
remain, some babbling plate or jewel.

I write you from the summer. The murmuring
leaves fill up the chinks through which the winter red
shone when Kate was here, and F—— was here, and
frogs sincerer than our own splash in their Maker's
pools. It's but a little past, dear, and yet how far
from here it seems, fled with the snow! So through
the snow go many loving feet parted by 'Alps.' How
brief, from vineyards and the sun!

Parents and Vinnie request love to be given girl.

EMILIE.

[1861 ?]

To the Same

KATIE, — Last year at this time I did not miss
you, but positions shifted, until I hold your black
in strong hallowed remembrance, and trust my colors
are to you tints slightly beloved.

You cease, indeed, to talk, which is a custom
prevalent among things parted and torn, but shall I
class this, dear, among elect exceptions, and bear
you just as usual unto the kind Lord?

We dignify our faith when we can cross the ocean
with it, though most prefer ships.

How do you do this year? . . . How many years,
I wonder, will sow the moss upon them, before we
bind again, a little altered, it may be, elder a little

it *will* be, and yet the same, as suns which shine between our lives and loss, and violets — not last year's, but having the mother's eyes.

Do you find plenty of food at home? Famine is unpleasant.

It is too late for frogs — or what pleases me better, dear, not quite early enough! The pools were full of you for a brief period, but that brief period blew away, leaving me with many stems, and but a few foliage! Gentlemen here have a way of plucking the tops of the trees, and putting the fields in their cellars annually, which in point of taste is execrable, and would they please omit, I should have fine vegetation and foliage all the year round, and never a winter month. Insanity to the sane seems so unnecessary — but I am only one, and they are ' four and forty,' which little affair of numbers leaves me impotent. Aside from this, dear Katie, inducements to visit Amherst are as they were — I am pleasantly located in the deep sea, but love will row you out, if her hands are strong, and don't wait till I land, for I 'm going ashore on the other side.

EMILIE.

Following are letters written to her sister, Miss Lavinia Dickinson, while Emily was receiving treatment for her eyes in Boston. She was there for this purpose twice, — during the summer of 1864, and again in 1865, usually

writing of these years as ' when I was sick so
long,' which has given many persons the idea
of an invalidism she never had.

[1864.]

DEAR VINNIE, — Many write that they do not
write because that they have too much to say, I that
I have enough.   Do you remember the whippoor-
will that sang one night on the orchard fence, and
then drove to the south, and we never heard of him
afterward?

He will go home, and I shall go home, perhaps
in the same train.   It is a very sober thing to keep
my summer in strange towns — what, I have not
told, but I have found friends in the wilderness.
You know Elijah did, and to see the ' ravens ' mend-
ing my stockings would break a heart long hard.

Fanny and Lou are solid gold, and Mrs B—— and
her daughter very kind, and the doctor enthusiastic
about my getting well.   I feel no gayness yet — I
suppose I had been discouraged so long.

You remember the prisoner of Chillon did not
know liberty when it came, and asked to go back to
jail.

C—— and A—— came to see me and brought
beautiful flowers.   Do you know what made them
remember me?   Give them my love and gratitude.

They told me about the day at Pelham, you,
dressed in daisies, and Mr McD——.   I could n't
see you, Vinnie.   I am glad of all the roses you find,

while your primrose is gone. How kind Mr C——
grew. Was Mr D—— dear?

Emily wants to be well — if any one alive wants
to get well more, I would let him, first.

Give my love to father and mother and Austin.
Tell Margaret I remember her, and hope Richard is
well. . . . How I wish I could rest all those who are
tired for me.

EMILY.

To the Same

[1865.]

DEAR VINNIE, — The hood is far under way, and
the girls think it a beauty. . . . I hope the chimneys
are done, and the hemlocks set, and the two teeth
filled in the front yard. How astonishing it will
be to me ! . . .

The pink lily you gave Lou has had five flowers
since I came, and has more buds. The girls think
it my influence. Lou wishes she knew father's view
of Jeff Davis' capture — thinks no one but him can
do it justice. She wishes to send a photograph of
the arrest to Austin, including the skirt and spurs,
but fears he will think her trifling with him. I
advised her not to be rash.

How glad I should be to see you all, but it won't
be long, Vinnie. You will be willing, won't you, for
a little while? It has rained and been very hot,
and mosquitoes, as in August. I hope the flowers are
well. The tea-rose I gave Aunt L—— has a flower

now. Is the lettuce ripe? Persons wear no bonnets here. Fanny has a blade of straw with handle of ribbon.

Affectionately,

EMILY.

To the Same

. . . Father told me you were going. I wept for the little plants, but rejoiced for you. Had I loved them as well as I did, I could have begged you to stay with them, but they are foreigners now, and all, a foreigner. I have been sick so long I do not know the sun. I hope they may be alive, for home would be strange except them, now the world is dead.

A—— N—— lives here since Saturday, and two new people more, a person and his wife, so I do little but fly, yet always find a nest. I shall go home in two weeks. You will get me at Palmer?

Love for E—— and Mr D——.

SISTER.

To the Same

. . . The Doctor will let me go Monday of Thanksgiving week. He wants to see me Sunday, so I cannot before. . . . Love for the Middletown pearls. Shall write E—— after Tuesday, when I go to the Doctor. Thank her for sweet note.

The drums keep on for the still man — but Emily must stop.

Love of Fanny and Lou.

SISTER.

Soon after the close of the war, a friend, Mrs Vanderbilt of Long Island, met with a very serious bodily accident. Upon her recovery she received the following welcome to the realm of health : —

> To this world she returned,
> But with a tingle of that ;
> A compound manner,
> As a sod
> Espoused a violet
> That chiefer to the skies
> Than to himself allied,
> Dwelt, hesitating,
> Half of dust,
> And half of day, the bride.
>
> EMILY.

On the occasion of another friend's departure from Amherst after a visit, Emily's good-by was embodied in the following lines, accompanied by an oleander blossom tied with black ribbon :

> We 'll pass without a parting,
> So to spare
> Certificate of absence,
> Deeming where
> I left her I could find her
> If I tried.
> This way I keep from missing
> Those who died.
>
> EMILY.

CHAPTER IV

To Dr J. G. Holland and Mrs Holland

THE dates of these letters can be approx-
imated only by the hand-writing —
which varies from the early style, about 1853,
to the latest — and by events mentioned, the
time of whose occurrence is known. Mrs Holland writes that there were many other letters,
even more quaint and original, but unhappily
not preserved.

[About 1853.]

Friday Evening.

Thank you, dear Mrs Holland — Vinnie and I
will come, if you would like to have us. We should
have written before, but mother has not been well,
and we hardly knew whether we could leave her,
but she is better now, and I write quite late this
evening, that if you still desire it, Vinnie and I will
come. Then, dear Mrs Holland, if agreeable to
you, we will take the Amherst train on Tuesday
morning, for Springfield, and be with you at noon.

The cars leave here at nine o'clock, and I think

reach Springfield at twelve. I can think just how we dined with you a year ago from now, and it makes my heart beat faster to think perhaps we 'll see you so little while from now.

To live a thousand years would not make me forget the day and night we spent there, and while I write the words, I don't believe I 'm coming, so sweet it seems to me. I hope we shall not tire you ; with all your other cares, we fear we should not come, but you *will* not let us trouble you, will you, dear Mrs Holland ?

Father and mother ask a very warm remembrance to yourself and Dr Holland.

We were happy the grapes and figs seemed acceptable to you, and wished there were many more. I am very sorry to hear that ' Kate ' has such excellent lungs. With all your other cares, it must be quite a trial to you.

It is also a source of pleasure to me that Annie goes to sleep, on account of the ' interregnum ' it must afford to you.

Three days and we are there — happy — very happy ! To-morrow I will sew, but I shall think of you, and Sunday sing and pray — yet I shall not forget you, and Monday 's very near, and here 's to me on Tuesday ! Good-night, dear Mrs Holland — I see I 'm getting wild — you will forgive me all, and not *forget* me all, though ? Vinnie is fast asleep, or her love would be here — though she is, it is. Once more, if it is fair, we will come on Tuesday,

and you love to have us, but if not convenient,
please surely tell us so.

Affectionately,

EMILIE.

Tuesday Evening.

DEAR DR AND MRS HOLLAND, — dear Minnie —
it is cold to-night, but the thought of you so warm,
that I sit by it as a fireside, and am never cold any
more.   I love to write to you — it gives my heart
a holiday and sets the bells to ringing.   If prayers
had any answers to them, you were all here to-night,
but I seek and I don't find, and knock and it is
not opened.   Wonder if God is just — presume He
is, however, and 't was only a blunder of Matthew's.

I think mine is the case, where when they ask an
egg, they get a scorpion, for I keep wishing for you,
keep shutting up my eyes and looking toward the
sky, asking with all my might for you, and yet you
do not come.   I wrote to you last week, but thought
you would laugh at me, and call me sentimental,
so I kept my lofty letter for 'Adolphus Hawkins,
Esq.'

If it was n't for broad daylight, and cooking-stoves,
and roosters, I'm afraid you would have occasion
to smile at my letters often, but so sure as 'this
mortal' essays immortality, a crow from a neighboring farm-yard dissipates the illusion, and I am
here again.

And what I mean is this — that I thought of you

all last week, until the world grew rounder than it sometimes is, and I broke several dishes.

Monday, I solemnly resolved I would be *sensible*, so I wore thick shoes, and thought of Dr Humphrey, and the Moral Law. One glimpse of *The Republican* makes me break things again — I read in it every night.

Who writes those funny accidents, where railroads meet each other unexpectedly, and gentlemen in factories get their heads cut off quite informally? The author, too, relates them in such a sprightly way, that they are quite attractive. Vinnie was disappointed to-night, that there were not more accidents — I read the news aloud, while Vinnie was sewing. *The Republican* seems to us like a letter from you, and we break the seal and read it eagerly. . . .

Vinnie and I talked of you as we sewed, this afternoon. I said — 'how far they seem from us,' but Vinnie answered me 'only a little way.' . . . I'd love to be a bird or bee, that whether hum or sing, still might be near you.

Heaven is large — is it not? Life is short too, isn't it? Then when one. is done, is there not another, and — and — then if God is willing, we are neighbors then. Vinnie and mother send their love. Mine too is here. My letter as a bee, goes laden. Please love us and remember us. Please write us very soon, and tell us how you are. . . .

Affectionately,

EMILIE.

... it is cold tonight,
but the thoughts of you ...
... that I sit by it as a
... and am never cold
any more. I love to write to you
it ... my heart a ...
and ... the ... to singing.
...

[Late Autumn, 1853.]

Sabbath Afternoon.

DEAR FRIENDS, — I thought I would write again. I write you many letters with pens which are not seen. Do you receive them?

I think of you all to-day, and dreamed of you last night.

When father rapped on my door to wake me this morning, I was walking with you in the most wonderful garden, and helping you pick — roses, and though we gathered with all our might, the basket was never full. And so all day I pray that I may walk with you, and gather roses again, and as night draws on, it pleases me, and I count impatiently the hours 'tween me and the darkness, and the dream of you and the roses, and the basket never full.

God grant the basket fill not, till, with hands purer and whiter, we gather flowers of gold in baskets made of pearl; higher — higher! It seems long since we heard from you — long, since how little Annie was, or any one of you — so long since Cattle Show, when Dr Holland was with us. Oh, it always seems a long while from our seeing you, and even when at your house, the nights seemed much more long than they 're wont to do, because separated from you. I want so much to know if the friends are all well in that dear cot in Springfield — and if well whether happy, and happy — *how* happy, and

-why, and what bestows the joy? And then those other questions, asked again and again, whose answers are so sweet, do they love — remember us — wish sometimes we were there? Ah, friends — dear friends — perhaps my queries tire you, but I so long to know.

The minister to-day, not our own minister, preached about death and judgment, and what would become of those, meaning Austin and me, who behaved improperly — and somehow the sermon scared me, and father and Vinnie looked very solemn as if the whole was true, and I would not for worlds have them know that it troubled me, but I longed to come to you, and tell you all about it, and learn how to be better. He preached such an awful sermon though, that I did n't much think I should ever see you again until the Judgment Day, and then you would not speak to me, according to his story. The subject of perdition seemed to please him, somehow. It seems very solemn to me. I 'll tell you all about it, when I see you again.

I wonder what you are doing to-day — if you have been to meeting? To-day has been a fair day, very still and blue. To-night the crimson children are playing in the west, and to-morrow will be colder. How sweet if I could see you, and talk of all these things ! Please write us very soon. The days with you last September seem a great way off, and to meet you again, delightful. I 'm sure it won't be long before we sit together.

Then will I not repine, knowing that bird of mine, though flown — learneth beyond the sea, melody new for me, and will return.

Affectionately,

EMILY.

This little poem was enclosed in the fore-going letter: —

> Truth is as old as God,
> His twin identity —
> And will endure as long as He,
> A co-eternity,
> And perish on the day
> That He is borne away
> From mansion of the universe,
> A lifeless Deity.

[Enclosing some leaves, 1854.]

January 2d.

May it come *to-day ?*

Then New Year the sweetest, and long life the merriest, and the Heaven highest — by and by !

EMILIE.

{Spring, 1854.]

PHILADELPHIA.

DEAR MRS HOLLAND AND MINNIE, and Dr Holland too — I have stolen away from company to write a note to you ; and to say that I love you still.

I am not at home — I have been away just five

weeks to-day, and shall not go quite yet back to
Massachusetts. Vinnie is with me here, and we
have wandered together into many new ways.

We were three weeks in Washington, while father
was there, and have been two in Philadelphia.   We
have had many pleasant times, and seen much that
is fair, and heard much that is wonderful — many
sweet ladies and noble gentlemen have taken us by
the hand and smiled upon us pleasantly — and the
sun shines brighter for our way thus far.

I will not tell you what I saw — the elegance,
the grandeur ; you will not care to know the value of
the diamonds my Lord and Lady wore, but if you
have n't been to the sweet Mount Vernon, then I *will*
tell you how on one soft spring day we glided down
the Potomac in a painted boat, and jumped upon
the shore — how hand in hand we stole along up a
tangled pathway till we reached the tomb of General
George Washington, how we paused beside it, and
no one spoke a word, then hand in hand, walked
on again, not less wise or sad for that marble story ;
how we went within the door — raised the latch
he lifted when he last went home — thank the Ones
in Light that he 's since passed in through a brighter
wicket !   Oh, I could spend a long day, if it did not
weary you, telling of Mount Vernon — and I will
sometime if we live and meet again, and God grant
we shall !

I wonder if you have all forgotten us, we have
stayed away so long.   I hope you have n't — I tried

to write so hard before I went from home, but the moments were so busy, and then they *flew* so. I was sure when days *did* come in which I was less busy, I should seek your forgiveness, and it did not occur to me that you might not forgive me. Am I too late to-day? Even if you are angry, I shall keep praying you, till from very weariness, you will take me in. It seems to me many a day since we were in Springfield, and Minnie and the *dumb-bells* seem as vague — as vague ; and sometimes I wonder if I ever dreamed — then if I 'm dreaming now, then if I *always* dreamed, and there is not a world, and not these darling friends, for whom I would not count my life too great a sacrifice. Thank God there is a world, and that the friends we love dwell forever and ever in a house above. I fear I grow incongruous, but to meet my friends does delight me so that I quite forget time and sense and so forth.

Now, my precious friends, if you won't forget me until I get home, and become more sensible, I will write again, and more properly. Why did n't I ask before, if you were well and happy?

Forgetful

Emilie.

[November, 1854.]

Saturday Eve.

I come in flakes, dear Dr Holland, for verily it snows, and as descending swans, here a pinion and

there a pinion, and anon a plume, come the bright
inhabitants of the white home.

I know they fall in Springfield; perhaps you see
them now — and therefore I look out again, to see if
you are looking.

How pleasant it seemed to hear your voice — so
said Vinnie and I, as we as individuals, and then
collectively, read your brief note. Why did n't you
speak to us before? We thought you had forgotten
us — we concluded that one of the bright things
had gone forever more. That is a sober feeling,
and it must n't come too often in such a world as
this. A violet came up next day, and blossomed in
our garden, and were it not for these same flakes,
I would go in the dark and get it, so to send to
you. Thank Him who is in Heaven, Katie Holland
lives! Kiss her on every cheek for me — I really
can't remember how many the bairn has — and give
my warmest recollection to Mrs Holland and Minnie, whom to love, this Saturday night, is no trifling
thing. I 'm very happy that you are happy — and
that you cheat the angels of another one.

I would the many households clad in dark attire
had succeeded so. You must all be happy and
strong and well. I love to have the lamps shine on
your evening table. I love to have the sun shine on
your daily walks.

The 'new house'! God bless it! You will leave
the 'maiden and married life of Mary Powell' behind.

Love and remember   EMILIE.

While the family lived for many years in the old mansion built by Emily Dickinson's grandfather, the Hon. Samuel Fowler Dickinson, they had moved away from it about 1840; and the following letter describes their return after fifteen years to their early home, where Emily was born, and where she died: —

[1855.]

Sabbath Day.

Your voice is sweet, dear Mrs Holland — I wish I heard it oftener.

One of the mortal musics Jupiter denies, and when indeed its gentle measures fall upon my ear, I stop the birds to listen. Perhaps you think I *have* no bird, and this is rhetoric — pray, Mr Whately, what is *that* upon the cherry-tree? Church is done, and the winds blow, and Vinnie is in that pallid land the simple call 'sleep.' They will be wiser by and by, we shall all be wiser! While I sit in the snows, the summer day on which you came and the bees and the south wind, seem fabulous as *Heaven* seems to a sinful world — and I keep remembering it till it assumes a *spectral* air, and nods and winks at me, and then all of you turn to phantoms and vanish slow away. We cannot talk and laugh more, in the parlor where we met, but we learned to love for aye, there, so it is just as well.

We shall sit in a parlor 'not made with hands' unless we are very careful!

I cannot tell you how we moved. I had rather not remember. I believe my ' effects ' were brought in a bandbox, and the ' deathless me,' on foot, not many moments after. I took at the time a memorandum of my several senses, and also of my hat and coat, and my best shoes — but it was lost in the *mêlée*, and I am out with lanterns, looking for myself.

Such wits as I reserved, are so badly shattered that repair is useless — and still I can't help laughing at my own catastrophe. I supposed we were going to make a ' transit,' as heavenly bodies did — but we came budget by budget, as our fellows do, till we fulfilled the pantomime contained in the word ' moved.' It is a kind of *gone-to-Kansas* feeling, and if I sat in a long wagon, with my family tied behind, I should suppose without doubt I was a party of emigrants!

They say that ' home is where the heart is.' I think it is where the *house* is, and the adjacent buildings.

But, my dear Mrs Holland, I have another story, and lay my laughter all away, so that I can sigh. Mother has been an invalid since we came *home*, and Vinnie and I ' regulated,' and Vinnie and I ' got settled,' and still we keep our father's house, and mother lies upon the lounge, or sits in her easy-chair. I don't know what her sickness is, for I am but a simple child, and frightened at myself. I often wish I was a grass, or a toddling daisy, whom all these problems of the dust might not terrify — and should my own machinery get slightly out of gear, *please*, kind ladies and gentlemen, some one stop the wheel, — for I know that with belts and bands of gold, I shall whizz triumphant on the new stream ! Love for you — love for Dr Holland — thanks for his exquisite hymn — tears for your sister in sable, and kisses for Minnie and the bairns.

From your mad

EMILIE.

[Spring, 1856?]

. . . February passed like a skate and I know March. Here is the 'light' the stranger said 'was not on sea or land.' Myself could arrest it, but will not chagrin him.

. . . Cousin Peter told me the Doctor would address Commencement — trusting it insure you both for papa's *fête* I endowed Peter. We do not always know the source of the smile that flows to us. . . .

My flowers are near and foreign, and I have but to cross the floor to stand in the Spice Isles.

The wind blows gay to-day and the jays bark like blue terriers.

I tell you what I see — the landscape of the spirit requires a lung, but no tongue. I hold you few I love, till my heart is red as February and purple as March.

Hand for the Doctor.   EMILY.

[Late Summer, 1856.]

Sabbath Night.

Don't tell, dear Mrs Holland, but wicked as I am, I read my Bible sometimes, and in it as I read to-day, I found a verse like this, where friends should ' go no more out ; ' and there were ' no tears,' and I wished as I sat down to-night that we were *there* — not *here* — and that wonderful world had commenced, which makes such promises, and rather than to write you, I were by your side, and the ' hundred and forty and four thousand' were chatting pleasantly, yet not disturbing us.   And I 'm half tempted to take my seat in that Paradise of which the good man writes, and begin forever and ever *now*, so wondrous does it seem.   My only sketch, profile, of Heaven is a large, blue sky, bluer and larger than the *biggest* I have seen in June, and in it are my friends — all of them — every one of them — those who are with me now, and those who were ' parted' as we walked, and ' snatched up to Heaven.'

If roses had not faded, and frosts had never come, and one had not fallen here and there whom I could not waken, there were no need of other Heaven than the one below — and if God had been here this summer, and seen the things that *I* have seen — I guess that He would think His Paradise superfluous.   Don't

tell Him, for the world, though, for after all He's
said about it, I should like to see what He *was*
building for us, with no hammer, and no stone, and
no journeyman either.   Dear Mrs Holland, I love,
to-night — love you and Dr Holland, and 'time and
sense' — and fading things, and things that do *not*
fade.

I'm so glad you are not a blossom, for those in
my garden fade, and then a 'reaper whose name is
Death' has come to get a few to help him make a
bouquet for himself, so I'm glad you are not a rose
— and I'm glad you are not a bee, for where they
go when summer's done, only the thyme knows, and
even were you a robin, when the west winds came,
you would coolly wink at me, and away, some
morning !

As 'little Mrs Holland,' then, I think I love you
most, and trust that tiny lady will dwell below while
we dwell, and when with many a wonder we seek
the new Land, *her* wistful face, *with* ours, shall look
the last upon the hills, and first upon — well, *Home!*

Pardon my sanity, Mrs Holland, in a world *in*sane,
and love me if you will, for I had rather *be* loved
than to be called a king in earth, or a lord in
Heaven.

Thank you for your sweet note — the clergy are
very well.   Will bring such fragments from them as
shall seem me good.   I kiss my paper here for you
and Dr Holland — would it were cheeks instead.

Dearly,   EMILIE.

P. S. The bobolinks have gone.

[1857 ?]

DEAR SISTER, — After you went, a low wind warbled through the house like a spacious bird, making it high but lonely. When you had gone the love came. I supposed it would. The supper of the heart is when the guest has gone.

Shame is so intrinsic in a strong affection we must all experience Adam's reticence. I suppose the street that the lover travels is thenceforth divine, incapable of turnpike aims.

That you be with me annuls fear and I await Commencement with merry resignation. Smaller than David you clothe me with extreme Goliath.

Friday I tasted life. It was a vast morsel. A circus passed the house — still I feel the red in my mind though the drums are out.

The book you mention, I have not met. Thank you for tenderness.

The lawn is full of south and the odors tangle, and I hear to-day for the first the river in the tree.

You mentioned spring's delaying — I blamed her for the opposite. I would eat evanescence slowly.

Vinnie is deeply afflicted in the death of her dappled cat, though I convince her it is immortal which assists her some. Mother resumes lettuce, involving my transgression — suggestive of yourself, however, which endears disgrace.

' House ' is being ' cleaned.' I prefer pestilence. That is more classic and less fell.

Yours was my first arbutus. It was a rosy boast.
I will send you the first witch hazel.

A woman died last week, young and in hope but
a little while — at the end of our garden. I thought
since of the power of Death, not upon affection, but
its mortal signal. It is to us the Nile.

You refer to the unpermitted delight to be with
those we love. I suppose that to be the license not
granted of God.

> Count not that far that can be had,
> Though sunset lie between —
> Nor that adjacent, that beside,
> Is further than the sun.

Love for your embodiment of it.   EMILY.

[1859.]

God bless you, dear Mrs Holland! I read it in
the paper.

I'm so glad it's a little boy, since now the little
sisters have some one to draw them on the sled —
and if a grand old lady you should live to be,
there's something sweet, they say, in a son's arm.

I pray for the tenants of that holy chamber, the
wrestler, and the wrestled for. I pray for distant
father's heart, swollen, happy heart!

Saviour keep them all!   EMILY.

[Autumn, 1859.]

DEAR HOLLANDS, — Belong to me! We have
no fires yet, and the evenings grow cold. To-morrow, stoves are set. How many barefoot shiver I

trust their Father knows who saw not fit to give them shoes.

Vinnie is sick to-night, which gives the world a russet tinge, usually so red. It is only a headache, but when the head aches next to you, it becomes important. When she is well, time leaps. When she is ill, he lags, or stops entirely.

Sisters are brittle things. God was penurious with me, which makes me shrewd with Him.

One is a dainty sum! One bird, one cage, one flight; one song in those far woods, as yet suspected by faith only!

This is September, and you were coming in September. Come! Our parting is too long. There has been frost enough. We must have summer now, and 'whole legions' of daisies.

The gentian is a greedy flower, and overtakes us all. Indeed, this world is short, and I wish, until I tremble, to touch the ones I love before the hills are red — are gray — are white — are 'born again'! If we knew how deep the crocus lay, we never should let her go. Still, crocuses stud many mounds whose gardeners till in anguish some tiny, vanished bulb.

We saw you that Saturday afternoon, but heedlessly forgot to ask where you were going, so did not know, and could not write. Vinnie saw Minnie flying by, one afternoon at Palmer. She supposed you were all there on your way from the sea, and untied her fancy! To say that her fancy wheedled her is superfluous.

We talk of you together, then diverge on life, then hide in you again, as a safe fold. Don't leave us long, dear friends! You know we 're children still, and children fear the dark.

Are you well at home? Do you work now? Has it altered much since I was there? Are the children women, and the women thinking it will soon be afternoon? We will help each other bear our unique burdens.

Is Minnie with you now? Take her our love, if she is. Do her eyes grieve her now? Tell her she may have half ours.

Mother's favorite sister is sick, and mother will have to bid her good-night. It brings mists to us all; — the aunt whom Vinnie visits, with whom she spent, I fear, her last inland Christmas. Does God take care of those at sea? My aunt is such a timid woman!

Will you write to us? I bring you all their loves — *many*.

They tire me.   EMILIE.

[1860.]

How is your little Byron? Hope he gains his foot without losing his genius. Have heard it ably argued that the poet's genius lay in his foot — as the bee's prong and his song are concomitant. Are you stronger than these? To assault so minute a creature seems to me malign, unworthy of Nature — but the frost is no respecter of persons.

I should be glad to be with you, or to open your letter. Blossoms belong to the bee, if needs be by *habeas corpus.*

EMILY.

Probably about 1861 came this brilliant, yet half pathetic, arraignment of the friends who had not written when Emily expected to hear. Who could resist such a plea?

Friday.

DEAR FRIENDS, — I write to you. I receive no letter.

I say 'they dignify my trust.' I do not disbelieve. I go again. *Cardinals* would n't do it. Cockneys would n't do it, but I can't *stop* to strut, in a world where bells toll. I hear through visitor in town, that 'Mrs Holland is not strong.' The little peacock in me, tells me not to inquire again. Then I remember my tiny friend — how brief she is — how dear she is, and the peacock quite dies away. Now, you need not speak, for perhaps you are weary, and 'Herod' requires all your thought, but if you are *well* — let Annie draw me a little picture of an erect flower; if you are *ill*, she can hang the flower a little on one side !

Then, I shall understand, and you need not stop to write me a letter. Perhaps you laugh at me ! Perhaps the whole United States are laughing at me too ! *I* can't stop for that ! *My* business is to love. I found a bird, this morning, down — down

— on a little bush at the foot of the garden, and wherefore sing, I said, since nobody *hears?*

One sob in the throat, one flutter of bosom — '*My* business is to *sing*' — and away she rose! How do I know but cherubim, once, themselves, as patient, listened, and applauded her unnoticed hymn?

EMILY.

[1864?]

DEAR SISTER, — Father called to say that our steel-yard was fraudulent, exceeding by an ounce the rates of honest men. He had been selling oats. I can-not stop smiling, though it is hours since, that even our steelyard will not tell the truth.

Besides wiping the dishes for Margaret, I wash them now, while she becomes Mrs Lawler, vicarious papa to four previous babes. Must she not be an adequate bride?

I winced at her loss, because I was in the habit of her, and even a new rolling-pin has an embarrass-ing element, but to all except anguish, the mind soon adjusts.

It is also November. The noons are more laconic and the sundowns sterner, and Gibraltar lights make the village foreign. November always seemed to me the Norway of the year. —— is still with the sister who put her child in an ice nest last Monday forenoon. The redoubtable God! I notice where Death has been introduced, he frequently calls, mak-ing it desirable to forestall his advances.

It is hard to be told by the papers that a friend is failing, not even know where the water lies. Incidentally, only, that he comes to land. Is there no voice for these? Where is Love to-day?

Tell the dear Doctor we mention him with a foreign accent, party already to transactions spacious and untold. Nor have we omitted to breathe shorter for our little sister. Sharper than dying is the death for the dying's sake.

News of these would comfort, when convenient or possible.

EMILY.

DEAR SISTER,— It was incredibly sweet that Austin had seen you, and had stood in the dear house which had lost its friend. To see one who had seen you was a strange assurance. It helped dispel the fear that you departed too, for notwithstanding the loved notes and the lovely gift, there lurked a dread that you had gone or would seek to go. 'Where the treasure is,' there is the prospective.

Austin spoke very warmly and strongly of you, and we all felt firmer, and drew a vocal portrait of Kate at Vinnie's request, so vivid that we saw her. . . .

> Not all die early, dying young,
> Maturity of fate
> Is consummated equally
> In ages or a night.
> A hoary boy I 've known to drop
> Whole-statured, by the side
> Of junior of fourscore — 't was act,
> Not period, that died.

EMILY.

Will some one lay this little flower on Mrs
Holland's pillow?

EMILIE.

In handwriting similar to the letters about
1862–68, are several poems, enclosed to the
Hollands, among them, —

> Away from home are some and I,
> An emigrant to be
> In a metropolis of homes
> Is common possibility.
> The habit of a foreign sky
> We, difficult, acquire,
> As children who remain in face,
> The more their feet retire.

And —

> Though my destiny be fustian
> Hers be damask fine —
> Though she wear a silver apron,
> I, a less divine,
>
> Still, my little gypsy being,
> I would far prefer,
> Still my little sunburnt bosom,
> To her rosier.
>
> For when frosts their punctual fingers
> On her forehead lay,
> You and I and Doctor Holland
> Bloom eternally,

Roses of a steadfast summer
In a steadfast land,
Where no autumn lifts her pencil,
And no reapers stand.

In addition to these, many other poems were
sent to the Hollands which have already been
published; all of them, however, showing slight
changes from copies which she retained.

[Autumn, 1876.]

Saturday Eve.

DEAR HOLLANDS, — Good-night! I can't stay
any longer in a world of death. Austin is ill of
fever. I buried my garden last week — our man,
Dick, lost a little girl through the scarlet fever. I
thought perhaps that *you* were dead, and not knowing the sexton's address, interrogate the daisies.
Ah! dainty — dainty Death! Ah! democratic
Death! Grasping the proudest zinnia from my
purple garden, — then deep to his bosom calling
the serf's child!

Say, is he everywhere? Where shall I hide my
things? Who is alive? The woods are dead. Is
Mrs H. alive? Annie and Katie — are they below,
or received to nowhere?

I shall not tell how short time is, for I was told
by lips which sealed as soon as it was said, and the
open revere the shut. You were not here in summer.
Summer? My memory flutters — had I — was there

a summer? You should have seen the fields go
— gay little entomology! Swift little ornithology!
Dancer, and floor, and cadence quite gathered away,
and I, a phantom, to you a phantom, rehearse
the story! An orator of feather unto an audience
of fuzz, — and pantomimic plaudits. 'Quite as good
as a play,' indeed! Tell Mrs Holland she is mine.

Ask her if *vice versa?* Mine is but just the
thief's request — 'Remember me to-day.' Such are
the bright chirographies of the 'Lamb's Book.' Good-
night! My ships are in! — My window overlooks
the wharf! One yacht, and a man-of-war; two
brigs and a schooner! 'Down with the topmast!
Lay her a' hold, a' hold!'   EMILIE.

A letter from Mrs Holland to Emily and her
sister jointly, in 1877, called forth this unique
protest.

SISTER, — A mutual plum is not a plum. I was
too respectful to take the pulp and do not like a
stone.

Send no union letters. The soul must go by
Death alone, so, it must by life, if it is a soul.

If a committee — no matter.

I saw the sunrise on the Alps since I saw you.
Travel why to Nature, when she dwells with us?
Those who lift their hats shall see her, as devout
do God.

I trust you are merry and sound. The chances

are all against the dear, when we are not with them,
though paws of principalities cannot affront if we
are by.

Dr Vaill called here Monday on his way to your
house to get the Doctor to preach for him. Shall
search *The Republican* for a brief of the sermon.
To-day is very homely and awkward as the homely
are who have not mental beauty.

Then follows, —

'The sky is low, the clouds are mean,'

printed at page 103 of the *Poems*, First Series.

[Spring, 1878.]

I thought that 'Birnam Wood' had 'come to
Dunsinane.' Where did you pick arbutus? In
Broadway, I suppose. They say that God is everywhere, and yet we always think of Him as somewhat
of a recluse. . . . It is hard not to hear again that
vital 'Sam is coming' — though if grief is a test of
a priceless life, he is compensated. He was not
ambitious for redemption — that was why it is his.
'To him that hath, shall be given.' Were it not for
the eyes, we would know of you oftener. Have
they no remorse for their selfishness? 'This taber-
nacle' is a blissful trial, but the bliss predominates.

I suppose you will play in the water at Alexandria
Bay, as the baby does at the tub in the drive. . . .
Speak to us when your eyes can spare you, and

'keep us, at home, or by the way,' as the clergyman says, when he folds the church till another
Sabbath.

Lovingly,

EMILY.

[August, 1879.]

LOVED AND LITTLE SISTER, — Vinnie brought in a
sweet pea to-day, which had a pod on the 'off'
side.   Startled by the omen, I hasten to you.

An unexpected impediment to my reply to your
dear last, was a call from my Aunt Elizabeth —' the
only male relative on the female side,' and though
many days since, its flavor of court-martial still sets
my spirit tingling.

With what dismay I read of those columns of
kindred in the Bible — the Jacobites and the Jebu-
sites and the Hittites and the Jacqueminots !

I am sure you are better, for no rheumatism in
its senses would stay after the thermometer struck
ninety !

We are revelling in a gorgeous drought.

The grass is painted brown, and how nature would
look in other than the standard colors, we can all
infer. . . . I bade —— call on you, but Vinnie said
you were 'the other side the globe,' yet Vinnie
thinks Vermont is in Asia, so I don't intend to be
disheartened by trifles.

Vinnie has a new pussy that catches a mouse an
hour.   We call her the 'minute hand.' . . .

Dr Holland's death, in October of 1881, brought grief to many loving hearts, but to the quiet Amherst household peculiar pain, voiced in the notes to follow.

We read the words but know them not. We are too frightened with sorrow. If that dear, tired one must sleep, could we not see him first?

Heaven is but a little way to one who gave it, here. 'Inasmuch,' to him, how tenderly fulfilled!

Our hearts have flown to you before — our breaking voices follow. How can we wait to take you all in our sheltering arms?

Could there be new tenderness, it would be for you, but the heart is full — another throb would split it — nor would we dare to speak to those whom such a grief removes, but we have somewhere heard 'A little child shall lead them.'

EMILY.

Thursday.

After a while, dear, you will remember that there is a heaven — but you can't now. Jesus will excuse it. He will remember his shorn lamb.

The lost one was on such childlike terms with the Father in Heaven. He has passed from confiding to comprehending — perhaps but a step.

The *safety* of a beloved lost is the first anguish. With you, that is peace.

I shall never forget the Doctor's prayer, my first

morning with you — so simple, so believing. *That*
God must be a friend — *that* was a different God —
and I almost felt warmer myself, in the midst of a
tie so sunshiny.

I am yearning to know if he knew he was fleeing
— if he spoke to you. Dare I ask if he suffered?
Some one will tell me a very little, when they have
the strength. . . . Cling tight to the hearts that will
not let you fall.

EMILY.

Panting to help the dear ones and yet not knowing how, lest any voice bereave them but that loved
voice that will not come, if I can rest them, here is
down — or rescue, here is power.

One who only said 'I am sorry' helped me the
most when father ceased — it was too soon for
language.

Fearing to tell mother, some one disclosed it unknown to us. Weeping bitterly, we tried to console
her. She only replied 'I loved him so.'

Had he a tenderer eulogy?

EMILY.

. . . I know you will live for our sake, dear,
you would not be willing to for your own. That is
the duty which saves. While we are trying for
others, power of life comes back, very faint at first,
like the new bird, but by and by it has wings.

How sweetly you have comforted me — the toil

to comfort you, I hoped never would come. A
sorrow on your sunny face is too dark a miracle —
but how sweet that he rose in the morning — accompanied by dawn. How lovely that he spoke with
you, that memorial time ! How gentle that he left
the pang he had not time to feel ! Bequest of
darkness, yet of light, since unborne by him.
'Where thou goest, *we* will go ' — how mutual, how
intimate ! No solitude receives him, but neighborhood and friend.

Relieved forever of the loss of those that must
have fled, but for his sweet haste. Knowing he
could not spare *them*, he hurried like a boy from
that unhappened sorrow. Death has mislaid his
sting — the grave forgot his victory. Because the
flake fell not on him, we will accept the drift, and
wade where he is lain.

Do you remember the clover leaf? The little
hand that plucked it will keep tight hold of mine.

Please give her love to Annie, and Kate, who also
gave a father.

                                        EMILY.

[To Mrs Holland, on the marriage of her daughter Annie,
                December 7, 1881]

SWEET SISTER, — We were much relieved to know
that the dear event had occurred without over-
whelming any loved one, and perhaps it is sweeter
and safer so. I feared much for the parting, to
you, to whom parting has come so thickly in the

last few days. I knew all would be beautiful, and rejoice it was. Few daughters have the immortality of a father for a bridal gift. Could there be one more costly?

As we never have ceased to think of you, we will more tenderly, now. Confide our happiness to Annie, in her happiness. We hope the unknown balm may ease the balm withdrawn.

You and Katie, the little sisters, lose her, yet obtain her, for each new width of love largens all the rest. Mother and Vinnie think and speak. Vinnie hopes to write. Would that mother could, but her poor hand is idle. Shall I return to you your last and sweetest words — 'But I love you all'?

EMILY.

[Christmas, 1881.]

Dare we wish the brave sister a sweet Christmas, who remembered us punctually in sorrow as in peace?

The broken heart is broadest. Had it come all the way in your little hand, it could not have reached us perfecter, though had it, we should have clutched the hand and forgot the rest.

Fearing the day had associations of anguish to you, I was just writing when your token came. Then, humbled with wonder at your self-forgetting, I delayed till now. Reminded again of gigantic Emily Brontë, of whom her Charlotte said 'Full of ruth for others, on herself she had no mercy.' The hearts that never lean, must fall.   To moan is justified.

To thank you for remembering under the piercing circumstances were a profanation.

God bless the hearts that suppose they are beating and are not, and enfold in His infinite tenderness those that do not know they are beating and are.

Shall we wish a triumphant Christmas to the brother withdrawn?   Certainly he possesses it.

> How much of Source escapes with thee —
> How chief thy sessions be —
> For thou hast borne a universe
> Entirely away.

With wondering love,

EMILY.

'Whom seeing not, we ' clasp.

EMILY.

[1883?]

Concerning the little sister, not to assault, not to adjure, but to obtain those constancies which exalt friends, we followed her to St Augustine, since which the trail was lost, or says George Stearns of his alligator, 'there was no such aspect.'

The beautiful blossoms waned at last, the charm of all who knew them, resisting the effort of earth or air to persuade them to root, as the great florist says 'The flower that never will in other climate grow.'

To thank you for its fragrance would be impossible, but then its other blissful traits are more than can be numbered.   And the beloved Christmas, too, for which I never thanked you.   I hope the little heart is well, — *big* would have been the width, — and the health solaced; any news of her as sweet as the first arbutus.

Emily and Vinnie give the love greater every hour.

CHAPTER V ✓

To Mr Samuel Bowles and Mrs Bowles

AS Emily Dickinson approached middle
life, and even before her thirtieth year,
it seemed to become more and more impossible for her to mingle in general society; and
a growing feeling of shyness, as early as 1862
or 1863, caused her to abstain, sometimes,
from seeing the dearest friends who came to
the house. In spite of her sympathy with
sadness, and her deep apprehension of the
tragic element in life, she was not only keenly
humorous and witty, as already said, but,
while made serious by the insistence of life's
pathos, she was yet at heart as ecstatic as
a bird. This combination of qualities made
her companionship, when she vouchsafed it,
peculiarly breezy and stimulating. Such a
nature must inevitably know more pain than
pleasure.

Passionately devoted to her friends, her happiness in their love and trust was at times
almost too intense to bear; and it will already

have been seen how disproportionately great pain was caused by even comparatively slight separations.   With her, pathos lay very near raillery and badinage, — sadness very near delight.

Whether, in writing her poems, the joy of creating was sufficient, or whether a thought of future and wider recognition ever came, it is certain that during life her friends made her audience. She cared more for appreciation and approval from the few who were dear than for any applause from an impersonal public. She herself writes, ' My friends are my estate.'

All her letters show this rare loyalty of soul, those in the preceding chapter particularly, but none perhaps more strongly than those to Mr and Mrs Bowles. Beginning about 1858, the letters cover a period of twenty-six or twenty-seven years. Often a single short poem comprises the entire letter, — sometimes only four lines, and without title, date, or signature, but unmistakably pertinent to a special occasion or subject.

[Late August, 1858 ?]
AMHERST.

DEAR MR BOWLES, — I got the little pamphlet. I think you sent it to me, though unfamiliar with your hand — I may mistake.

Thank you, if I am right. Thank you, if not, since here I find bright pretext to ask you how you are to-night, and for the health of four more, elder and minor Mary, Sallie and Sam, tenderly to inquire.

I hope your cups are full.

I hope your vintage is untouched. In such a porcelain life one likes to be *sure* that all is well lest one stumble upon one's hopes in a pile of broken crockery.

My friends are my estate. Forgive me then the avarice to hoard them! They tell me those were poor early have different views of gold. I don't know how that is.

God is not so wary as we, else He would give us no friends, lest we forget Him! The charms of the heaven in the bush are superseded, I fear, by the heaven in the hand, occasionally.

Summer stopped since you were here. Nobody noticed her — that is, no men and women. Doubtless, the fields are rent by petite anguish, and 'mourners go about' the woods. But this is not for us. Business enough indeed, our stately resurrection! A special courtesy, I judge, from what the clergy say! To the 'natural man' bumblebees would seem an improvement, and a spicing of birds, but far be it from me to impugn such majestic tastes!

Our pastor says we are a 'worm.' How is that reconciled? 'Vain, sinful worm' is possibly of another species.

Do you think we shall 'see God'?   Think of Abraham strolling with Him in genial promenade !

The men are mowing the second hay.   The cocks are smaller than the first, and spicier.   I would distil a cup, and bear to all my friends, drinking to her no more astir, by beck, or burn, or moor !

Good-night, Mr Bowles.   This is what they say who come back in the morning ; also the closing paragraph on repealed lips.   Confidence in day-break modifies dusk.

Blessings for Mrs Bowles, and kisses for the bairns' lips.   We want to see you, Mr Bowles, but spare you the rehearsal of 'familiar truths.'

Good-night,

EMILY.

[Winter, 1858 ?]

Monday Eve.

DEAR MRS BOWLES, — You send sweet messages. Remembrance is more sweet than robins in May orchards.

I love to trust that round bright fires, some, braver than I, take my pilgrim name.   How are papa, mamma, and the little people? . . .

It storms in Amherst five days — it snows, and then it rains, and then soft fogs like veils hang on all the houses, and then the days turn topaz, like a lady's pin.

Thank you for bright bouquet, and afterwards verbena.   I made a plant of a little bough of yellow heliotrope which the bouquet bore me, and call it Mary Bowles. It is many days since the summer day when you came with Mr Bowles, and before another summer day it will be many days. My garden is a little knoll with faces under it, and only the pines sing tunes, now the birds are absent. I cannot walk to the distant friends on nights piercing as these, so I put both hands on the window-pane, and try to think how birds fly, and imitate, and fail, like Mr 'Rasselas.' I could make a balloon of a dandelion, but the fields are gone, and only 'Professor Lowe' remains to weep with me. If I built my house I should like to call you. I talk of all these things with Carlo, and his eyes grow meaning, and his shaggy feet keep a slower pace. Are you safe to-night? I hope you may be glad. I ask God on my knee to send you much prosperity, few winter days, and long suns. I have a childish hope to gather all I love together and sit down beside and smile. . . .

Will you come to Amherst? The streets are very cold now, but we will make you warm. But if you never came, perhaps you could write a letter, saying how much you would like to, if it were 'God's will.' I give good-night, and daily love to you and Mr Bowles.   EMILIE.

[1859.]
                                       AMHERST.

I should like to thank dear Mrs Bowles for the little book, except my cheek is red with shame because I write so often.   Even the ' lilies of the field ' have their dignities.

Why did you bind it in green and gold?   The *immortal* colors.   I take it for an emblem.   I never read before what Mr Parker wrote.

I heard that he was ' poison.'   Then I like poison very well.   Austin stayed from service yesterday afternoon, and I . . . found him reading my Christmas gift. . . . I wish the ' faith of the fathers ' did n't wear brogans, and carry blue umbrellas.   I give you all ' New Year ! '   I think you kept gay Christmas, from the friend's account, and can only sigh with one not present at ' John Gilpin,' ' and when he next doth ride a race,' etc.   You picked your berries from my holly.   Grasping Mrs Bowles !

To-day is very cold, yet have I much bouquet upon the window-pane of moss and fern.   I call them saints' flowers, because they do not romp as other flowers do, but stand so still and white.

The snow is very tall, . . . which makes the trees so low that they tumble my hair, when I cross the bridge.

I think there will be no spring this year, the flowers are gone so far.   Let us have spring in our heart, and never mind the orchises ! . . . Please have my love, mother's, and Vinnie's.   Carlo sends a brown kiss, and pussy a gray and white one, to each of the children.

Please, now I write so often, make lamplighter of me, then I shall not have lived in vain.

Dear Mrs Bowles, dear Mr Bowles, dear Sally —
Sam and Mamie, now all shut your eyes, while I do
benediction !

Lovingly,   EMILY.

[Written in 1861, on the birth of a son.]

DEAR MARY, — Can you leave your flower long
enough just to look at mine?

Which is the prettiest? I shall tell you myself,
some day. I used to come to comfort you, but now
to tell you how glad I am, and how glad we all are.
. . . You must not stay in New York any more —
you must come back now, and bring the blanket to
Massachusetts where we can all look. What a
responsible shepherd ! Four lambs in one flock !
Shall you be glad to see us, or shall we seem old-
fashioned, by the face in the crib?

Tell him I 've got a pussy for him, with a spotted
gown ; and a dog with ringlets.

We have very cold days since you went away, and
I think you hear the wind blow far as the Brevoort
House, it comes from so far, and crawls so. Don't
let it blow baby away. Will you call him Robert
for me? He is the bravest man alive, but *his* boy
has no mamma. That makes us all weep, don't it?

Good-night, Mary.

EMILY.

One of the very few of Emily Dickinson's
verses named by herself was sent Mrs Bowles
soon after the preceding letter.

BABY.

Teach him, when he makes the names,
Such an one to say
On his babbling, berry lips
As should sound to me —
Were my ear as near his nest
As my thought, to-day —
As should sound — ' forbid us not ' —
Some like ' Emily.'

[August, 1861.]

MARY, — I do not know of you, a long while.
I remember you — several times. I wish I knew if
you kept me? The doubt, like the mosquito,
buzzes round my faith. We are all human, Mary,
until we are divine, and to some of us, that is far
off, and to some as near as the lady ringing at the
door; perhaps *that's* what alarms. I say I will go
myself — I cross the river, and climb the fence —
now I am at the gate, Mary — now I am in the hall
— now I am looking your heart in the eye !

Did it wait for me — did it go with the company?
Cruel company, who have the stocks, and farms,
and creeds — and *it* has just its heart ! I hope you
are glad, Mary; no pebble in the brook to-day — no
film on noon.

I can think how you look; you can't think how I
look; I 've got more freckles, since you saw me,

playing with the school-boys; then I pare the
' Juneating ' to make the pie, and get my fingers
' tanned.'

Summer went very fast — she got as far as the
woman from the hill, who brings the blueberry, and
that is a long way. I shall have no winter this
year, on account of the soldiers. Since I cannot
weave blankets or boots, I thought it best to
omit the season. Shall present a ' memorial ' to
God when the maples turn. Can I rely on your
' name '?

How is your garden, Mary? Are the pinks true,
and the sweet williams faithful? I 've got a geranium like a sultana, and when the humming-
birds come down, geranium and I shut our eyes,
and go far away.

Ask ' Mamie ' if I shall catch her a butterfly with
a vest like a Turk? I will, if she will build him a
house in her ' morning-glory.'

Vinnie would send her love, but she put on a
white frock, and went to meet to-morrow — a few
minutes ago; mother would send her love, but she
is in the ' eave spout,' sweeping up a leaf that blew
in last November; I brought my own, myself, to
you and Mr Bowles.

Please remember me, because I remember you —
always.

Then follows the poem beginning ' My river
runs to thee,' published in the First Series of
the _Poems_, page 54.

Don't cry, dear Mary. Let us do that for you, because you are too tired now. We don't know how dark it is, but if you are at sea, perhaps when we say that we are there, you won't be as afraid.

The waves are very big, but every one that covers you, covers us, too.

Dear Mary, you can't see us, but we are close at your side. May we comfort you?

Lovingly,

EMILY.

[Autumn, 1861.]

FRIEND, SIR, — I did not see you. I am very sorry. Shall I keep the wine till you come again, or send it in by Dick? It is now behind the door in the library, also an unclaimed flower. I did not know you were going so soon. Oh! my tardy feet.

Will you not come again?

Friends are gems, infrequent. Potosi is a care, sir. I guard it reverently, for I could not afford to be poor now, after affluence. I hope the hearts in Springfield are not so heavy as they were. God bless the hearts in Springfield.

I am happy you have a horse. I hope you will get stalwart, and come and see us many years.

I have but two acquaintance, the 'quick and the dead' — and would like more.

I write you frequently, and am much ashamed. My voice is not quite loud enough to cross so many fields, which will, if you please, apologize for my pencil.

Will you take my love to Mrs Bowles, whom I remember every day?

EMILIE.

Vinnie hallos from the world of night-caps, 'don't forget her love.'

[January, 1862.]

DEAR FRIEND, — Are you willing? I am so far from land. To offer you the cup, it might some Sabbath come *my* turn. Of wine how solemn-full!

Did you get the doubloons — did you vote upon 'Robert'? You said you would come in February. Only three weeks more to wait at the gate!

While you are sick, we — are homesick. Do you look out to-night? The moon rides like a girl through a topaz town. I don't think we shall ever be merry again — you are ill so long. When did the dark happen?

I skipped a page to-night, because I come so often, now, I might have tired you.

That page is fullest, though.

Vinnie sends her love. I think father and mother care a great deal for you, and hope you may be well. When you tire with pain, to know that eyes would cloud, in Amherst — might that comfort, *some?*

EMILY.

We never forget Mary.

DEAR MR BOWLES, — Thank you.

> Faith is a fine invention
> When gentlemen can see!
> But microscopes are prudent
> In an emergency![1]

You spoke of the ʻEast.ʼ   I have thought about it this winter.

Donʼt you think you and I should be shrewder to take the mountain road?

That bareheaded life, under the grass, worries one like a wasp.

The rose is for Mary.

EMILY.

> The zeros taught us phosphorus —
> We learned to like the fire
> By playing glaciers when a boy,
> And tinder guessed by power
>
> Of opposite to balance odd,
> If white, a red must be ![2]
> Paralysis, our primer dumb
> Unto vitality.

I couldnʼt let Austinʼs note go, without a word.

EMILY.

[1] Second Series, page 53.

[2] The poems enclosed in letters to friends are often slightly different from her own copies preserved in the manuscript volumes.   This line, for instance, in another place reads ʻEclipses suns imply.ʼ

Sunday Night.

DEAR MARY, — Could you leave 'Charlie' long enough? Have you time for *me*? I sent Mr Bowles a little note, last Saturday morning, asking him to do an errand for me.

I forgot he was going to Washington, or I should n't have troubled him, so late. Now, Mary, I fear he did not get it, and *you* tried to do the errand for me — and it troubled you. Did it? Will you tell me? Just say with your pencil ' It did n't tire me, Emily,' and then I shall be sure, for with all your care, I would not have taxed you for the world.

You never refused me, Mary, you cherished me many times, but I thought it must seem so selfish to ask the favor of Mr Bowles just as he went from home, only I forgot that. Tell me to-night just a word, Mary, with your own hand, so I shall know I harassed none — and I will be *so* glad.

Austin told us of Charlie — I send a rose for his small hands.

Put it in, when he goes to sleep, and then he will dream of Emily, and when you bring him to Amherst we shall be ' old friends.' Don't love him so well, you know, as to forget us. We shall wish he was n't *there*, if you do, I 'm afraid, sha'n't we?

I 'll remember you, if you like me to, while Mr Bowles is gone, and that will stop the lonely, some, but I cannot agree to stop when he gets home from Washington.

Good-night, Mary. You won't forget my little note, to-morrow, in the mail. It will be the first one you ever wrote me in your life, and yet, was I the little friend a long time? *Was* I, Mary?

EMILY.

[March, 1862.]

Perhaps you thought I did n't care — because I stayed out, yesterday. I *did* care, Mr Bowles. I pray for your sweet health to Allah every morning, but something troubled me, and I knew you needed light and air, so I did n't come. Nor have I the conceit that you *noticed* me — but I could n't bear that you, or Mary, so gentle to me, should think me forgetful.

It 's little at the most, we can do for ours, and we must do *that* flying, or our things are flown !

Dear friend, I wish you were well.

It grieves me till I cannot speak, that you are suffering. Won't you come back? Can't I bring you something? My little balm might be o'erlooked by wiser eyes, you know. Have you tried the breeze that swings the sign, or the hoof of the dandelion? *I* own 'em — wait for mine ! This is all I have to say. Kinsmen need say nothing, but 'Swiveller' may be sure of the

'MARCHIONESS.'

Love for Mary.

DEAR FRIEND, — . . . Austin is disappointed — he expected to see you to-day. He is sure you

won't go to sea without first speaking to him. I
presume if Emily and Vinnie knew of his writing,
they would entreat him to ask you not.

Austin is chilled by Frazer's murder.[1] He says
his brain keeps saying over ' Frazer is killed ' —
' Frazer is killed,' just as father told it to him. Two
or three words of lead, that dropped so deep they
keep weighing. Tell Austin how to get over them !

He is very sorry you are not better. He cares
for you when at the office, and afterwards, too, at
home ; and sometimes wakes at night, with a worry
for you he did n't finish quite by day. He would
not like it that I betrayed him, so you 'll never
tell. . . .

Mary sent beautiful flowers. Did she tell you ?

[Spring, 1862.]

DEAR FRIEND, — The hearts in Amherst ache to-
night — you could not know how hard. They
thought they could not wait, last night, until the
engine sang a pleasant tune that time, because that
you were coming. The flowers waited, in the vase,
and love got peevish, watching. A railroad person
rang, to bring an evening paper — Vinnie tipped
pussy over, in haste to let you in, and I, for joy and
dignity, held tight in my chair. My hope put out a
petal.

You would come, to-day, — but . . . we don't be-

---

[1] A son of President Stearns of Amherst College, who
was killed during the war, 13th March, 1862.

lieve it, now; 'Mr Bowles not coming!' Would n't you, to-morrow, and this but be a bad dream, gone by next morning?

Please do not take our *spring* away, since you blot summer out! We cannot count our tears for this, because they drop so fast. . . .

Dear friend, we meant to make *you* brave, but moaned before we thought. . . . If you'll be sure and get well, we'll try to bear it. If we could only care the less, it would be so much easier. Your letter troubled my throat. It gave that little scalding we could not know the reason for till we grew far up.

I must do my good-night in crayon I meant to in red.

Love for Mary.

                                        EMILY.

After Mr Bowles had sailed for Europe, Emily sent this quaintly consoling note to Springfield.

[Early Summer, 1862.]

DEAR MARY, — When the best is gone, I know that other things are not of consequence. The heart wants what it wants, or else it does not care.

You wonder why I write so. Because I cannot help. I like to have you know some care — so when your life gets faint for its other life, you can lean on us. We won't break, Mary. We look very small, but the reed can carry weight.

Not to see what we love is very terrible, and talking does n't ease it, and nothing does but just itself. The eyes and hair we chose are all there are — to us. Is n't it so, Mary?

I often wonder how the love of Christ is done when that below holds so.

I hope the little 'Robert' coos away the pain. Perhaps your flowers help, some. . . .

The frogs sing sweet to-day — they have such pretty, lazy times — how nice to be a frog ! . . .

Mother sends her love to you — she has a sprained foot, and can go but little in the house, and not abroad at all.

Don't dishearten, Mary, we 'll keep thinking of you. Kisses for all.

EMILY.

[To Mr Bowles, June, 1862.]

DEAR FRIEND, — You go away — and where you go we cannot come — but then the months have names — and each one comes but once a year — and though it seems they never could, they sometimes do, go by.

We hope you are more well than when you lived in America, and that those foreign people are kind, and true, to you. We hope you recollect each life you left behind, even ours, the least.

We wish we knew how Amherst looked, in your memory. Smaller than it did, maybe, and yet things swell, by leaving, if big in themselves.

We hope you will not alter, but be the same we grieved for when the *China* sailed.

If you should like to hear the news, we did not die here — we did not change. We have the guests we did, except yourself — and the roses hang on the same stems as before you went. Vinnie trains the honeysuckle, and the robins steal the string for nests — quite, quite as they used to.

I have the errand from my heart — I might forget to tell it. Would you please to come home? The long life's years are scant, and fly away, the Bible says, like a told story — and sparing is a solemn thing, somehow, it seems to me — and I grope fast, with my fingers, for all out of my sight I own, to get it nearer.

I had one letter from Mary. I think she tries to be patient — but you would n't want her to succeed, would you, Mr Bowles?

It 's fragrant news, to know they pine, when we are out of sight.

It is 'most Commencement. The little cousin from Boston has come, and the hearts in Pelham have an added thrill. We shall miss you, most, dear friend, who annually smiled with us, at the gravities. I question if even Dr Vaill have his wonted applause.

Should anybody, where you go, talk of Mrs Browning, you must hear for us, and if you touch her grave, put one hand on the head, for me — her unmentioned mourner.

Father and mother, and Vinnie and Carlo, send
their love to you, and warm wish for your health —
and I am taking lessons in prayer, so to coax God
to keep you safe. Good-night, dear friend. You
sleep so far, how can I know you hear?

EMILY.

DEAR FRIEND, — I cannot see you. You will not
less believe me. That you return to us alive is
better than a summer, and more to hear your voice
below than news of any bird.

EMILY.

[August, 1862.]

DEAR MR BOWLES, — Vinnie is trading with a tin
peddler — buying water-pots for me to sprinkle
geraniums with when you get home next winter,
and she has gone to the war.

Summer is n't so long as it was, when we stood
looking at it before you went away; and when I
finish August, we 'll hop the autumn very soon, and
then 't will be yourself.

I don't know how many will be glad to see you, —
because I never saw your whole friends, but I have
heard that in large cities noted persons chose you —
though how glad those I know will be, is easier told.

I tell you, Mr Bowles, it is a suffering to have a sea
— no care how blue — between your soul and you.

The hills you used to love when you were in
Northampton, miss their old lover, could they

speak; and the puzzled look deepens in Carlo's forehead as the days go by and you never come.

I 've learned to read the steamer place in newspapers now. It 's 'most like shaking hands with you, or more like your ringing at the door.

We reckon your coming by the fruit. When the grape gets by, and the pippin and the chestnut — when the days are a little short by the clock, and a little long by the want — when the sky has new red gowns, and a purple bonnet — then we say you will come. I am glad that kind of time goes by.

It is easier to look behind at a pain, than to see it coming.

A soldier called, a morning ago, and asked for a nosegay to take to battle. I suppose he thought we kept an aquarium.

How sweet it must be to one to come home, whose home is in so many houses, and every heart a 'best room.' I mean you, Mr Bowles. . . . Have not the clovers names to the bees?

EMILY.

Before he comes
We weigh the time,
'T is heavy, and 't is light.
When he departs
An emptiness
Is the superior freight.

EMILY.

While asters
On the hill
Their everlasting fashions set,
And covenant gentians frill !

EMILY.

[Late Autumn, 1862.]

So glad we are, a stranger 'd deem
'T was sorry that we were ;
For where the holiday should be
There publishes a tear ;
Nor how ourselves be justified,
Since grief and joy are done
So similar, an optizan
Could not decide between.

[Early Winter, 1862.]

DEAR FRIEND, — Had we the art like you, to
endow so many, by just recovering our health,
't would give us tender pride, nor could we keep
the news, but carry it to you, who seem to us to
own it most.

So few that live have life, it seems of quick im-
portance not one of those escape by death. And
since you gave us fear, congratulate us for ourselves
— you give us safer peace.

How extraordinary that life's large population
contain so few of power to us — and those a vivid
species who leave no mode, like Tyrian dye.

Remembering these minorities, permit our gratitude for you. We ask that you be cautious, for many sakes, excelling ours. To recapitulate the stars were useless as supreme. Yourself is yours, dear friend, but ceded, is it not, to here and there a minor life? Do not defraud these, for gold may be bought, and purple may be bought, but the sale of the spirit never did occur.

Do not yet work. No public so exorbitant of any as its friend, and we can wait your health. Besides, there is an idleness more tonic than toil.

> The loss of sickness — was it loss?
> Or that ethereal gain
> You earned by measuring the grave,
> Then measuring the sun.

Be sure, dear friend, for want you have estates of lives.

EMILY.

[With Flowers.]

> If she had been the mistletoe,
> And I had been the rose,
> How gay upon your table
> My velvet life to close !
> Since I am of the Druid,
> And she is of the dew,
> I 'll deck tradition's buttonhole,
> And send the rose to you.

E.

DEAR MR BOWLES, — I can't thank you any more. You are thoughtful so many times you grieve me always; *now* the old words are numb, and there are n't any new ones.

Brooks are useless in freshet time. When you come to Amherst— please God it were to-day — I will tell you about the picture — if I *can,* I will.

> *Speech* is a prank of Parliament,
> *Tears* a trick of the nerve, —
> But the heart with the heaviest freight on
> Does n't always swerve.
>
> EMILY.

Perhaps you think me stooping !
I 'm not ashamed of that !
Christ stooped until he touched the grave !
Do those at sacrament
Commemorate dishonor —
Or love, annealed of love,
Until it bend as low as death
Re-royalized above ?

> The juggler's hat her country is,
> The mountain gorse the bee 's.

> I stole them from a bee,
> Because — thee !
> Sweet plea —
> He pardoned me !
>
> EMILY.

Besides the verses given here, many others were sent to Mr and Mrs Bowles, as to the Hollands, which, having already been published in one or the other volume of the *Poems*, will not be reprinted.

[Summer, 1863.]

DEAR FRIENDS, — I am sorry you came, because you went away.

Hereafter, I will pick no rose, lest it fade or prick me.

I would like to have you dwell here.

Though it is almost nine o'clock, the skies are gay and yellow, and there's a purple craft or so, in which a friend could sail. To-night looks like 'Jerusalem'! . . . I hope we may all behave so as to reach Jerusalem.

How are your hearts to-day? Ours are pretty well. I hope your tour was bright, and gladdened Mrs Bowles. Perhaps the retrospect will call you back some morning.

You shall find us all at the gate if you come in a hundred years, just as we stood that day. If it become of 'jasper' previously, you will not object, so that we lean there still, looking after you.

I rode with Austin this morning. He showed me mountains that touched the sky, and brooks that sang like bobolinks. Was he not very kind? I will give them to you, for they are mine, and 'all things are mine,' excepting 'Cephas and Apollos,' for whom I have no taste. Vinnie's love brims mine.

Take

EMILIE.

DEAR MRS BOWLES, — Since I have no sweet flower to send you, I enclose my heart. A little one, sunburnt, half broken sometimes, yet close as the spaniel to its friends. Your flowers come from heaven, to which, if I should ever go, I will pluck you palms.

My words are far away when I attempt to thank you, so take the silver tear instead, from my full eye.

You have often remembered me.

I have little dominion. Are there not wiser than I, who, with curious treasure, could requite your gift?

Angels fill the hand that loaded

EMILY'S.

> Nature and God, I neither knew,
> Yet both, so well knew me
> They startled, like executors
> Of an identity.
> Yet neither told, that I could learn;
> My secret as secure
> As Herschel's private interest,
> Or Mercury's affair.

[1863.]

DEAR FRIEND, — You remember the little 'meeting' we held for you last spring? We met again, Saturday.

'T was May when we 'adjourned,' but then adjourns are all. The meetings were alike, Mr Bowles.

The topic did not tire us, so we chose no new. We voted to remember you so long as both should live, including immortality; to count you as ourselves, except sometimes more tenderly, as now, when you are ill, and we, the haler of the two — and so I bring the bond we sign so many times, for you to read when chaos comes, or treason, or decay, still witnessing for morning. . . . We hope our joy to see you gave of its own degree to you. We pray for your new health, the prayer that goes not down when they shut the church. We offer you our cups — stintless, as to the bee, — the lily, her new liquors.

Would you like summer?   Taste of ours.

Spices? Buy here!

Ill!   We have berries, for the parching!

Weary!   Furloughs of down!

Perplexed!   Estates of violet trouble ne'er looked on!

Captive!   We bring reprieve of roses!

Fainting!   Flasks of air!

Even for Death, a fairy medicine.

But, which is it, sir?   EMILY.

I 'll send the feather from my hat!
Who knows but at the sight of *that*
My sovereign will relent?
As trinket, worn by faded child,
Confronting eyes long comforted
Blisters the adamant!

                    EMILY.

Her breast is fit for pearls,
But I was not a diver.
Her brow is fit for thrones,
But I had not a crest.
Her heart is fit for rest —
I, a sparrow, build there
Sweet of twigs and twine,
My perennial nest.

[1864?]

DEAR FRIEND, — How hard to thank you — but the large heart requites itself. Please to need me. I wanted to ask you to receive Mr Browning from me, but you denied my Brontë — so I did not dare.

Is it too late now? I should like so much to remind you how kind you had been to me.

You could choose — as you did before — if it would not be obnoxious — except where you 'measured by your heart,' you should measure this time by mine. I wonder which would be biggest !

Austin told, Saturday morning, that you were not so well. 'T was sundown, all day, Saturday — and Sunday such a long bridge no news of you could cross !

Teach us to miss you less because the fear to miss you more haunts us all the time. We did n't care so much, once. I wish it was then, now, but you kept tightening, so it can't be stirred to-day. You did n't mean to be worse, did you? Was n't it a mistake?

Won't you decide soon to be the strong man we first knew? 'T would lighten things so much — and yet that man was not so dear — I guess you'd better not.

We pray for you, every night. A homely shrine our knee, but Madonna looks at the heart first.

Dear friend — don't discourage !

> Affectionately,
>
> EMILY.

> No wilderness can be
> Where *this* attendeth thee —
> No desert noon,
> No fear of frost to come
> Haunt the perennial bloom,
> But certain June !
>
> EMILY.

The following lines, sent with flowers, have almost as quaint and 'seventeenth century' a flavor as the now famous quatrain beginning, —

'A death-blow is a life-blow to some.'

> If recollecting were forgetting
> Then I remember not.
> And if forgetting, recollecting,
> How near I had forgot !
> And if to miss were merry,
> And if to mourn were gay,
> How very blithe the fingers
> That gathered this, to-day !
>
> EMILIE.

. Other verses, sent at different times, were
written in the same general hand, — that of
the early middle period, from about 1863 to
1870; among them : —

> ' They have not chosen me,' he said,
> ' But I have chosen them.'
> Brave, broken-hearted statement
> Uttered in Bethlehem !
>
> *I* could not have told it,
> But since Jesus dared,
> Sovereign ! know a daisy
> Thy dishonor shared.   EMILY.

Saturday.

Mother never asked a favor of Mr Bowles before
— that he accept from her the little barrel of apples.
' Sweet apples,' she exhorts me, with an occasional
Baldwin for Mary and the squirrels.

                              EMILY.

> Just once — oh ! least request !
> Could adamant refuse
> So small a grace,
> So scanty put,
> Such agonizing terms?
>
> Would not a God of flint
> Be conscious of a sigh,
> As down his heaven dropt remote,
> ' Just once, sweet Deity ? '

Saturday
Mother never asked
a favor of Mr Bowles
before – that he'd
accept from her
the little Barrel
of Apples.
"Sweet Apples". She
exhorts me – with an
occasional Baldwin
in Trays, and the
Squirrels   Emily

A spray of white pine was enclosed with this note : —

> A feather from the whippoorwill
> That everlasting sings !
> Whose galleries are sunrise,
> Whose opera the springs,
> Whose emerald nest the ages spin
> Of mellow, murmuring thread,
> Whose beryl egg, what school boys-hunt
> In ' recess ' overhead !
>
> EMILY.

We part with the river at the flood through a timid custom, though with the same waters we have often played.

EMILY.

[1865?]

DEAR FRIEND, — Vinnie accidentally mentions that you hesitated between the *Theophilus* and the *Junius.*

Would you confer so sweet a favor as to accept that too, when you come again?

I went to the room as soon as you left, to confirm your presence, recalling the Psalmist's sonnet to God beginning

> I have no life but this —
> To lead it here,
> Nor any death but lest
> Dispelled from there.
> Nor tie to earths to come,
> Nor action new,
> Except through this extent —
> The love of you.

It is strange that the most intangible thing is the most adhesive.

Your ' rascal.'

I washed the adjective.

[1868 ?]

I should think you would have few letters, for your own are so noble that they make men afraid. And sweet as your approbation is, it is had in fear, lest your depth convict us.

You compel us each to remember that when water ceases to rise, it has commenced falling. That is the law of flood.

The last day that I saw you was the newest and oldest of my life.

Resurrection can come but once, first, to the same house.   Thank you for leading us by it.

Come always, dear friend, but refrain from going. You spoke of not liking to be forgotten.   Could you, though you would?

Treason never knew you.

EMILY.

[1869?]

DEAR FRIEND, — You have the most triumphant face out of Paradise, probably because you are there constantly, instead of ultimately.

Ourselves we do inter with sweet derision the channel of the dust; who once achieves, invalidates the balm of that religion, that doubts as fervently as it believes.

EMILY.

Wednesday.

Dear Mr Bowles's note, of itself a blossom, came
only to-night.

I am glad it lingered, for each was all the heart
could hold.

EMILY.

Of your exquisite act there can be no acknowledgment but the ignominy that grace gives.

EMILY.

> Could mortal lip divine
> The undeveloped freight
> Of a delivered syllable,
> 'T would crumble with the weight !

[1873.]

DEAR FRIEND, — It was so delicious to see you
— a peach before the time — it makes all seasons
possible, and zones a caprice.

We, who arraign the *Arabian Nights* for their un-
derstatement, escape the stale sagacity of supposing
them sham.

We miss your vivid face, and the besetting accents
you bring from your Numidian haunts.

Your coming welds anew that strange trinket of
life which each of us wear and none of us own ;
and the phosphorescence of yours startles us for its
permanence.

Please rest the life so many own — for gems
abscond.

In your own beautiful words — for the voice is
the palace of all of us, —

'Near, but remote.'

EMILY.

[1874.]

DEAR FRIEND, — The paper wanders so I cannot
write my name on it, so I give you father's portrait
instead.

> As summer into autumn slips
> And yet we sooner say
> 'The summer' than 'the autumn,' lest
> We turn the sun away,
>
> And almost count it an affront
> The presence to concede
> Of one however lovely, not
> The one that we have loved, —
>
> So we evade the charge of years,
> One, one attempting shy
> The circumvention of the shaft
> Of life's declivity.　　EMILY.

If we die, will you come for us, as you do for
father?

'Not born,' yourself ' to die,' you must reverse us
all.

> Last to adhere
> When summers swerve away —
> Elegy of
> Integrity.

To remember our own Mr Bowles is all we can do.
With grief it is done, so warmly and long, it can
never be new.

EMILY.

In January of 1878, Mr Bowles died, leaving
a sense of irreparable loss, not only to his
friends, but to his great constituency through
The Republican, into whose success he had
woven the very tissue of his own magnetic
personality.

[January, 1878.]

I hasten to you, Mary, because no moment must
be lost when a heart is breaking, for though it broke
so long, each time is newer than the last, if it broke
truly.   To be willing that I should speak to you was
so generous, dear.

Sorrow almost resents love, it is so inflamed.

I am glad if the broken words helped you.   I
had not hoped so much, I felt so faint in uttering
them, thinking of your great pain.   Love makes us
' heavenly ' without our trying in the least.   'T is
easier than a Saviour — it does not stay on high and
call us to its distance; its low ' Come unto me '
begins in every place.   It makes but one mistake,
it tells us it is ' rest ' — perhaps its toil is rest, but
what we have not known we shall know again, that
divine ' again ' for which we are all breathless.

I am glad you ' work.'   Work is a bleak redeemer, but it does redeem; it tires the flesh so that can't tease the spirit.

Dear 'Mr Sam' is very near, these midwinter days. When purples come on Pelham, in the afternoon, we say 'Mr Bowles's colors.' I spoke to him once of his Gem chapter, and the beautiful eyes rose till they were out of reach of mine, in some hallowed fathom.

Not that he goes — we love him more who led us while he stayed. Beyond earth's trafficking frontier, for what he moved, he made.

Mother is timid and feeble, but we keep her with us. She thanks you for remembering her, and never forgets you. . . . Your sweet 'and left me all alone,' consecrates your lips.

EMILY.

[Spring, 1878.]

Had you never spoken to any, dear, they would not upbraid you, but think of you more softly, as one who had suffered too much to speak. To forget you would be impossible, had we never seen you; for you were his for whom we moan while consciousness remains. As he was himself Eden, he is with Eden, for we cannot become what we were not.

I felt it sweet that you needed me — though but a simple shelter I will always last. I hope your boys and girls assist his dreadful absence, for sorrow does not stand so still on their flying hearts.

How fondly we hope they look like him — that his beautiful face may be abroad.

Was not his countenance on earth graphic as a spirit's? The time will be long till you see him, dear, but it will be short, for have we not each our heart to dress — heavenly as his?

He is without doubt with my father. Thank you for thinking of him, and the sweet, last respect you so faithfully paid him.

Mother is growing better, though she cannot stand, and has not power to raise her head for a glass of water. She thanks you for being sorry, and speaks of you with love. . . . Your timid 'for his sake,' recalls that sheltering passage, 'for his sake who loved us, and gave himself to die for us.'

EMILY.

[1879.]

How lovely to remember! How tenderly they told of you! Sweet toil for smitten hands to console the smitten!

Labors as endeared may engross our lost. Buds of other days quivered in remembrance. Hearts of other days lent their solemn charm.

Life of flowers lain in flowers — what a home of dew! And the bough of ivy; was it as you said? Shall I plant it softly?

There were little feet, white as alabaster.

Dare I chill them with the soil?

VOL. I. — 15

Nature is our eldest mother, she will do no harm.

Let the phantom love that enrolls the sparrow shield you softer than a child.

[April, 1880.]

DEAR MARY, — The last April that father lived, lived I mean below, there were several snow-storms, and the birds were so frightened and cold, they sat by the kitchen door. Father went to the barn in his slippers and came back with a breakfast of grain for each, and hid himself while he scattered it, lest it embarrass them. Ignorant of the name or fate of their benefactor, their descendants are singing this afternoon.

As I glanced at your lovely gift, his April returned. I am powerless toward your tenderness.

Thanks of other days seem abject and dim, yet antiquest altars are the fragrantest. The past has been very near this week, but not so near as the future — both of them pleading, the latter priceless.

David's grieved decision haunted me when a little girl. I hope he has found Absalom.

Immortality as a guest is sacred, but when it becomes as with you and with us, a member of the family, the tie is more vivid. . . .

If affection can reinforce, you, dear, shall not fall.

EMILY.

[Probably the famous ' Yellow Day,' September 6, 1881.]
Tuesday.

DEAR MARY, — I give you only a word this mysterious morning in which we must light the lamps to see each other's faces, thanking you for the trust too confiding for speech.

You spoke of enclosing the face of your child. As it was not there, forgive me if I tell you, lest even the copy of sweetness abscond ; and may I trust you received the flower the mail promised to take you, my foot being incompetent?

The timid mistake about being ' forgotten,' shall I caress or reprove? Mr Samuel's ' sparrow ' does not ' fall ' without the fervent ' notice.'

' Would you see us, would Vinnie?' Oh, my doubting Mary! Were you and your brave son in my father's house, it would require more prowess than mine to resist seeing you.

Shall I still hope for the picture? And please address to my full name, as the little note was detained and opened, the name being so frequent in town, though not an Emily but myself.

Vinnie says ' give her my love, and tell her I would delight to see her ;' and mother combines.

There should be no tear on your cheek, dear, had my hand the access to brush it away.

EMILY.

[1881.]

DEAR MARY, — To have been the mother of the beautiful face, is of itself fame, and the look of

Arabia in the eyes is like Mr Samuel. ' Mr Samuel' is his memorial name. 'Speak, that we may see thee,' and Gabriel no more ideal than his swift eclipse. Thank you for the beauty, which I reluctantly return, and feel like committing a ' startling fraud' in that sweet direction. If her heart is as magical as her face, she will wreck many a spirit, but the sea is ordained.

Austin looked at her long and earnestly.

' Yes, it is Sam's child.'   His Cashmere confederate. It is best, dear, you have so much to do. Action is redemption.

' And again a little while and ye shall not see me,' Jesus confesses is temporary.

Thank you indeed.

EMILY.

END OF VOLUME I.

LETTERS

OF

EMILY DICKINSON

Volume II

LETTERS

OF

EMILY DICKINSON

Volume II

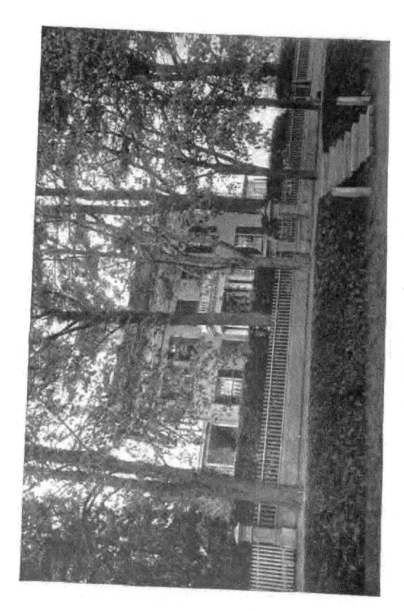

EMILY DICKINSON'S HOME.

LETTERS

OF

EMILY DICKINSON

EDITED BY

MABEL LOOMIS TODD

IN TWO VOLUMES

VOLUME II

BOSTON

ROBERTS BROTHERS

1894

University Press
JOHN WILSON AND SON, CAMBRIDGE, U.S.A.

TABLE OF CONTENTS

VOLUME II

———◆———

LIST OF ILLUSTRATIONS

LETTERS OF EMILY DICKINSON

———•———

CHAPTER VI

To the Misses ———•

AMONG the most natural and spontaneous of Emily Dickinson's letters are these to her cousins. They are, perhaps, more than usually full of her real self, or one unmistakable phase of that elusive individuality. Many, indeed, are so completely personal that they are of necessity omitted, and the final letter has been reserved for the closing chapter.

[January, 1859.]

Since it snows this morning, dear L———, too fast for interruption, put your brown curls in a basket, and come and sit with me.

I am sewing for Vinnie, and Vinnie is flying through the flakes to buy herself a little hood. It's quite a fairy morning, and I often lay down my needle, and 'build a castle in the air' which seriously impedes the sewing project. What if I pause a little longer, and write a note to you! Who will

be the wiser? I have known little of you, since
the October morning when our families went out
driving, and you and I in the dining-room decided
to be distinguished. It 's a great thing to be 'great,'
L——, and you and I might tug for a life, and never
accomplish it, but no one can stop our looking on,
and you know some cannot sing, but the orchard
is full of birds, and we all can listen. What if we
learn, ourselves, some day! Who indeed knows?
—— said you had many little cares; I hope they do
not fatigue you. I would not like to think of L——
as weary, now and then. Sometimes *I* get tired,
and I would rather none I love would understand
the word. . . .

Do you still attend Fanny Kemble? 'Aaron
Burr' and father think her an 'animal,' but I fear
zoölogy has few such instances. I have heard
many notedly *bad* readers, and a fine one would
be almost a fairy surprise. When will you come
again, L——? For you remember, dear, you are
one of the ones from whom I do not run away! I
keep an ottoman in my heart exclusively for you.
My love for your father and F——.

EMILY.

[March, 1859.]

The little 'apple of my eye,' is not dearer than
L——; she knows I remember her, — why waste an
instant in defence of an absurdity? My birds fly
far off, nobody knows where they go to, but you

see I know they are coming back, and other people
don't, that makes the difference.

I 've had a curious winter, very swift, sometimes
sober, for I have n't felt well, much, and March
amazes me ! I did n't think of it, that 's all ! Your
' hay ' don't look so dim as it did at one time. I
hayed a little for the horse two Sundays ago, and
mother thought it was summer, and set one plant
outdoors which she brought from the deluge, but
it snowed since, and we have fine sleighing, now,
on *one* side of the road, and wheeling on the other,
a kind of variegated turnpike quite picturesque to
see !

You are to have Vinnie, it seems, and I to tear my
hair, or engage in any other vocation that seems
fitted to me. Well, the earth is round, so if Vinnie
rolls your side sometimes, 't is n't strange ; I wish I
were there too, but the geraniums felt so I could n't
think of leaving them, and one minute carnation
pink cried, till I shut her up — see box !

Now, my love, robins, for both of you, and when
you and Vinnie sing at sunrise on the apple boughs,
just cast your eye to my twig.

POOR PLOVER.

[Early Summer, 1859.]

DEAR L——, — You did not acknowledge my
vegetable ; perhaps you are not familiar with it. I was
reared in the garden, you know. It was to be eaten
with mustard ! Bush eighty feet high, just under

chamber window — much used at this season when other vegetables are gone. You should snuff the hay if you were here to-day, infantile as yet, homely, as cubs are prone to be, but giving brawny promise of hay-cocks by and by. 'Methinks I see you,' as school-girls say, perched upon a cock with the 'latest work,' and confused visions of bumblebees tugging at your hat. Not so far off, cousin, as it used to be, that vision and the hat. It makes me feel so hurried, I run and brush my hair so to be all ready.

I enjoy much with a precious fly, during sister's absence, not one of your blue monsters, but a timid creature, that hops from pane to pane of her white house, so very cheerfully, and hums and thrums, a sort of speck piano. Tell Vinnie I 'll kill him the day she comes, for I sha'n't need him any more, and she don't mind flies!

Tell F—— and papa to come with the sweet-williams.

Tell Vinnie I counted three peony noses, red as Sammie Matthews's, just out of the ground, and get her to make the accompanying face. 'By-Bye.'

EMILY.

Miss Lavinia Dickinson was visiting her cousins when their mother died, and Emily's letter to her sister at that time seems more appropriate here than in any other connection: —

[April, 1860.]

VINNIE, — I can't believe it, when your letters come, saying what Aunt L—— said 'just before she died.' Blessed Aunt L—— now; all the world goes out, and I see nothing but her room, and angels bearing her into those great countries in the blue sky of which we don't know anything.

Then I sob and cry till I can hardly see my way 'round the house again; and then sit still and wonder if she sees us now, if she sees *me*, who said that she 'loved Emily.' Oh! Vinnie, it is dark and strange to think of summer afterward! How she loved the summer! The birds keep singing just the same. Oh! The thoughtless birds!

Poor little L——! Poor F——! You must comfort them!

If you were with me, Vinnie, we could talk about her together.

And I thought she would live! I wanted her to live so, I thought she could not die! To think how still she lay while I was making the little loaf, and fastening her flowers! Did you get my letter in time to tell her how happy I would be to do what she requested? Mr Brady is coming to-morrow to bring arbutus for her. Dear little aunt! Will she look down?

You must tell me all you can think about her. Did she carry my little bouquet? So many brokenhearted people have got to hear the birds sing, and see all the little flowers grow, just the same as if the sun had n't stopped shining forever ! . . . How I wish I could comfort you ! How I wish you could comfort me, who weep at what I did not see and never can believe. I will try and share you a little longer, but it is so long, Vinnie.

We did n't think, that morning when I wept that you left me, and you, for other things, that we should weep more bitterly before we saw each other.

Well, she is safer now than 'we know or even think.' Tired little aunt, sleeping ne'er so peaceful ! Tuneful little aunt, singing, as we trust, hymns than which the robins have no sweeter ones.

Good-night, broken hearts, L——, and F——, and Uncle L——. Vinnie, remember

SISTER.

[Autumn, 1860.]

Bravo, L——, the cape is a beauty, and what shall I render unto F——, for all her benefits? I will take my books and go into a corner and give thanks ! Do you think I am going 'upon the boards' that I wish so smart attire? Such are my designs, though. I beg you not to disclose them ! May I not secure L—— for drama, and F—— for comedy? You are a brace of darlings, and it would give me joy to see you both, in any capacity. . . . Will treasure all till I see you. Never fear that I shall forget ! In event of my decease, I will still exclaim 'Dr Thompson,' and he will reply 'Miss Montague.'

My little L—— pined for the hay in her last com-
munication.   Not to be saucy, dear, we sha'n't have
any more before the first of March, Dick having hid
it all in the barn in a most malicious manner; but
he has not brought the sunset in, so there is still an
inducement to my little girls.   We have a sky or
two, well worth consideration, and trees so fashion-
able they make us all *passée.*

I often remember you both, last week.   I thought
that flown mamma could not, as was her wont,
shield from crowd, and strangers, and was glad Eliza
was there.   I knew she would guard my children,
as she has often guarded me, from publicity, and
help to fill the deep place never to be full.   Dear
cousins, I know you both better than I did, and
love you both better, and always I have a chair
for you in the smallest parlor in the world, to wit,
my heart.

This world is just a little place, just the red in
the sky, before the sun rises, so let us keep fast
hold of hands, that when the birds begin, none of
us be missing.

'Burnham' must think F—— a scholastic female.
I would n't be in her place!   If she feels delicate
about it, she can tell him the books are for a friend
in the East Indies.

Won't F—— give my respects to the 'Bell and
Everett party' if she passes that organization on her
way to school?   I hear they wish to make me
Lieutenant-Governor's daughter.   Were they cats

I would pull their tails, but as they are only patriots, I must forego the bliss. . . .

Love to papa.   EMILY.

[Winter, 1860–61.]

DEAR FRIENDS, — L——'s note to Miss W—— only stopped to dine. It went out with a beautiful name on its face in the evening mail. 'Is there nothing else,' as the clerk says? So pleased to enact a trifle for my little sister. It is little sisters you are, as dear F—— says in the hallowed note. Could mamma read it, it would blur her light even in Paradise.

It was pretty to lend us the letters from the new friends. It gets us acquainted. We will preserve them carefully. . . . I regret I am not a scholar in the Friday class. I believe the love of God may be taught not to seem like bears. Happy the reprobates under that loving influence.

I have one new bird and several trees of old ones. A snow slide from the roof, dispelled mother's 'sweetbrier.' You will of course feel for her, as you were named for him! There are as yet no streets, though the sun is riper, and these small bells have rung so long I think it 'tea-time' always.

[Spring, 1861.]

. . . Send a sundown for L——, please, and a crocus for F——. Shadow had no stem, so they could not pick him.

. . . —— fed greedily upon *Harper's Magazines* while here. Suppose he is restricted to Martin Luther's works at home. It is a criminal thing to be a boy in a godly village, but maybe he will be forgiven.

. . . The seeing pain one can't relieve makes a demon of one. If angels have the heart beneath their silver jackets, I think such things could make them weep, but Heaven is so cold! It will never look kind to me that God, who causes all, denies such little wishes. It could not hurt His glory, unless it were a lonesome kind. I 'most conclude it is.

. . . Thank you for the daisy. With nature in my ruche I shall not miss the spring. What would become of us, dear, but for love to reprieve our blunders?

. . . I'm afraid that home is 'most done, but do not say I fear so. Perhaps God will be better. They're happy, you know. That makes it doubtful. Heaven hunts round for those that find itself below, and then it snatches.

. . . Think Emily lost her wits — but she found 'em, likely. Don't part with wits long in this neighborhood.

. . . Your letters are all real, just the tangled road children walked before you, some of them to

the end, and others but a little way, even as far as
the fork in the road.   That Mrs Browning fainted,
we need not read *Aurora Leigh* to know, when
she lived with her English aunt; and George Sand
' must make no noise in her grandmother's bed-
room.'   Poor children !   Women, now, queens, now !
And one in the Eden of God.   I guess they both
forget that now, so who knows but we, little stars
from the same night, stop twinkling at last?   Take
heart, little sister, twilight is but the short bridge, and
the moon stands at the end.   If we can only get to
her !   Yet, if she sees us fainting, she will put out
her yellow hands. . . .

[December, 1861.]

DEAR PEACOCK, — I received your feather with
profound emotion.   It has already surmounted a
work, and crossed the Delaware.   Doubtless you
are moulting *à la* canary bird — hope you will not
suffer from the reduction of plumage these December
days.   The latitude is quite stiff for a few nights,
and gentlemen and ladies who go barefoot in our
large cities must find the climate uncomfortable.   A
land of frosts and zeros is not precisely the land for
me ; hope you find it congenial.   I believe it is
several hundred years since· I met you and F——,
yet I am pleased to say, you do not become dim ;
I think you rather brighten as the hours fly.   I should
love to see you dearly, girls ; perhaps I may, before

south winds, but I feel rather confused to-day, and the future looks 'higglety-pigglety.'

You seem to take a smiling view of my finery. If you knew how solemn it was to me, you might be induced to curtail your jests. My sphere is doubt-less calicoes, nevertheless I thought it meet to sport a little wool. The mirth it has occasioned will deter me from further exhibitions! Wòn't you tell 'the public' that at present I wear a brown dress with a cape if possible browner, and carry a parasol of the same! We have at present one cat, and twenty-four hens, who do nothing so vulgar as lay an egg, which checks the ice-cream tendency.

I miss the grasshoppers much, but suppose it is all for the best. I should become too much at-tached to a trotting world.

My garden is all covered up by snow; picked ↙ gilliflower Tuesday, now gilliflowers are asleep. The hills take off their purple frocks, and dress in long white nightgowns.

There is something fine and something sad in the year's toilet. . . .

We often talk of you and your father these new winter days. Write, dear, when you feel like it.
Lovingly,
EMILY.

[December 29, 1861.]

. . . Your letter did n't surprise me, L——; I brushed away the sleet from eyes familiar with it —

looked again to be sure I read it right —and then took up my work hemming strings for mother's gown. I think I hemmed them faster for knowing you were n't coming, my fingers had nothing else to do. . . . Odd, that I, who say ' no ' so much, cannot bear it from others. Odd, that I, who run from so many, cannot brook that one turn from me. Come when you will, L——, the hearts are never shut here. I don't remember ' May.' Is that the one that stands next April? And is that the month for the river-pink?

Mrs Adams had news of the death of her boy to-day, from a wound at Annapolis. Telegram signed by Frazer Stearns. You remember him. Another one died in October — from fever caught in the camp. Mrs Adams herself has not risen from bed since then. ' Happy new year ' step softly over such doors as these ! ' Dead ! Both her boys ! One of them shot by the sea in the East, and one of them shot in the West by the sea.' . . . Christ be merciful ! Frazer Stearns is just leaving Annapolis. His father has gone to see him to-day. I hope that ruddy face won't be brought home frozen. Poor little widow's boy, riding to-night in the mad wind, back to the village burying-ground where he never dreamed of sleeping ! Ah ! the dreamless sleep !

Did you get the letter I sent a week from Monday? You did not say, and it makes me anxious, and I sent a scrap for Saturday last, that

too?   L——, I wanted you very much, and I put you
by with sharper tears than I give to many.   Won't
you tell me about the chills — what the doctor says? I
must not lose you, sweet.   Tell me if I could send a
tuft to keep the cousin warm, a blanket of a thistle,
say, or something !

Much love and Christmas, and sweet year, for you
and F—— and papa.

EMILIE.

Dear little F——'s note received, and shall write
her soon.

Meanwhile, we wrap her in our heart to keep her
tight and warm.

. . . Uncle told us you were too busy. Fold your
little hands — the heart is the only workman we
cannot excuse.

. . . Gratitude is not the mention of a tenderness, but its mute appreciation, deeper than we
reach — all our LORD demands, who sizes better
knows than we.   Willing unto death, if only we per-
ceive He die.

[February, 1862.]

DEAR F——, — I fear you are getting as driven
as Vinnie. We consider her standard for super-
human effort erroneously applied.   Dear L——
remembers the basket Vinnie ' never got to.'   But
we must blame with lenience.   Poor Vinnie has

been very sick, and so have we all, and I feared one day our little brothers would see us no more, but God was not so hard. Now health looks so beautiful, the tritest 'How do you do' is living with meaning. No doubt you 'heard a bird,' but which route did he take? Has n't reached here yet. Are you sure it was n't a 'down brakes'? Best of ears will blunder! Unless he come by the first of April, I sha'n't countenance him. We have had fatal weather — thermometer two below zero all day, without a word of apology. Summer was always dear, but such a kiss as she 'll get from me if I ever see her again, will make her cry, I know. . . .

[April, 1862.]

DEAR CHILDREN, — You have done more for me — 't is least that I can do, to tell you of brave Frazer — 'killed at Newbern,' darlings. His big heart shot away by a 'Minie ball.'

I had read of those — I did n't think that Frazer would carry one to Eden with him. Just as he fell, in his soldier's cap, with his sword at his side, Frazer rode through Amherst. Classmates to the right of him, and classmates to the left of him, to guard his narrow face! He fell by the side of Professor Clark, his superior officer — lived ten minutes in a soldier's arms, asked twice for water — murmured just, 'My God!' and passed! Sanderson, his classmate, made a box of boards in the night, put the brave boy in, covered with a blanket, rowed six miles to reach the boat, — so poor Frazer came. They tell that Colonel Clark cried like a little child when he missed his pet, and could hardly resume his post. They loved each other very much. Nobody here could look on Frazer — not even his father. The doctors would not allow it.

The bed on which he came was enclosed in a large casket shut entirely, and covered from head to foot with the sweetest flowers. He went to sleep from the village church. Crowds came to tell him good-night, choirs sang to him, pastors told how brave he was — early-soldier heart. And the family bowed their heads, as the reeds the wind shakes.

So our part in Frazer is done, but you must come next summer, and we will mind ourselves of this young crusader — too brave that he could fear to die. We will play his tunes — maybe he can hear them ; we will try to comfort his broken-hearted Ella, who, as the clergyman said, 'gave him peculiar confidence.' . . . Austin is stunned completely. Let us love better, children, it 's most that 's left to do.

Love from   EMILY.

. . . Sorrow seems more general than it did, and not the estate of a few persons, since the war began ; and if the anguish of others helped one with one's own, now would be many medicines.

'T is dangerous to value,. for only the precious can alarm. I noticed that Robert Browning had made another poem, and was astonished — till I remembered that I, myself, in my smaller way, sang off charnel steps. Every day life feels mightier, and what we have the power to be, more stupendous.

[May, 1862.]

When you can leave your little children, L——, you must tell us all you know about dear Myra's going, so sudden, and shocking to us all, we are only bewildered and cannot believe the telegrams. I want so much to see you, and ask you what it means, and why this young life's sacrifice should come so soon, and not far off. I wake in the morning saying 'Myra, no more Myra in this world,' and the thought of that young face in the dark, makes the whole so sorrowful, I cover my face with the blanket, so the robins' singing cannot get through — I had rather not hear it. Was Myra willing to leave us all? I want so much to know if it was very hard, husband and babies and big life and sweet home by the sea. I should think she would rather have stayed. . . . She came to see us first in May. I remember her frock, and how prettily she fixed her hair, and she and Vinnie took long walks, and got home to tea at sundown; and now remembering is all there is, and no more Myra. I wish 't was plainer, L——, the anguish in this world. I wish one could be sure the suffering had a loving side. The thought to look down some day, and see the crooked steps we came, from a safer place, must be a precious thing. . . .

L——, you are a dear child to go to Uncle J——, and all will thank you, who love him. We will remember you every day, and the little children, and make a picture to ourself, of the small mamma. . . . Father and Vinnie would have gone immediately to Lynn, but got the telegram too late. Tell Uncle they wanted to. But what can Emily say? Their Father in Heaven remember them and her.

My little girls have alarmed me so that notwithstanding the comfort of Austin's assurance that 'they will come,' I am still hopeless and scared, and regard Commencement as some vast anthropic bear, ordained to eat me up. What made 'em scare 'em so? Did n't they know Cousin Aspen could n't stand alone? I remember a tree in McLean Street, when you and we were a little girl, whose leaves went topsy-turvy as often as a wind, and showed an ashen side — that 's fright, that 's Emily. L—— and F—— were that wind, and the poor leaf, who? Won't they stop a' blowing? . . . Commencement would be a dreary spot without my double flower, that sows itself, and just comes up, when Emily seeks it most. Austin gives excellent account, I trust not overdrawn. 'Health and aspect admirable, and lodgings very fine.' Says the rooms were marble, even to the flies. Do they dwell in Carrara? Did they find the garden in the gown? Should have

sent a farm, but feared for our button-hole. Hope
to hear favorable news on receipt of this. Please
give date of coming, so we might prepare our heart.

EMILY.

[July, 1862?]

. . . Just a word for my children, before the mails
shut. L—— left a tumbler of sweet-peas on the
green room bureau. I am going to leave them there
till they make pods and sow themselves in the
upper drawer, and then I guess they'll blossom
about Thanksgiving time. There was a thunder-
shower here Saturday at car-time, and Emily was
glad her little ones had gone before the hail and
rain, lest it frighten them. . . . We wish the visit had
just begun instead of ending now; next time we'll
leave 'the mountains' out, and tell good Dr Gregg
to recommend the orchards. I defrauded L—— of
1 spool of thread; we will 'settle,' however — and
F——'s ruff is set high in my book of remembrance.
They must be good children and recollect, as they
agreed, and grow so strong in health that Emily
won't know them when they show again. . . . Such
a purple morning — even to the morning-glory that
climbs the cherry-tree. The cats desire love to
F——.   EMILY.

[About May 30, 1863.]

I said I should come 'in a day.' Emily never
fails except for a cause; that you know, dear L——.

The nights turned hot, when Vinnie had gone, and I must keep no window raised for fear of prowling 'booger,' and I must shut my door for fear front door slide open on me at the 'dead of night,' and I must keep 'gas' burning to light the danger up, so I could distinguish it — these gave me a snarl in the brain which don't unravel yet, and that old nail in my breast pricked me; these, dear, were my cause. Truth is so best of all I wanted you to know. Vinnie will tell of her visit. . . .

About Commencement, children, I can have no doubt, if you should fail me then, my little life would fail of itself. Could you only lie in your little' bed and smile at me, that would be support. Tell the doctor I am inexorable, besides I shall heal you quicker than he. You need the balsam word. And who is to cut the cake, ask F——, and chirp to those trustees? Tell me, dears, by the coming mail, that you will not fail me. . . .

Jennie Hitchcock's mother was buried yesterday, so there is one orphan more, and her father is very sick besides. My father and mother went to the service, and mother said while the minister prayed, a hen with her chickens came up, and tried to fly into the window. I suppose the dead lady used to feed them, and they wanted to bid her good-by.

> Life is death we 're lengthy at,
> Death the hinge to life.

Love from all,

EMILY.

[Autumn, 1863.]

Wednesday.

DEAR CHILDREN, — Nothing has happened but loneliness, perhaps too daily to relate. Carlo is consistent, has asked for nothing to eat or drink, since you went away. Mother thinks him a model dog, and conjectures what he might have been, had not Vinnie 'demoralized' him. Margaret objects to furnace heat on account of bone decrepitudes, so I dwell in my bonnet and suffer comfortably. . . .

Miss Kingman called last evening to inspect your garden; I gave her a lanthorn, and she went out, and thanks you very much. No one has called so far, but one old lady to look at a house. I directed her to the cemetery to spare expense of moving.

I got down before father this morning, and spent a few moments profitably with the South Sea rose. Father detecting me, advised wiser employment, and read at devotions the chapter of the gentleman with one talent. I think he thought my conscience would adjust the gender.

Margaret washed to-day, and accused Vinnie of calicoes. I put her shoe and bonnet in to have them nice when she got home. I found a milliner's case in Miss N——'s wardrobe, and have opened business. I have removed a geranium leaf, and supplied a lily in Vinnie's parlor vase. The sweet-peas are unchanged. Cattle-show is to-morrow. The coops and committees are passing now. . . . They are picking the Baldwin apples. Be good children,

and mind the vicar. Tell me precisely how Wakefield
looks, since I go not myself.

· :{   :   EMILY.

[Autumn, 1863.]

. . . I should be wild with joy to see my little
lovers. The writing them is not so sweet as their
two faces that seem so small way off, and yet have
been two weeks from me — *two* wishful, wandering
weeks. Now, I begin to doubt if they ever came.

I bid the stiff ' good-night ' and the square ' good-
morning' to the lingering guest, I finish mamma's
sack, all but the overcasting — that fatal sack, you
recollect. I pick up tufts of mignonette, and sweet
alyssum for winter, dim as winter seems these red,
and gold, and ribbon days.

I am sure I feel as Noah did, docile, but somewhat sceptic, under the satinet.

No frost at our house yet. Thermometer frost,
I mean. Mother had a new tooth Saturday. You
know Dr S—— had promised her one for a long
time. 'Teething' did n't agree with her, and she
kept her bed, Sunday, with a face that would take
a premium at any cattle-show in the land. Came
to town next morning with slightly reduced features,
but no eye on the left side. Doubtless we are
' fearfully and wonderfully made,' and occasionally
grotesquely.

L—— goes to Sunderland, Wednesday, for a
minute or two ; leaves here at half-past six — what
a fitting hour — and will breakfast the night before ;

such a smart atmosphere! The trees stand right
up straight when they hear her boots, and will bear
crockery wares instead of fruit, I fear. She has n't
starched the geraniums yet, but will have ample
time, unless she leaves before April. Emily is very
mean, and her children in dark must n't remember
what she says about damsel.

Grateful for little notes, and shall ask for longer
when my birds locate. Would it were here. Three
sisters are prettier than one. . . . Tabby is a continual shrine, and her jaunty ribbons put me in mind
of fingers far out at sea. F——'s admonition made
me laugh and cry too. In the hugest haste, and the
engine waiting.   EMILY.

[After the death of the Misses ——'s father, Jan. 1864.]

What shall I tell these darlings except that my
father and mother are half their father and mother,
and my home half theirs, whenever, and for as long
as, they will. And sometimes a dearer thought than
that creeps into my mind, but it is not for to-night.
Was n't dear papa so tired always after mamma
went, and was n't it almost sweet to think of the two
together these new winter nights? The grief is our
side, darlings, and the glad is theirs. Vinnie and I
sit down to-night, while mother tells what makes us
cry, though we know it is well and easy with uncle
and papa, and only our part hurts. Mother tells
how gently he looked on all who looked at him —
how he held his bouquet sweet, as he were a guest

in a friend's parlor and must still do honor. The meek, mild gentleman who thought no harm, but peace toward all.

Vinnie intended to go, but the day was cold, and she wanted to keep Uncle L—— as she talked with him, always, instead of this new way. She thought too, for the crowd, she could not see you, children, and she would be another one to give others care. Mother said Mr V——, yes, dears, even Mr V——, at whom we sometimes smile, talked about 'Lorin' and Laviny' and his friendship towards them, to your father's guests. We won't smile at him any more now, will we? Perhaps he 'll live to tell some gentleness of us, who made merry of him.

But never mind that now. When you have strength, tell us how it is, and what we may do for you, of comfort, or of service. Be sure you crowd all others out, precious little cousins. Good-night. Let Emily sing for you because she cannot pray : —

> It is not dying hurts us so, —
> 'T is living hurts us more;
> But dying is a different way,
> A kind, behind the door, —
> The southern custom of the bird
> That soon as frosts are due
> Adopts a better latitude.
> We are the birds that stay,
> The shiverers round farmers' doors,
> For whose reluctant crumb
> We stipulate, till pitying snows
> Persuade our feathers home.
>
> EMILY.

[1864.]

So many ask for the children that I must make a separate letter to tell them what they say, and leave my kisses till next time.

Eliza wrote last week, faint note in pencil — dressed in blankets, and propped up, having been so sick — and yet too weak to talk much, even with her slate.   She said this of you, I give it in her own word, 'Make them know I love them,' and added, should have written immediately herself, except for weakness.

Mr Dwight asks for you in the phrase 'Of your sweet cousins.' He does not yet know papa is asleep — only very weary.

The milliner at the head of the street wipes her eye for F—— and L——, and a tear rumples her ribbons. Mr and Mrs Sweetser care — Mrs Sweetser most tenderly.

. . . Even Dick's wife, simple dame, with a kitchen full, and the grave besides, of little ragged ones, wants to know 'more about' you, and follows mother to the door, who has called with bundle.

Dick says, in his wise way, he 'shall always be interested in them young ladies.'   One little young lady of his own, you know, is in Paradise.   That makes him tenderer-minded.

Be sure you don't doubt about the sparrow.

Poor —— and ——, in their genteel, antique way, express their sympathy, mixing admiring anecdotes of your father and mother's youth, when they, God help them, were not so sere. Besides these other, children, shall we tell them who else cherishes, every day the same, the bright one and the black one too? Could it be Emily?

Would it interest the children to know that crocuses come up, in the garden off the dining-room, and a fuchsia, that pussy partook, mistaking it for strawberries? And that we have primroses, like the little pattern sent in last winter's note, and heliotrope by the aprons full — the mountain colored one — and a jasmine bud, you know the little odor like Lubin — and gilliflowers, magenta, and few mignonette, and sweet alyssum bountiful, and carnation buds?

Will it please them to know that the ice-house is filled, to make their tumblers cool next summer, and once in a while a cream?

And that father has built a new road round the pile of trees between our house and Mr S——'s, where they can take the soldier's shirt to make, or a sweet poem, and no man find them but the fly, and he such a little man?

Love, dears, from us all, and won't you tell us how you are?

We seem to hear so little.　　　　　　EMILY.

[January, 1865.]

. . . I am glad my little girl is at peace. Peace is a deep place. Some, too faint to push, are assisted by angels.

I have more to say to you all than March has to the maples, but then I cannot write in bed. I read a few words since I came home — John Talbot's parting with his son, and Margaret's with Suffolk. I read them in the garret, and the rafters wept.

Remember me to your company, their Bedouin guest.

Every day in the desert, Ishmael counts his tents. New heart makes new health, dear.

Happiness is haleness. I dreamed last night I heard bees fight for pond-lily stamens, and waked with a fly in my room.

Shall you be strong enough to lift me by the first of April? I won't be half as heavy as I was before. I will be good and chase my spools.

I shall think of my little Eve going away from Eden. Bring me a jacinth for every finger, and an onyx shoe.   EMILY.

[1865.]

DEAR SISTER, — Brother has visited, and the night is falling, so I must close with a little hymn.

I had hoped to express more. Love more I never can, sweet D—— or yourself.

> This was in the white of the year,
> That was in the green.
> Drifts were as difficult then to think,
> As daisies now to be seen.
> Looking back is best that is left,
> Or if it be before,
> Retrospection is prospect's half,
> Sometimes almost more.
>   EMILY.

[February, 1865.]

All that my eyes will let me shall be said for L——, dear little solid gold girl. I am glad to the foot of my heart that you will go to M——. It will make you warm. Touches 'from home,' tell Gungl, are better than ' sounds.' [1]

You persuade me to speak of my eyes, which I shunned doing, because I wanted you to rest. I could not bear a single sigh should tarnish your vacation, but, lest through me one bird delay a change of latitude, I will tell you, dear.

The eyes are as with you, sometimes easy, sometimes sad. I think they are not worse, nor do I think them better than when I came home.

The snow-light offends them, and the house is bright; notwithstanding, they hope some. For the first few weeks I did nothing but comfort my plants, till now their small green cheeks are covered with smiles. I chop the chicken centres when we have roast fowl, frequent now, for the hens contend and the Cain is slain. . . . Then I make the yellow to the pies, and bang the spice for cake, and knit the soles to the stockings I knit the bodies to last June. They say I am a 'help.' Partly because it is true, I suppose, and the rest applause. Mother and Margaret are so kind, father as gentle as he knows how, and Vinnie good to me, but 'cannot see why I don't get well.' This makes me think I am long

---

[1] Referring to an old piece of piano-forte music.

sick, and this takes the ache to my eyes. I shall try to stay with them a few weeks more before going to Boston, though what it would be to see you and have the doctor's care — that cannot be told. You will not wait for me. Go to M—— now. I wish I were there, myself, to start your little feet ' lest they seem to come short of it.' I have so much to tell I can tell nothing, except a sand of love. When I dare I shall ask if I may go, but that will not be now.

Give my love to my lamp and spoon, and the small lantana. Kindest remembrance for all the house, and write next from M——. Go, little girl, to M——. Life is so fast it will run away, notwithstanding our sweetest *whoa*.

Already they love you. Be but the maid you are to me, and they will love you more.

Carry your heart and your curls, and nothing more but your fingers. Mr D—— will ask for these every candle-light. How I miss ten robins that never flew from the rosewood nest !

DEAR L——, — This is my letter — an ill and peevish thing, but when my eyes get well I 'll send you thoughts like daisies, and sentences could hold the bees. . . .

[1866.]

. . . Oh, L——, why were the children sent too faint to stand alone ? . . . Every hour is anxious now, and heaven protect the lamb who shared her fleece with a timider, even Emily.

[1868.]

DEAR CHILDREN, — The little notes shall go as
fast as steam can take them.

Our hearts already went. Would we could mail
our faces for your dear encouragement.

Remember

> The longest day that God appoints
> Will finish with the sun.
> Anguish can travel to its stake,
> And then it must return.

I am in bed to-day — a curious place for me, and
cannot write as well as if I was firmer, but love as
well, and long more. Tell us all the load. Amherst's
little basket is never so full but it holds more. That's
a basket's cause. Not a flake assaults my birds but
it freezes me. Comfort, little creatures — whatever
befall us, this world is but this world. Think of that
great courageous place we have never seen !

Write at once, please, I am so full of grief and
surprise and physical weakness. I cannot speak
until I know.

                    Lovingly,   EMILY.

Of this letter her cousin writes, ' All this
trouble has become only a myth now; it must
have been some illness, or other forgotten
calamity.'

[Autumn, 1869.]

Vinnie was ' gone ' indeed and is due to-day, and before the tumult that even the best bring we will take hold of hands. It was sweet and antique as birds to hear L——'s voice, worth the lying awake from five o'clock summer mornings to hear. I rejoice that my wren can rise and touch the sky again. We all have moments with the dust, but the dew is given. Do you wish you heard ' A—— talk'? Then I would you did, for then you would be here always, a sweet premium. Would you like to ' step in the kitchen '? Then you shall by faith, which is the first sight. Mr C—— is not in the tree, because the rooks won't let him, but I ate a pear as pink as a plum that he made last spring, when he was ogling you. Mother has on the petticoat you so gallantly gathered while he sighed and grafted.

Tabby is eating a stone dinner from a stone plate, . . . Tim is washing Dick's feet, and talking to him now and then in an intimate way. Poor fellow, how he warmed when I gave him your message ! The red reached clear to his beard, he was so gratified ; and Maggie stood as still for hers as a puss for patting. The hearts of these poor people lie so unconcealed you bare them with a smile.

Thank you for recollecting my weakness. I am not so well as to forget I was ever ill, but better and working. I suppose we must all ' ail till evening.'

Read Mr Lowell's *Winter*. One does not often meet anything so perfect.

In many little corners how much of L—— I have.

Maggie 'dragged' the garden for this bud for you. You have heard of the 'last rose of summer.' This is that rose's son.

Into the little port you cannot sail unwelcome at any hour of day or night. Love for F——, and stay close to   EMILY.

[Spring, 1870.]

DEAR CHILDREN, — I think the bluebirds do their work exactly like me. They dart around just so, with little dodging feet, and look so agitated. I really feel for them, they seem to be so tried.

The mud is very deep — up to the wagons' stomachs — arbutus making pink clothes, and everything alive.

Even the hens are touched with the things of Bourbon, and make republicans like me feel strangely out of scene.

Mother went rambling, and came in with a burdock on her shawl, so we know that the snow has perished from the earth. Noah would have liked mother.

I am glad you are with Eliza. It is next to shade to know that those we love are cool on a parched day.

Bring my love to —— and Mr ——. You will

not need a hod. C—— writes often, full of joy
and liberty. I guess it is a case of peace. . . .

Pussy has a daughter in the shavings barrel.

Father steps like Cromwell when he gets the
kindlings.

Mrs —— gets bigger, and rolls down the lane to
church like a reverend marble. Did you know
little Mrs Holland was in Berlin for her eyes? . . .

Did you know about Mrs J——? She fledged
her antique wings. 'T is said that 'nothing in her
life became her like the leaving it.'

'Great streets of silence led away,' etc. [1]

EMILY.

[May.]

This little sheet of paper has lain for several years
in my Shakespeare, and though it is blotted and
antiquated is endeared by its resting-place.

I always think of you peculiarly in May, as it is
the peculiar anniversary of your loving kindness to
me, though you have always been dear cousins, and
blessed me all you could.

I cooked the peaches as you told me, and they
swelled to beautiful fleshy halves and tasted quite
magic. The beans we fricasseed and they made a
savory cream in cooking that 'Aunt Emily' liked to
sip. She was always fonder of julep food than of
more substantial. Your remembrance of her is very
sweetly touching.

[1] Second Series, page 225.

Maggie is ironing, and a cotton and linen and ruffle heat makes the pussy's cheeks red. It is lonely without the birds to-day, for it rains badly, and the little poets have no umbrellas. . . .

. . . Fly from Emily's window for L——. Botanical name unknown.

[Enclosing a pressed insect.]

[September, 1870.]

LITTLE SISTERS, — I wish you were with me, not precisely here, but in those sweet mansions the mind likes to suppose. Do they exist or nay? We believe they may, but do they, how know we? 'The light that never was on sea or land' might just as soon be had for the knocking.

F——'s rustic note was as sweet as fern; L——'s token also tenderly estimated. Maggie and I are fighting which shall give L—— the 'plant,' though it is quite a pleasant war. . . . A—— went this morning, after a happy egg and toast provided by Maggie, whom he promised to leave his sole heir.

The 'pussum' is found. 'Two dollars reward' would return John Franklin. . . .

Love for Aunt O——. Tell her I think to instruct flowers will be her labor in heaven. . . .

Nearly October, sisters! No one can keep a sumach and keep a secret too. That was my 'pipe' F—— found in the woods.

Affectionately,

MODOC.

[1870.]

UNTIRING LITTLE SISTERS, — What will I ever do
for you, yet have done the most, for love is that one
perfect labor nought can supersede.   I suppose the
pain is still there, for pain that is worthy does not go
so soon.   The small can crush the great, however,
only temporarily.   In a few days we examine, muster
our forces, and cast it away.   Put it out of your
hearts, children.   Faith is too fair to taint it so.
There are those in the morgue that bewitch us with
sweetness, but that which is dead must go with the
ground.   There is a verse in the Bible that says
there are those who shall not see death.   I suppose
them to be the faithful.   Love will not expire.
There was never the instant when it was lifeless in
the world, though the quicker deceit dies, the better
for the truth, who is indeed our dear friend.

I am sure you will gain, even from this wormwood.
The martyrs may not choose their food.

> God made no act without a cause,
>   Nor heart without an aim,
> Our inference is premature,
>   Our premises to blame.

. . . Sweetest of Christmas to you both, and a
better year.   EMILY.

DEAR CHILDREN, — When I think of your little
faces I feel as the band does before it makes its first
shout. . . .   EMILY.

[1870.]

. . . Mother drives with Tim to carry pears to settlers. Sugar pears with hips like hams, and the flesh of bonbons. Vinnie fastens flowers from the frosts. . . .

Lifetime is for two, never for committee.

I saw your Mrs H——. She looks a little tart, but Vinnie says makes excellent pies after one gets acquainted.

[Spring, 1871.]

The will is always near, dear, though the feet vary. The terror of the winter has made a little creature of me, who thought myself so bold.

Father was very sick. I presumed he would die, and the sight of his lonesome face all day was harder than personal trouble. He is growing better, though physically reluctantly. I hope I am mistaken, but I think his physical life don't want to live any longer. You know he never played, and the straightest engine has its leaning hour. Vinnie was not here. Now we will turn the corner. All this while I was with you all, much of every hour, wishing we were near enough to assist each other. Would you have felt more at home, to know we were both in extremity? That would be my only regret that I had not told you.

As regards the 'pine' and the 'jay,' it is a long tryst, but I think they are able. I have spoken with them.

Of the 'thorn,' dear, give it to me, for I am strongest. Never carry what I can carry, for though I think I bend, something straightens me. Go to the ' wine-press,' dear, and come back and say has the number altered. I descry but one. What I would, I cannot say in so small a place.

Interview is acres, while the broadest letter feels a bandaged place. . . .

Tell F—— we hold her tight. Tell L—— love is oldest and takes care of us, though just now in a piercing place.

EMILY.

[Written to Milwaukee, just after the Chicago fire, 1871.]

We have the little note and are in part relieved, but have been too alarmed and grieved to hush immediately. The heart keeps sobbing in its sleep. It is the speck that makes the cloud that wrecks the vessel, children, yet no one fears a speck. I hope what is not lost is saved. Were any angel present, I feel it could not be allowed. So grateful that our little girls are not on fire too. Amherst would have quenched them. Thank you for comforting innocent blamed creatures. We are trying, too. The mayor of Milwaukee cuts and you and L—— sew, don't you ? The *New York Times* said so. Sorrow is the ' funds ' never quite spent, always a little left to be loaned kindly. We have a new cow. I wish I could give Wisconsin a little pail of milk. Dick's Maggie is wilting. Awkward little flower, but transplanting

makes it fair.   How are the long days that made
the fresh afraid?

BROTHER EMILY.

[March, 1872.]

Thank you, own little girls, for the sweet remembrance — sweet specifically.   Be sure it was pondered
with loving thoughts not unmixed with palates.

But love, like literature, is ' its exceeding great
reward.' . . . I am glad you heard ' Little Em'ly.'   I
would go far to hear her, except I have lost the run of
the roads. . . . Infinite March is here, and I ' hered '
a bluebird.   Of course I am standing on my head !

> Go slow, my soul, to feed thyself
> Upon his rare approach.
> Go rapid, lest competing death
> Prevail upon the coach.
> Go timid, should his testing eye
> Determine thee amiss,
> Go boldly, for thou paidst the price,
> Redemption for a kiss.

Tabby is singing *Old Hundred*, which, by the
way, is her maiden name.   Would they address and
mail the note to their friend J—— W——?

Tidings of a book.

EMILY.

[1872.]

I like to thank you, dear, for the annual candy.
Though you make no answer, I have no letter from
the dead, yet daily love them more.   No part of

mind is permanent.   This startles the happy, but it
assists the sad.

This is a mighty morning.   I trust that L—— is
with it, on hill or pond or wheel.   Too few the
mornings be, too scant the nights.   No lodging can
be had for the delights that come to earth to stay,
but no apartment find and ride away.   F—— was
brave and dear, and helped as much by counsel as
by actual team.   Whether we missed L—— we will
let her guess ; riddles are healthful food.

Eliza was not with us, but it was owing to the
trains.   We know she meant to come.

Oh! Cruel Paradise!   We have a chime of bells
given for brave Frazer.   You 'll stop and hear them,
won't you?

' We conquered, but Bozzaris fell.'   That sentence
always chokes me.   EMILY.

The new College church was given in 1870
by Mr William French Stearns, brother of the
Frazer so mourned ; and its chime of bells was
a memorial[1] to the Amherst students who were

---

[1] Following is the inscription on the fundamental bell : —

THESE BELLS ARE PLACED HERE BY
GEORGE HOWE OF BOSTON AND ARE
TO BE MADE TO CHIME ON ALL SUITABLE
OCCASIONS IN COMMEMORATION OF THE
BRAVE PATRIOTS CONNECTED WITH
AMHERST COLLEGE WHO LOST THEIR
LIVES IN THE WAR AGAINST THE
GREAT REBELLION OF 1861

killed in the war.   A cannon, now in Williston
Hall, Amherst College, was given by General
Burnside at the request of Colonel Clark, in
loving memory of Frazer Stearns, the first of
all the Amherst students who enlisted, nearly
two hundred and fifty in number.

An ill heart, like a body, has its more comfortable days, and then its days of pain, its long
relapse, when rallying requires more effort than to
dissolve life, and death looks choiceless.

Of Miss P —— I know but this, dear.   She wrote
me in October, requesting me to aid the world by
my chirrup more.   Perhaps she stated it as my
duty, I don't distinctly remember, and always burn
such letters, so I cannot obtain it now.   I replied
declining.   She did not write to me again — she
might have been offended, or perhaps is extricating
humanity from some hopeless ditch. . . .

Emily was often besieged by different persons, literary and otherwise, to benefit the world
by her 'chirrup,' but she steadily refused to
publish during her lifetime.   In all these years
she was constantly writing verses ; and while,
as already apparent, she frequently enclosed
poems in letters to friends, the fact that scores
in addition were being written every year was
her own secret.   Her literary methods were also
her own, — she must frequently have tossed

off, many times daily, the stray thoughts which
came to her. The box of 'scraps' found by
her sister after her death proves this conclu-
sively, as some of Emily's rarest flashes were
caught upon the margins of newspapers, backs
of envelopes, or whatever bit of paper was
nearest at hand, in the midst of other occupations. In the more carefully copied poems
are many alterations, but it is a curious fact
that not one change has reference to improvement in rhyme or rhythm. Every suggestion for a different word or phrase was in
the evident hope that by some one of them
the thought might be made clearer, and not in
a single instance merely to smooth the form.

Whether Emily Dickinson had any idea that
her work would ever be published cannot be
known. Except when a friend occasionally
'turned love to larceny' as some one has aptly
said, nothing was printed before her death.
One of the poems, indeed, begins, —

> Publication is the auction
> Of the mind of man.

But the *Prelude* to the *Poems*, First Series,
almost seems to indicate the thought of a possible future public, when she herself should
be beyond the reach of the praise or criticism
which her writing might call forth.

[Early Summer, 1872.]

DEAR CHILDREN, — We received the news of your
loving kindness through Uncle J—— last evening,
and Vinnie is negotiating with neighbor Gray, who
goes to a wedding in Boston next week, for the
procuring of the nest. Vinnie's views of expressage do not abate with time. The crocuses are with
us and several other colored friends. Cousin H——
broke her hip, and is in a polite bed, surrounded by
mint juleps. I think she will hate to leave it as badly
as *Marian Erle* did. Vinnie says there is a tree in
Mr Sweetser's woods that shivers. I am afraid it is
cold. I am going to make it a little coat. . I must
make several, because it is tall as the barn, and put
them on as the circus men stand on each other's
shoulders. . . . There is to be a ' show ' next week,
and little Maggie's bed is to be moved to the door
so she can see the tents. Folding her own like
the Arabs gives her no apprehension. While I
write, dear children, the colors Eliza loved quiver
on the pastures, and day goes gay to the northwest,
innocent as she.   EMILY.

. . . Thank you for the passage. How long to
live the truth is ! A word is dead when it is said,
some say. I say it just begins to live that day.

[July 27, 1872.]

Little Irish Maggie went to sleep this morning at six o'clock, just the time grandpa rises, and

will rest in the grass at Northampton to-morrow. She has had a hard sickness, but her awkward little life is saved and gallant now.   Our Maggie is helping her mother put her in the cradle. . . .

Month aft·r this — after that is October, is n't it? That is n't much long.   Joy to enfold our little girls in so close a future.   That was a lovely letter of F——'s.   It put the cat to playing and the kettle to purring, and two or three birds in plush teams reined nearer to the window. . . . You will miss the nasturtiums, but you will meet the chestnuts.   You also will miss the south wind, but I will save the west. . . .

Of course we shall have a telegram that you have left for Nebraska. . . .   EMILY.

. . . J—— is coming to put away her black hair on the children's pillow.   I hoped she 'd come while you were here, to help me with the starch, but Satan's ways are not as our ways.   I 'm straightening all the property, and making things erect and smart, and to-morrow, at twilight, her little heel boots will thump into Amherst.   It being summer season she will omit the sleigh-bell gown, and that 's a palliative. Vinnie is all disgust, and I shall have to smirk for two to make the manners even.

[1872, or 1873.]

Thank you, dear, for the love.   I am progressing timidly.

Experiment has a stimulus which withers its
fear.

> This is the place they hoped before,
> Where I am hoping now.
> The seed of disappointment grew,,:
> Within a capsule gay,
> Too distant to arrest the feet
> That walk this plank of balm —
> Before them lies escapeless sea — -
> The way is closed they came.

Since you so gently ask, I have had but one
serious adventure — getting a nail in my foot, but
Maggie pulled it out. It only kept me awake one
night, and the birds insisted on sitting up, so it
became an occasion instead of a misfortune. There
was a circus, too, and I watched it away at half-past
three that morning. They said ' hoy, hoy ' to their
horses.

Glad you heard Rubinstein. Grieved L—— could
not hear him. He makes me think of polar nights
Captain Hall could tell ! Going from ice to ice !
What an exchange of awe !

I am troubled for L——'s eye. Poor little girl !
Can I help her? She has so many times saved
me. Do take her to Arlington Street.[1] Xerxes must
go now and see to her worlds. You shall ' taste,'
dear.   Lovingly.

[1] To the physician who had already done so much for
Emily's eyes.

[Winter, 1873.]

. . . I know I love my friends — I feel it far in here where neither blue nor black eye goes, and fingers cannot reach. I know 't is love for them that sets the blister in my throat, many a time a day, when winds go sweeter than their wont, or a different cloud puts my brain from home.

> I cannot see my soul, but know 't is there,
> Nor ever saw his house nor furniture,
> Who has invited me with him to dwell;
> But a confiding guest consult as well,
> What raiment honor him the most,
> That I be adequately dressed,
> For he insures to none
> Lest men specifical adorn
> Procuring him perpetual drest
> By dating it a sudden feast.

Love for the glad if you know them, for the sad if they know you.

[March, 1873.]

. . . I open my window, and it fills the chamber with white dirt. I think God must be dusting; and the wind blows so I expect to read in *The Republican* 'Cautionary signals for Amherst,' or, 'No ships ventured out from Phœnix Row.' . . . Life is so rotatory that the wilderness falls to each, sometime. It is safe to remember that. . . .

[Autumn, 1873.]

. . . I think of your little parlor as the poets once thought of Windermere, — peace, sunshine, and books.

> There is no frigate like a book
> To take us lands away,
> Nor any coursers like a page
> Of prancing poetry.
> This traverse may the poorest take,
> Without oppress of toll;
> How frugal is the chariot
> That bears the human soul!

What words could more vividly express the uplift, the expansion, the wider horizon which books bring! To Emily Dickinson, they were always solace and delight, — 'frigates' and 'coursers' indeed, to her quiet life, taking her over the world and into the infinite spaces, bringing Cathay and Brazil, Cashmere and Teneriffe, into an intimacy as near and familiar as the summer bees and butterflies of her own home noon. Without the help of books even, her nimble fancy leaped intervening leagues as if it commanded the magic carpet of Prince Houssain; but her love for books and indebtedness to them are many times expressed in the poems, both published and unpublished.

[Autumn, 1873.]

DEAR BERKELEYS, — I should feel it my duty to lay my 'net' on the national altar, would it appease finance, but as Jay Cooke can't wear it, I suppose it won't. I believe he opened the scare. M——says D—— pulled her hair, and D—— says M—— pulled her hair, but the issue at court will be, which pulled the preliminary hair. I am not yet 'thrown out of employment,' nor ever receiving 'wages' find them materially 'reduced,' though when bread may be a 'tradition' Mr C—— alone knows. I am deeply indebted to F——, also to her sweet sister *Mrs Ladislaw;* add the funds to the funds, please. Keep the cap till I send — I could not insult my country by incurring expressage now. . . . Buff sings like a nankeen bumble-bee, and a bird's nest on the syringa is just in a line with the conservatory fence, so I have fitted a geranium to it and the effect is deceitful.

I see by the paper that father spends the winter with you. Will you be glad to see him? . . . Tell L—— when I was a baby father used to take me to mill for my health. I was then in consumption! While he obtained the 'grist,' the horse looked round at me, as if to say ' " eye hath not seen nor ear heard the things that " I would do to you if I were n't tied ! ' That is the way I feel toward her. . . .

Maggie will write soon, says it was Mount Holyoke, and not sweet-brier she gave you ! Thanks for the little 'news.' Did get F——'s note and thank it.

Have thousands of things to say as also ten thousands, but must abate now.

Lovingly,

EMILY.

[1874.]

DEAR CHILDREN, — Father is ill at home. I think it is the 'Legislature' reacting on an otherwise obliging constitution. Maggie is ill at Tom's — a combination of cold and superstition of fever — of which her enemy is ill — and longing for the promised land, of which there is no surplus. 'Apollyon' and the 'Devil' fade in martial lustre beside Lavinia and myself. 'As thy day is so shall thy' stem 'be.' We can all of us sympathize with the man who wanted the roan horse to ride to execution, because he said 'twas a nimble hue, and 'twould be over sooner. . . .

Dear L——, shall I enclose the slips, or delay till father? Vinnie advises the latter. I usually prefer formers, latters seeming to me like Dickens's hero's dead mamma, 'too some weeks off' to risk. Do you remember the 'sometimes' of childhood, which invariably never occurred ? . . .

Be pleased you have no cat to detain from justice. Ours have taken meats, and the wife of the 'general court' is trying to lay them out, but as she has but two wheels and they have four, I would accept their chances. Kitties eat kindlings now. Vinnie thinks they are 'cribbers.' I wish I could make you as long a call as De Quincey made North, but that morning cannot be advanced.

EMILY.

[1874.]

. . . I was sick, little sister, and write you the first that I am able.

The loveliest sermon I ever heard was the disappointment of Jesus in Judas. It was told like a mortal story of intimate young men. I suppose no surprise we can ever have will be so sick as that. The last 'I never knew you' may resemble it. I would your hearts could have rested from the first severity before you received this other one, but 'not as I will.' I suppose the wild flowers encourage themselves in the dim woods, and the bird that is bruised limps to his house in silence, but we have human natures, and these are different. It is lovely that Mrs W—— did not disappoint you; not that I thought it possible, but you were so much grieved. . . . A finite life, little sister, is that peculiar garment that were it optional with us we might decline to wear. Tender words to L——, not most, I trust, in need of them.

Lovingly,   EMILY.

. . . How short it takes to go, dear, but afterward to come so many weary years — and yet 't is done as cool as a general trifle. Affection is like bread, unnoticed till we starve, and then we dream of it, and sing of it, and paint it, when every urchin in the street has more than he can eat. We turn not older with years, but newer every day.

Of all these things we tried to talk, but the time refused us. Longing, it may be, is the gift no other gift supplies. Do you remember what you said the night you came to me? I secure that sentence. If I should see your face no more it will be your portrait, and if I should, more vivid than your mortal face. We must be careful what we say. No bird resumes its egg.

> A word left careless on a page
> May consecrate an eye,
> When folded in perpetual seam
> The wrinkled author lie.
>
>   EMILY.

. . . A tone from the old bells, perhaps, might wake the children.

> We send the wave to find the wave,
> An errand so divine
> The messenger enamored too,
> Forgetting to return,
> We make the sage decision still
> Soever made in vain,
> The only time to dam the sea
> Is when the sea is gone.
>
>   EMILY, with love.

[Spring, 1874.]

SISTERS, — I hear robins a great way off, and wagons a great way off, and rivers a great way off,

and all appear to be hurrying somewhere undis-
closed to me.   Remoteness is the founder of sweetness; could we see all we hope, or hear the whole
we fear told tranquil, like another tale, there would
be madness near.   Each of us gives or takes heaven
in corporeal person, for each of us has the skill of
life.   I am pleased by your sweet acquaintance.   It
is not recorded of any rose that it failed of its bee,
though obtained in specific instances through scarlet
experience.   The career of flowers differs from ours
only in inaudibleness.   I feel more reverence as I
grow for these mute creatures whose suspense or
transport may surpass my own.   Pussy remembered
the judgment, and remained with Vinnie.   Maggie
preferred her home to 'Miggles' and 'Oakhurst,'
so with a few spring touches, nature remains
unchanged.

> The most triumphant bird
> I ever knew or met,
> Embarked upon a twig to-day, —
> And till dominion set
> I perish to behold
> So competent a sight —
> And sang for nothing scrutable
> But impudent delight.
> Retired and resumed
> His transitive estate;
> To what delicious accident
> Does finest glory fit!

EMILY.

. . . There is that which is called an 'awakening' in the church, and I know of no choicer ecstasy than to see Mrs —— roll out in crape every morning, I suppose to intimidate antichrist; at least it would have that effect on me. It reminds me of Don Quixote demanding the surrender of the wind-mill, and of Sir Stephen Toplift, and of Sir Alexander Cockburn.

Spring is a happiness so beautiful, so unique, so unexpected, that I don't know what to do with my heart. I dare not take it, I dare not leave it — what do you advise?

Life is a spell so exquisite that everything conspires to break it.

'What do I think of *Middlemarch*?' What do I think of glory — except that in a few instances this 'mortal has already put on immortality.'

George Eliot is one. The mysteries of human nature surpass the 'mysteries of redemption,' for the infinite we only suppose, while we see the finite. . . . I launch Vinnie on Wednesday; it will require the combined efforts of Maggie, Providence and myself, for whatever advances Vinnie makes in nature and art, she has not reduced departure to a science. . . .

Your loving   EMILY.

When, in June of 1874, Emily's father died suddenly in Boston, — taken ill, indeed, while making a speech in the Legislature, and dying within a few hours, — the effect upon her was as if the foundations of her world had given way. She gathered herself together in a measure, and after a few days wrote to her cousins : —

You might not remember me, dears. I cannot recall myself. I thought I was strongly built, but this stronger has undermined me.

We were eating our supper the fifteenth of June, and Austin came in. He had a despatch in his hand, and I saw by his face we were all lost, though I did n't know how. He said that father was very sick, and he and Vinnie must go. The train had already gone. While horses were dressing, news came he was dead.

Father does not live with us now — he lives in a new house. Though it was built in an hour it is better than this. He has n't any garden because he moved after gardens were made, so we take him the best flowers, and if we only knew he knew, perhaps we could stop crying. . . . The grass begins after Pat has stopped it.

I cannot write any more, dears. Though it is many nights, my mind never comes home. Thank you each for the love, though I could not notice it. Almost the last tune that he heard was, ‘Rest from thy loved employ.’

EMILY.

[April, 1875.]

I have only a buttercup to offer for the centennial, as an 'embattled farmer' has but little time.

Begging you not to smile at my limited meadows, I am modestly

Yours.

[Summer, 1875.]

DEAR CHILDREN, — I decide to give you one more package of lemon drops, as they only come once a year. It is fair that the bonbons should change hands, you have so often fed me. This is the very weather that I lived with you those amazing years that I had a father. W. D——'s wife came in last week for a day and a night, saying her heart drove her. I am glad that you loved Miss W—— on knowing her nearer. Charlotte Brontë said 'Life is so constructed that the event does not, cannot, match the expectation.'

The birds that father rescued are trifling in his trees. How flippant are the saved! They were even frolicking at his grave, when Vinnie went there yesterday. Nature must be too young to feel, or many years too old.

Now children, when you are cutting the loaf, a crumb, peradventure a crust, of love for the sparrows' table. . . .

[August, 1876.]

DEAR COUSINS, — Mr S—— had spoken with pleasure of you, before you spoke of him. Good times are always mutual; that is what makes good times. I am glad it cheered you.

We have had no rain for six weeks except one thunder shower, and that so terrible that we locked the doors, and the clock stopped — which made it like Judgment day. The heat is very great, and the grass so still that the flies speck it. I fear L—— will despair. The notices of the 'fall trade' in the hurrying dailies, have a whiff of coolness.

Vinnie has a new pussy the color of Branwell Brontë's hair. She thinks it a little 'lower than the angels,' and I concur with her. You remember my ideal cat has always a huge rat in its mouth, just going out of sight — though going out of sight in itself has a peculiar charm. It is true that the unknown is the largest need of the intellect, though for it, no one thinks to thank God. . . . Mother is worn with the heat, but otherwise not altering. I dream about father every night, always a different dream, and forget what I am doing daytimes, wondering where he is. Without anybody, I keep thinking. What kind can that be?

Dr Stearns died homelike, asked Eliza for a saucer of strawberries, which she brought him, but he had no hands. 'In such an hour as ye think not' means something when you try it.

Lovingly,   EMILY.

[November.]

. . . Oh that beloved witch-hazel which would not reach me till part of the stems were a gentle brown, though one loved stalk as hearty as if just placed in the mail by the woods. It looked like tinsel fringe combined with staider fringes, witch and witching too, to my joyful mind.

I never had seen it but once before, and it haunted me like childhood's Indian pipe, or ecstatic puff-balls, or that mysterious apple that sometimes comes on river-pinks; and is there not a dim suggestion of a dandelion, if her hair were ravelled and she grew on a twig instead of a tube, — though this is timidly submitted. For taking Nature's hand to lead her to me, I am softly grateful — was she willing to come? Though her reluctances are sweeter than other ones' avowals.

> Trusty as the stars
> Who quit their shining working
> Prompt as when I lit them
> In Genesis' new house,
> Durable as dawn
> Whose antiquated blossom
> Makes a world's suspense
> Perish and rejoice.

Love for the cousin sisters, and the lovely alien. . . .

Lovingly,

EMILY.

[About July 4, 1879.]

DEAR COUSINS, — Did you know there had been a fire here, and that but for a whim of the wind Austin and Vinnie and Emily would have all been homeless? But perhaps you saw *The Republican.*

We were waked by the ticking of the bells, — the bells tick in Amherst for a fire, to tell the firemen.

I sprang to the window, and each side of the curtain saw that awful sun. The moon was shining high at the time, and the birds singing like trumpets.

Vinnie came soft as a moccasin, ' Don't be afraid, Emily, it is only the fourth of July.'

I did not tell that I saw it, for I thought if she felt it best to deceive, it must be that it was.

She took hold of my hand and led me into mother's room. Mother had not waked, and Maggie was sitting by her. Vinnie left us a moment, and I whispered to Maggie, and asked her what it was.

' Only Stebbins's barn, Emily ; ' but I knew that the right and left of the village was on the arm of Stebbins's barn. I could hear buildings falling, and oil exploding, and people walking and talking gayly, and cannon soft as velvet from parishes that did not know that we were burning up.

And so much lighter than day was it, that I saw a caterpillar measure a leaf far down in the orchard ; and Vinnie kept saying bravely, ' It 's only the fourth of July.'

It seemed like a theatre, or a night in London, or perhaps like chaos. The innocent dew falling 'as if it thought no evil,' . . . and sweet frogs prattling in the pools as if there were no earth.

At seven people came to tell us that the fire was stopped, stopped by throwing sound houses in as one fills a well.

Mother never waked, and we were all grateful; we knew she would never buy needle and thread at Mr Cutler's store, and if it were Pompeii nobody could tell her.

The post-office is in the old meeting-house where L—— and I went early to avoid the crowd, and —— fell asleep with the bumble-bees and the Lord God of Elijah.

Vinnie's 'only the fourth of July' I shall always remember. I think she will tell us so when we die, to keep us from being afraid.

· Footlights cannot improve the grave, only immortality.

Forgive me the personality; but I knew, I thought, our peril was yours.

Love for you each.

EMILY.

[1880.]

. . . Did the 'stars differ' from each other in anything but 'glory,' there would be often envy. The competitions of the sky corrodeless ply.

. . . We asked Vinnie to say in the rear of one of her mental products that we had neuralgia, but evidently her theme or her time did not admit of trifles. . . . I forget no part of that sweet, smarting visit, not even the nettle that stung my rose.

When Macbeth asked the physician what could be done for his wife, he made the mighty answer, 'That sort must heal itself;' but, sister, that was guilt, and love, you know, is God, who certainly 'gave the love to reward the love,' even were there no Browning.

. . . The slips of the last rose of summer repose in kindred soil with waning bees for mates. How softly summer shuts, without the creaking of a door, abroad for evermore.

. . . Vinnie has also added a pilgrim kitten to her flock, which besides being jet black, is, I think, a lineal descendant of the 'beautiful hearse horse' recommended to Austin.

[December, 1880.]

. . . The look of the words [stating the death of George Eliot] as they lay in the print I shall never forget. Not their face in the casket could have had the eternity to me. Now, *my* George Eliot. The gift of belief which her greatness denied her, I trust she receives in the childhood of the kingdom of heaven. As childhood is earth's confiding time,

perhaps having no childhood, she lost her way to
the early trust, and no later came.   Amazing human
heart, a syllable can make to quake like jostled tree,
what infinite for thee? . . .

[February, 1881.]

. . . God is rather stern with his 'little ones.'
'A cup of cold water in my name' is a shivering
legacy February mornings.

. . . Maggie's brother is killed in the mine, and
Maggie wants to die, but Death goes far around to
those that want to see him.   If the little cousins
would give her a note — she does not know I ask
it — I think it would help her begin, that bleeding
beginning that every mourner knows.

[Spring, 1881.]

The divine deposit came safely in the little bank.
We have heard of the 'deeds of the spirit,' but are
his acts gamboge and pink?   A morning call from
Gabriel is always a surprise.   Were we more fresh
from Eden we were expecting him — but Genesis is
a 'far journey.'   Thank you for the loveliness.

We have had two hurricanes within as many hours,
one of which came near enough to untie my apron —
but this moment the sun shines, Maggie's hens are
warbling, and a man of anonymous wits is making a
garden in the lane to set out slips of bluebird.
The moon grows from the seed. . . . Vinnie's pussy

slept in grass Wednesday — a Sicilian symptom —
the sails are set for summer, East India wharf.
Sage and saucy ones talk of an equinoctial, and are
trying the chimneys, but I am 'short of hearing,'
as the deaf say. Blessed are they that play, for
theirs is the kingdom of heaven. Love like a rose
from each one, and Maggie's a Burgundy one she
ardently asks.

EMILY.

[1881.]

MY DEAR LITTLE COUSINS, — I bring you a robin
who is eating a remnant oat on the sill of the barn.
The horse was not as hungry as usual, leaving an
ample meal for his dulcet friend. . . .

Maggie was charmed with her donkeys, and has
long been talking of writing, but has not quite cul-
minated. They stand on the dining-room side-board,
by the side of an orange, and a *Springfield Republican.* It will please you to know that the clover in
the bill of the brown one is fresh as at first, notwithstanding the time, though the only 'pastures' I
know gifted with that duration, are far off as the
psalms.

Mr C—— called with a twilight of you. It reminded me of a supper I took, with the pictures on
Dresden china. Vinnie asked him 'what he had for
supper,' and he said he 'could easier describe the
nectar of the gods.' . . . We read in a tremendous
Book about 'an enemy,' and armed a confidential

fort to scatter him away. The time has passed, and years have come, and yet not any 'Satan.' I think he must be making war upon some other nation.

EMILY.

[1881.]

The dear ones will excuse — they knew there was a cause. Emily was sick, and Vinnie's middle name restrained her loving pen.

These are my first words since I left my pillow — that will make them faithful, although so long withheld. We had another fire — it was in Phœnix Row, Monday a week ago, at two in the night. The horses were harnessed to move the office — Austin's office, I mean. After a night of terror, we went to sleep for a few moments, and I could not rise. The others bore it better. The brook from Pelham saved the town. The wind was blowing so, it carried the burning shingles as far as Tom's piazza. We are weak and grateful. The fire-bells are oftener now, almost, than the church-bells. Thoreau would wonder which did the most harm.

The little gifts came sweetly. The bulbs are in the sod — the seeds in homes of paper till the sun calls them. It is snowing now. . . . 'Fine sleighing we have this summer,' says Austin with a scoff. The box of dainty ones — I don't know what they were, buttons of spice for coats of honey — pleased the weary mother. Thank you each for all.

The beautiful words for which L—— asked were

that genius is the ignition of affection — not intellect, as is supposed, — the exaltation of devotion, and in proportion to our capacity for that, is our experience of genius. Precisely as they were uttered I cannot give them, they were in a letter that I do not find, but the suggestion was this.

It is startling to think that the lips, which are keepers of thoughts so magical, yet at any moment are subject to the seclusion of death.

. . . I must leave you, dear, to come perhaps again, —

> We never know we go — when we are going
> We jest and shut the door —
> Fate following behind us bolts it
> And we accost no more.

I give you my parting love.

EMILY.

[Autumn, 1881.]

Saturday.

DEAR ONES, — If I linger, this will not reach you before Sunday ; if I do not, I must write you much less than I would love. 'Do unto others as ye would that they should do unto you.' I would rather they would do unto me *so*.

After infinite wanderings the little note has reached us. It was mailed the twelfth — we received it the twenty-third. The address 'Misses Dickinson' misled the rustic eyes — the postmaster knows

Vinnie, also by faith who Emily is, because his little girl was hurt, and Emily sent her juleps — but he failed of the intellectual grasp to combine the names. So after sending it to all the *Mrs* Dickinsons he could discover, he consigned it to us, with the request that we would speedily return it if not ours, that he might renew his research. Almost any one under the circumstances would have doubted if it were theirs, or indeed if they were themself — but to us it was clear. Next time, dears, direct Vinnie, or Emily, and perhaps Mr ——'s astuteness may be adequate. I enclose the battered remains for your Sabbath perusal, and tell you we think of you tenderly, which I trust you often believe.

Maggie is making a flying visit to cattle-show, on her very robust wings — for Maggie is getting corpulent. Vinnie is picking a few seeds — for if a pod ' die, shall he not live again '; and with the shutting mail I go to read to mother about the President. When we think of the lone effort to live, and its bleak reward, the mind turns to the myth ' for His mercy endureth forever,' with confiding revulsion. Still, when Professor Fisk died on Mount Zion, Dr Humphrey prayed ' to whom shall we turn but thee?' 'I have finished,' said Paul, ' the faith.' We rejoice that he did not say discarded it.

The little postman has come — Thomas's ' second oldest,' and I close with reluctant and hurrying love.

EMILY.

[1881.]

What is it that instructs a hand lightly created, to impel shapes to eyes at a distance, which for them have the whole area of life or of death? Yet not a pencil in the street but has this awful power, though nobody arrests it. An earnest letter is or should be life-warrant or death-warrant, for what is each instant but a gun, harmless because 'unloaded,' but that touched 'goes off'?

Men are picking up the apples to-day, and the pretty boarders are leaving the trees, birds and ants and bees. I have heard a chipper say 'dee' six times in disapprobation. How should we like to have our privileges wheeled away in a barrel? . . .

The Essex visit was lovely. Mr L—— remained a week. Mrs —— re-decided to come with her son Elizabeth. Aunt L—— shouldered arms. I think they lie in my memory, a muffin and a bomb. Now they are all gone, and the crickets are pleased. Their bombazine reproof still falls upon the twilight, and checks the softer uproars of the departing day.

Earnest love to F——. This is but a fragment, but wholes are not below.

EMILY.

DEAR L——, — Thank you, with love, for the kindness; it would be very sweet to claim if we needed it, but we are quite strong, and mother well as usual, and Vinnie spectacular as Disraeli and sincere

as Gladstone, — was only sighing in fun. When
she sighs in earnest, Emily's throne will tremble, and
she will need both L—— and F——; but Vinnie
' still prevails.'   When one or all of us are lain on
' *Marian Erle's* dim pallet,' so cool that she deplored
to live because that she must leave it, L—— and the
ferns, and F—— and her fan shall supplement the
angels, if they have not already joined them.

Lovingly,   EMILY.

[October, 1881.]

Did the little sisters know that Dr Holland had
died — the dark man with the doll-wife, whom they
used to see at 'Uncle Edward's' before 'Uncle
Edward' went too?

Do they know any of the circumstances?

Did they know that the weary life in the second
story had mourned to hear from them, and whether
they were 'comfortable'? 'Comfortable' seems
to comprise the whole to those whose days are weak.
'Happiness' is for birds and other foreign nations,
in their faint esteem.

Mother heard F—— telling Vinnie about her
graham bread. She would like to taste it. Will
F—— please write Emily how, and not too inconvenient? Every particular, for Emily is dull, and
she will pay in gratitude, which, though not canned
like quinces, is fragrantest of all we know.

Tell us just how and where they are, and if October
sunshine is thoughtful of their heads.

EMILY.

. . . Thank you, dear, for the quickness which is the blossom of request, and for the definiteness — for a new rule is a chance.   The bread resulted charmingly, and such pretty little proportions, quaint as a druggist's formula — 'I do remember an apothecary.'   Mother and Vinnie think it the nicest they have ever known, and Maggie so extols it.

Mr Lathrop's poem was piteously sweet.[1]

To know of your homes is comforting.   I trust they are both peace.   Home is the riddle of the wise — the booty of the dove.   God bless the sunshine in L——'s room, and could he find a sweeter task than to 'temper the wind' to her curls? . . .

Tell us when you are happy, but be sure and tell us when you are sad, for Emily's heart is the edifice where the 'wicked cease from troubling.'

[January, 1882.]

I have only a moment, exiles, but you shall have the largest half.   Mother's dear little wants so engross the time, — to read to her, to fan her, to tell her health will come to-morrow, to explain to her *why* the grasshopper is a burden, because he is not so new a grasshopper as he was, — this is so ensuing, I hardly have said 'Good-morning, mother,' when I hear myself saying 'Mother, good-night.'

---

[1] This reference is to the pathetic verses to his little boy, by Mr George Parsons Lathrop, beginning, —

'Do you remember, my sweet absent son.'

[November, 1882.]

DEAR COUSINS, — I hoped to write you before, but mother's dying almost stunned my spirit.

I have answered a few inquiries of love, but written little intuitively. She was scarcely the aunt you knew. The great mission of pain had been ratified — cultivated to tenderness by persistent sorrow, so that a larger mother died than had she died before. There was no earthly parting. She slipped from our fingers like a flake gathered by the wind, and is now part of the drift called 'the infinite.'

We don't know where she is, though so many tell us.

I believe we shall in some manner be cherished by our Maker — that the One who gave us this remarkable earth has the power still farther to surprise that which He has caused. Beyond that all is silence. . . .

Mother was very beautiful when she had died. Seraphs are solemn artists. The illumination that comes but once paused upon her features, and it seemed like hiding a picture to lay her in the grave ; but the grass that received my father will suffice his guest, the one he asked at the altar to visit him all his life.

I cannot tell how Eternity seems. It sweeps around me like a sea. . . . Thank you for remembering me. Remembrance — mighty word.

'Thou gavest it to me from the foundation of the world.'

Lovingly,

EMILY.

[Spring, 1883.]

Thank you, dears, for the sympathy. I hardly dare to know that I have lost another friend, but anguish finds it out.

> Each that we lose takes part of us;
> A crescent still abides,
> Which like the moon, some turbid night,
> Is summoned by the tides.

. . . I work to drive the awe away, yet awe impels the work.

I almost picked the crocuses, you told them so sincerely. Spring's first conviction is a wealth beyond its whole experience.

The sweetest way I think of you is when the day is done, and L—— sets the 'sunset tree' for the little sisters. Dear F—— has had many stormy mornings ; . . . I hope they have not chilled her feet, nor dampened her heart. I am glad the little visit rested you. Rest and water are most we want.

I know each moment of Miss W—— is a gleam of boundlessness. 'Miles and miles away,' said Browning, 'there's a girl;' but 'the colored end of evening smiles' on but few so rare.

Thank you once more for being sorry. Till the
first friend dies, we think ecstasy impersonal, but
then discover that he was the cup from which we
drank it, itself as yet unknown. Sweetest love for
each, and a kiss besides for Miss W——'s cheek,
should you again meet her.

EMILY.

[July, 1884.]

DEAR COUSINS, — I hope you heard Mr Sanborn's
lecture. My *Republican* was borrowed before I
waked, to read till my own dawn, which is rather
tardy, for I have been quite sick, and could claim
the immortal reprimand, 'Mr Lamb, you come
down very late in the morning.' Eight Saturday
noons ago, I was making a loaf of cake with Maggie,
when I saw a great darkness coming and knew no
more until late at night. I woke to find Austin and
Vinnie and a strange physician bending over me,
and supposed I was dying, or had died, all was so
kind and hallowed. I had fainted and lain unconscious for the first time in my life. Then I grew
very sick and gave the others much alarm, but am
now staying. The doctor calls it 'revenge of the
nerves;' but who but Death had wronged them?
F——'s dear note has lain unanswered for this long
season, though its 'Good-night, my dear,' warmed
me to the core. I have all to say, but little strength
to say it; so we must talk by degrees. I do want to
know about L——, what pleases her most, book or
tune or friend.

I am glad the housekeeping is kinder; it is a prickly art. Maggie is with us still, warm and wild and mighty, and we have a gracious boy at the barn. We remember you always, and one or the other often comes down with a 'we dreamed of F—— and I.—— last night;' then that day we think we shall hear from you, for dreams are couriers.

The little boy we laid away never fluctuates, and his dim society is companion still. But it is growing damp and I must go in. Memory's fog is rising.

> The going from a world we know
>   To one a wonder still
> Is like the child's adversity
>   Whose vista is a hill,
> Behind the hill is sorcery
>   And everything unknown,
> But will the secret compensate
>   For climbing it alone?

Vinnie's love and Maggie's, and mine is presupposed.   EMILY.

[January 14, 1885.]

Had we less to say to those we love, perhaps we should say it oftener, but the attempt comes, then the inundation, then it is all over, as is said of the dead.

Vinnie dreamed about F—— last night, and designing for days to write dear L——, — dear, both of you, — indeed, with the astounding nearness which a dream brings, I must speak this morning.

I do hope you are well, and that the last enchanting days have refreshed your spirits, and I hope the poor little girl is better, and the sorrow at least adjourned.

L—— asked 'what books' we were wooing now — watching like a vulture for Walter Cross's life of his wife. A friend sent me *Called Back*. It is a haunting story, and as loved Mr Bowles used to say, 'greatly impressive to me.' Do you remember the little picture with his deep face in the centre, and Governor Bross on one side, and Colfax on the other? The third of the group died yesterday, so somewhere they are again together.

Moving to Cambridge seems to me like moving to Westminster Abbey, as hallowed and as un-believed, or moving to Ephesus with Paul for a next-door neighbor.

Holmes's *Life of Emerson* is sweetly commended, but you, I know, have tasted that. . . . But the whistle calls me — I have not begun — so with a moan, and a kiss, and a promise of more, and love from Vinnie and Maggie, and the half-blown carnation, and the western sky, I stop.

That we are permanent temporarily, it is warm to know, though we know no more.

EMILY.

CHAPTER VII

To Mr Thomas Wentworth Higginson

IN his article upon Emily Dickinson in
The Atlantic Monthly for October, 1891,
Colonel Higginson has already given many
of her letters to himself. The rest are here
added.

The first one, enclosing four of her now
widely known poems for his criticism, was
without signature, but accompanied by a card
bearing her name. Her wish for an impartial
and extrinsic judgment from a stranger may,
perhaps, illustrate Mrs Ford's suggestion that
'she was longing for poetic sympathy.' At a
time when she was but newly trying her own
wings, she must have felt something warmly
and essentially human in Colonel Higginson's
writing to be thus led to ask his help rather
than another's, — an intuition most happily
justified.

He received the first of her unique letters
at the beginning of 'war time.' Unfortunately
his answers cannot now be found:

[April 16, 1862.]

MR HIGGINSON, — Are you too deeply occupied to say if my verse is alive?

The mind is so near itself it cannot see distinctly, and I have none to ask.

Should you think it breathed, and had you the leisure to tell me, I should feel quick gratitude.

If I make the mistake, that you dared to tell me would give me sincerer honor toward you.

I enclose my name, asking you, if you please, sir, to tell me what is true?

That you will not betray me it is needless to ask, since honor is its own pawn.

[April 26, 1862.]

MR HIGGINSON, — Your kindness claimed earlier gratitude, but I was ill, and write to-day from my pillow.

Thank you for the surgery; it was not so painful as I supposed. I bring you others, as you ask, though they might not differ. While my thought is undressed, I can make the distinction; but when I put them in the gown, they look alike and numb.

You asked how old I was? I made no verse, but one or two, until this winter, sir.

I had a terror since September, I could tell to none; and so I sing, as the boy does of the burying ground, because I am afraid.

You inquire my books. For poets, I have Keats,

and Mr and Mrs Browning.   For prose, Mr Ruskin,
Sir Thomas Browne, and the *Revelations*.   I went
to school, but in your manner of the phrase had no
education.   When a little girl, I had a friend who
taught me Immortality; but venturing too near,
himself, he never returned.   Soon after my tutor
died, and for several years my lexicon was my only
companion.   Then I found one more, but he was
not contented I be his scholar, so he left the land.

You ask of my companions.   Hills, sir, and the
sundown, and a dog large as myself, that my father
bought me.   They are better than beings because
they know, but do not tell; and the noise in the
pool at noon excels my piano.

I have a brother and sister; my mother does not
care for thought, and father, too busy with his briefs
to notice what we do.   He buys me many books,
but begs me not to read them, because he fears they
joggle the mind.   They are religious, except me,
and address an eclipse, every morning, whom they
call their ' Father.'

But I fear my story fatigues you.   I would like
to learn.   Could you tell me how to grow, or is it
unconveyed, like melody or witchcraft?

You speak of Mr Whitman.   I never read his
book, but was told that it was disgraceful.

I read Miss Prescott's *Circumstance*, but it followed me in the dark, so I avoided her.

Two editors of journals came to my father's house
this winter, and asked me for my mind, and when I

asked them 'why' they said I was penurious, and they would use it for the world.

I could not weigh myself, myself. My size felt small to me. I read your chapters in *The Atlantic,* and experienced honor for you. I was sure you would not reject a confiding question.

Is this, sir, what you asked me to tell you?

Your friend,

E. DICKINSON.

[June 8, 1862.]

DEAR FRIEND, — Your letter gave no drunkenness, because I tasted rum before. Domingo comes but once ; yet I have had few pleasures so deep as your opinion, and if I tried to thank you, my tears would block my tongue.

My dying tutor told me that he would like to live till I had been a poet, but Death was much of mob as I could master, then. And when, far afterward, a sudden light on orchards, or a new fashion in the wind troubled my attention, I felt a palsy, here, the verses just relieve.

Your second letter surprised me, and for a moment, swung. I had not supposed it. Your first gave no dishonor, because the true are not ashamed. I thanked you for your justice, but could not drop the bells whose jingling cooled my tramp. Perhaps the balm seemed better, because you bled me first. I smile when you suggest that I delay 'to publish,' that being foreign to my thought as firmament to fin.

If fame belonged to me, I could not escape her ; if she did not, the longest day would pass me on the chase, and the approbation of my dog would forsake me then.   My barefoot rank is better.

You think my gait 'spasmodic.'   I am in danger, sir.   You think me 'uncontrolled.'   I have no tribunal.

Would you have time to be the 'friend' you should think I need?   I have a little shape : it would not crowd your desk, nor make much racket as the mouse that dents your galleries.

If I might bring you what I do — not so frequent to trouble you — and ask you if I told it clear, 't would be control to me.   The sailor cannot see the north, but knows the needle can.   The 'hand you stretch me in the dark' I put mine in, and turn away.   I have no Saxon now : —

> As if I asked a common alms,
> And in my wondering hand
> A stranger pressed a kingdom,
> And I, bewildered, stand ;
> As if I asked the Orient
> Had it for me a morn,
> And it should lift its purple dikes
> And shatter me with dawn!

But, will you be my preceptor, Mr Higginson?

After these startling letters it was but natural that Mr Higginson should have asked to see a photograph of his 'enigmatical correspondent.'   But there was none.   She had an

unconquerable aversion to seeing herself re-
produced in any sort of ' mould.' The frontis-
piece to the first volume of these *Letters* is
taken from an oil painting of Emily, when
she was but eight years old, in a group with
her brother and sister. The only other known
representation of her face is a daguerrotype
made a few years later; but it is entirely un-
satisfactory, both in expression and individuality. Instead of her photograph, she sent this
verbal portrait. Her coy avoidance of Mr
Higginson's request was as characteristically
piquant as her answer to his question of her
age : —

[July, 1862.]

Could you believe me without? I had no portrait, now, but am small, like the wren; and my
hair is bold, like the chestnut burr; and my eyes,
like the sherry in the glass that the guest leaves.
Would this do just as well?

It often alarms father. He says death might
occur, and he has moulds of all the rest, but has
no mould of me; but I noticed the quick wore off
those things in a few days, and forestall the dishonor. You will think no caprice of me.

You said 'dark.' I know the butterfly, and the
lizard, and the orchis. Are not those *your*
countrymen?

I am happy to be your scholar, and will deserve
the kindness I cannot repay.

If you truly consent, I recite now. Will you tell me my fault, frankly, as to yourself, for I had rather wince than die. Men do not call the surgeon to commend the bone, but to set it, sir, and fracture within is more critical. And for this, preceptor, I shall bring you obedience, the blossom from my garden, and every gratitude I know.

Perhaps you smile at me. I could not stop for that. My business is circumference. An ignorance, not of customs, but if caught with the dawn, or the sunset see me, myself the only kangaroo among the beauty, sir, if you please, it afflicts me, and I thought that instruction would take it away.

Because you have much business, beside the growth of me, you will appoint, yourself, how often I shall come without your inconvenience.

And if at any time you regret you received me, or I prove a different fabric to that you supposed, you must banish me.

When I state myself, as the representative of the verse, it does not mean me, but a supposed person.

You are true about the ' perfection.' To-day makes yesterday mean.

You spoke of *Pippa Passes*. I never heard anybody speak of *Pippa Passes* before. You see my posture is benighted.

To thank you baffles me. Are you perfectly powerful? Had I a pleasure you had not, I could delight to bring it.

YOUR SCHOLAR.

Colonel Higginson wrote, 'It would seem that at first I tried a little — a very little — to lead her in the direction of rules and traditions; but I fear it was only perfunctory, and that she interested me more in her — so to speak — unregenerate condition. Still, she recognizes the endeavor. In this case, as will be seen, I called her attention to the fact that while she took pains to correct the spelling of a word, she was utterly careless of greater irregularities. It will be seen by her answer that with her usual naïve adroitness she turns my point ': —

DEAR FRIEND, — Are these more orderly? I thank you for the truth.

I had no monarch in my life, and cannot rule myself; and when I try to organize, my little force explodes and leaves me bare and charred.

I think you called me 'wayward.' Will you help me improve?

I suppose the pride that stops the breath, in the core of woods, is not of ourself.

You say I confess the little mistake, and omit the large. Because I can see orthography; but the ignorance out of sight is my preceptor's charge.

Of 'shunning men and women,' — they talk of hallowed things, aloud, and embarrass my dog. He and I don't object to them, if they 'll exist their side. I think Carl would please you. He is dumb, and brave. I think you would like the chestnut-tree I met in my walk. It hit my notice suddenly, and I thought the skies were in blossom.

Then there 's a noiseless noise in the orchard that I let persons hear.

You told me in one letter you could not come to see me ' now,' and I made no answer; not because I had none, but did not think myself the price that you should come so far.

I do not ask so large a pleasure, lest you might deny me.

You say, ' Beyond your knowledge.' You would not jest with me, because I believe you; but, preceptor, you cannot mean it?

All men say ' What ' to me, but I thought it a fashion.

When much in the woods, as a little girl, I was told that the snake would bite me, that I might pick a poisonous flower, or goblins kidnap me; but I went along and met no one but angels, who were far shyer of me than I could be of them, so I have n't that confidence in fraud which many exercise.

I shall observe your precept, though I don't understand it, always.

I marked a line in one verse, because I met it after I made it, and never consciously touch a paint mixed by another person. I do not let go it, because it is mine.

Have you the portrait of Mrs Browning? Persons sent me three. If you had none, will you have mine?

YOUR SCHOLAR.

After entering the volunteer army of the Civil War, Colonel Higginson received the following letter while in camp in South Carolina, early in 1863: —

AMHERST.

DEAR FRIEND, — I did not deem that planetary forces annulled, but suffered an exchange of territory, or world.

I should have liked to see you before you became improbable. War feels to me an oblique place. Should there be other summers, would you perhaps come?

I found you were gone, by accident, as I find systems are, or seasons of the year, and obtain no cause, but suppose it a treason of progress that dissolves as it goes. Carlo still remained, and I told him

> Best gains must have the losses' test,
> To constitute them gains.

My shaggy ally assented.

Perhaps death gave me awe for friends, striking sharp and early, for I held them since in a brittle love, of more alarm than peace. I trust you may pass the limit of war; and though not reared to prayer, when service is had in church for our arms, I include yourself. . . . I was thinking to-day, as I noticed, that the 'supernatural' was only the natural disclosed.

> Not 'Revelation' 't is that waits,
> But our unfurnished eyes.

But I fear I detain you.   Should you, before this reaches you, experience Immortality, who will inform me of the exchange?   Could you, with honor, avoid death, I entreat you, sir.   It would bereave

YOUR GNOME.

I trust the *Procession of Flowers* was not a premonition.

Of this curious letter Colonel Higginson wrote: 'Mr Howells reminds me that Swedenborg somewhere has an image akin to her "oblique place," where he symbolizes evil as simply an oblique angle.'
In the summer of 1863 Colonel Higginson was wounded; in September of the same year began Emily's trouble with her eyes, frequently referred to.   In the April following she went to Boston, — her mention of Hawthorne's death (May, 1864) of itself placing the date: —

[Summer, 1864.]

DEAR FRIEND, — Are you in danger?   I did not know that you were hurt.   Will you tell me more? Mr Hawthorne died.

I was ill since September, and since April in Boston for a physician's care. He does not let me go, yet I work in my prison, and make guests for myself.

Carlo did not come, because that he would die in jail; and the mountains I could not hold now, so I brought but the gods.

I wish to see you more than before I failed. Will you tell me your health? I am surprised and anxious since receiving your note.

> The only news I know
> Is bulletins all day
> From Immortality.

Can you render my pencil? The physician has taken away my pen. I enclose the address from a letter, lest my figures fail.

Knowledge of your recovery would excel my own.

E. DICKINSON.

[1865.]

AMHERST.

DEAR FRIEND, — You were so generous to me, that if possible I offended you, I could not too deeply apologize.

To doubt my high behavior is a new pain. I could be honorable no more, till I asked you about it. I know not what to deem myself — yesterday 'your scholar,' but might I be the one you to-night forgave, 't is a better honor. Mine is but just the thief's request.

Please, sir, hear

'BARABBAS.'

> The possibility to pass
> Without a moment's bell
> Into conjecture's presence,
> Is like a face of steel
> That suddenly looks into ours
> With a metallic grin;
> The cordiality of Death
> Who drills his welcome in.

[1868.]

AMHERST.

DEAR FRIEND, — Whom my dog understood could not elude others.

I should be so glad to see you, but think it an apparitional pleasure, not to be fulfilled. I am uncertain of Boston.

I had promised to visit my physician for a few days in May, but father objects because he is in the habit of me.

Is it more far to Amherst?

You will find a minute host, but a spacious welcome. . . .

If I still entreat you to teach me, are you much displeased? I will be patient, constant, never reject your knife, and should my slowness goad you, you knew before myself that

> Except the smaller size
> No lives are round.
> These hurry to a sphere
> And show and end.
> The larger slower grow
> And later hang;
> The summers of Hesperides
> Are long.

[1868.]

AMHERST.

DEAR FRIEND, — A letter always feels to me like
Immortality because it is the mind alone without
corporeal friend.   Indebted in our talk to attitude
and accent, there seems a spectral power in thought
that walks alone.   I would like to thank you for
your great kindness, but never try to lift the words
which I cannot hold.

Should you come to Amherst, I might then succeed, though gratitude is the timid wealth of those
who have nothing.   I am sure that you speak the
truth, because the noble do, but your letters always
surprise me.

My life has been too simple and stern to embarrass
any.   'Seen of angels,' scarcely my responsibility.

It is difficult not to be fictitious in so fair a place,
but tests' severe repairs are permitted all.

When a little girl I remember hearing that remarkable passage and preferring the 'power,' not
knowing at the time that 'kingdom' and 'glory'
were included.

You noticed my dwelling alone.   To an emigrant,
country is idle except it be his own.   You speak
kindly of seeing me ; could it please your conven-
ience to come so far as Amherst, I should be very
glad, but I do not cross my father's ground to any
house or town.

Of our greatest acts we are ignorant.   You were
not aware that you saved my life.   To thank you in

person has been since then one of my few requests.
. . . You will excuse each that I say, because no
one taught me.

[August, 1870.]

DEAR FRIEND, — I will be at home and glad.

I think you said the 15th. The incredible never
surprises us, because it is the incredible.

E. DICKINSON.

Of his meeting Emily Dickinson in her own
home, and of his first impressions of her,
Colonel Higginson has told in the pages of
The Atlantic.

Withdrawing more and more constantly from
accumulated humanity, no thought of the pos-
sibility of a lack of congenial occupation ever
crossed her mind. During their first interview,
indeed, Colonel Higginson asked her ' if she
never felt any want of employment, not going
off the grounds, and rarely seeing a visitor; ' to
which she replied, ' I never thought of con-
ceiving that I could ever have the slightest
approach to such a want in all future time.'

Among the strong and remarkable things
she said to him are several sentences which
it seems not irrelevant to insert here: —

' Is it oblivion or absorption when things pass
from our minds? '

'Truth is such a rare thing, it is delightful to tell it.'

'I find ecstasy in living; the mere sense of living is joy enough.'

One or two others Colonel Higginson has called 'the very wantonness of over-statement,' as, —

'How do most people live without any thoughts? There are many people in the world, — you must have noticed them in the street, — how do they live? How do they get strength to put on their clothes in the morning?'

And this, 'a crowning extravaganza,' —

'If I read a book and it makes my whole body so cold no fire can ever warm me, I know that is poetry. If I feel physically as if the top of my head were taken off, I know that is poetry. These are the only ways I know it. Is there any other way?'

After the visit she wrote: —

[August, 1870.]

Enough is so vast a sweetness, I suppose it never occurs, only pathetic counterfeits.

Fabulous to me as the men of the *Revelations* who 'shall not hunger any more.' Even the possible has its insoluble particle.

After you went, I took Macbeth and turned to 'Birnam Wood.' Came *twice* 'to Dunsinane.' I thought and went about my work. . . .

The vein cannot thank the artery, but her solemn indebtedness to him, even the stolidest admit, and so of me who try, whose effort leaves no sound.

You ask great questions accidentally. To answer them would be events. I trust that you are safe.

I ask you to forgive me for all the ignorance I had. I find no nomination sweet as your low opinion.

Speak, if but to blame your obedient child.

You told me of Mrs Lowell's poems. Would you tell me where I could find them, or are they not for sight? An article of yours, too, perhaps the only one you wrote that I never knew. It was about a 'Latch.' Are you willing to tell me?[1]

If I ask too much, you could please refuse. Shortness to live has made me bold.

Abroad is close to-night and I have but to lift my hands to touch the 'Heights of Abraham.'

DICKINSON.

[Winter, 1871.]

To live is so startling, it leaves but little room for other occupations, though friends are, if possible, an event more fair.

I am happy you have the travel you so long desire, and chastened that my master met neither accident nor Death.

[1] Perhaps *A Shadow.*

Our own possessions, though our own, 't is well
to hoard anew, remembering the dimensions of pos-
sibility. I often saw your name in illustrious mention, and envied an occasion so abstinent to me.
Thank you for having been to Amherst. Could you
come again that would be far better, though the
finest wish is the futile one.

When I saw you last, it was mighty summer —
now the grass is glass, and the meadov ʼucco, and
' still waters ' in the pool where the frog drinks.

These behaviors of the year hurt almost like
music, shifting when it ease us most. Thank you
for the ' lesson.'

I will study it, though hitherto, —

> Menagerie to me
> My neighbor be.

YOUR SCHOLAR.

Her father's death (June 16) swept away all
her landmarks. To this friend she wrote: —

[July, 1874.]

The last afternoon that my father lived, though
with no premonition, I preferred to be with him,
and invented an absence for mother, Vinnie being
asleep. He seemed peculiarly pleased, as I oftenest
stayed with myself; and remarked, as the afternoon
withdrew, he ' would like it to not end.'

His pleasure almost embarrassed me, and my
brother coming, I suggested they walk. Next

morning I woke him for the train, and saw him no more.

His heart was pure and terrible, and I think no other like it exists.

I am glad there is Immortality, but would have tested it myself, before intrusting him. Mr Bowles was with us. With that exception, I saw none. I have wished for you, since my father died, and had you an hour unengrossed, it would be almost priceless. Thank you for each kindness. . . . Your beautiful hymn, was it not prophetic? It has assisted that pause of space which I call ' father.'

[August, 1874]

When I think of my father's lonely life and lonelier death, there is this redress, —

> Take all away;
> The only thing worth larceny
> Is left — the Immortality.

My earliest friend wrote me the week before he died, ' If I live, I will go to Amherst; if I die, I certainly will.'

Is your house deeper off?

YOUR SCHOLAR.

DEAR FRIEND, — I find you with dusk, for day is tired, and lays her antediluvian cheek to the hill like a child.

Nature confides now.

I hope you are joyful frequently, these beloved days, and the health of your friend bolder.

I remember her with my blossoms and wish they were hers

> Whose pink career may have a close
> Portentous as our own, who knows?
> To imitate these neighbors fleet,
> In awe and innocence, were meet.

Summer is so kind I had hoped you might come. Since my father's dying, everything sacred enlarged so it was dim to own.   When a few years old, I was taken to a funeral which I now know was of peculiar distress, and the clergyman asked, ' Is the arm of the Lord shortened, that it cannot save?'

He italicised the ' cannot.'   I mistook the accent for a doubt of Immortality, and not daring to ask, it besets me still, though we know that the mind of the heart must live if its clerical part do not.   Would you explain it to me? . . . It comforts an instinct if another have felt it too.   I was re-reading your *Decoration*.   You may have forgotten it.

[June, 1875.]

DEAR FRIEND, — Mother was paralyzed Tuesday, a year from the evening father died.   I thought perhaps you would care.

YOUR SCHOLAR.

> A death-blow is a life-blow to some
> Who, till they died, did not alive become;
> Who, had they lived, had died, but when
> They died, vitality begun.

[1875.]

DEAR FRIEND, — The flower was jasmine. I am glad if it pleased your friend. It is next dearest to daphne, except wild-flowers — those are dearer.

I have a friend in Dresden, who thinks the love of the field a misplaced affection — and says he will send me a meadow that is better than summer's. If he does, I will send it to you.

I have read nothing of Tourguéneff's, but thank you for telling me — and will seek him immediately. I did not read Mr Miller because I could not care about him.

Mrs Hunt's poems are stronger than any written by women since Mrs Browning, with the exception of Mrs Lewes's; but truth like ancestors' brocades can stand alone. You speak of *Men and Women*. That is a broad book.

Bells and Pomegranates I never saw, but have Mrs Browning's endorsement. While Shakespeare remains, literature is firm.

An insect cannot run away with Achilles's head. Thank you for having written the *Atlantic Essays*. They are a fine joy, though to possess the ingredient for congratulation renders congratulation superfluous.

Dear friend, I trust you as you ask. If I exceed permission, excuse the bleak simplicity that knew no tutor but the north. Would you but guide

DICKINSON?

[1875.]

DEAR FRIEND, — I am sorry your brother is dead. I fear he was dear to you. I should be glad to know you were painlessly grieved.

> Of Heaven above the firmest proof
> We fundamental know —
> Except for its marauding hand
> It had been heaven below.

DICKINSON.

As already shown, Emily had effectively resisted all importunity to publish. Even the eloquent pleading of her long-time friend 'H. H.' was of no avail; but apparently reinforcement in her decision was sometimes sought: —

[Early in 1876.]

DEAR FRIEND, — Are you willing to tell me what is right ? Mrs Jackson, of Colorado, was with me a few moments this week, and wished me to write for this.[1] I told her I was unwilling, and she asked me why? I said I was incapable, and she seemed not to believe me and asked me not to decide for a few days. Meantime, she would write to me. She was so sweetly noble, I would regret to estrange her, and if you would be willing to give me a note saying you disapproved it and

---

[1] A circular of the *No Name Series* was enclosed.

thought me unfit, she would believe you. I am sorry to flee so often to my safest friend, but hope he permits me.

[Acknowledging a photograph, 1876.]

DEAR FRIEND, — Except your coming I know no gift so great, and in one extent it exceeds that, — it is permanent.

Your face is more joyful when you speak, and I miss an almost arrogant look that at times haunts you, but with that exception, it is so real I could think it you.

Thank you with delight, and please to thank your friend for the lovely suggestion.

I hope she has no suffering now.

Was it Browning's flower that ' ailed till evening ' ? I shall think of your ' keeping house ' at night when I close the shutter — but to be Mrs Higginson's guest is the boon of birds.

Judge Lord was with us a few days since, and told me that the joy we most revere we profane in taking. I wish that was wrong.

Mrs Jackson has written. It was not stories she asked of me. But may I tell her just the same that you don't prefer it? Thank you if I may, for it almost seems sordid to refuse from myself again.

My brother and sister speak of you, and covet your remembrance, and perhaps you will not reject my own to Mrs Higginson?

Summer laid her supple glove
In its sylvan drawer —
Wheresoe'er, or was she
The demand of awe ?

YOUR SCHOLAR.

[March, 1876.]

. . . But two had mentioned the 'spring' to me
— yourself and the *Revelations*. 'I, Jesus, have
sent mine angel.'

I inferred your touch in the papers on Lowell and
Emerson. It is delicate that each mind is itself,
like a distinct bird.

I was lonely there was an 'or' in that beautiful
'I would go to Amherst,' though grieved for its
cause. I wish your friend had my strength, for I
don't care for roving — she perhaps might, though
to remain with you is journey.

To abstain from *Daniel Deronda* is hard — you
are very kind to be willing. . . . I am glad *Immortality* pleased you. I believed it would. I suppose
even God Himself could not withhold that now.

To disappear enhances,
The man that runs away
Is tinctured for an instant
With Immortality.

But yesterday a vagrant,
To-day in memory lain
With superstitious value —
We tamper with again.

But 'never' far as honor
Withdraws the worthless thing,
And impotent to cherish
We hasten to adorn.

Of Death the sternest function
That just as we discern
The excellence defies us —
Securest gathered then

The fruit perverse to plucking,
But leaning to the sight
With the ecstatic limit
Of unobtained delight.

In sending a volume of George Eliot to Mrs Higginson, Emily wrote, 'I am bringing you a little granite book to lean on.'

[Autumn, 1876.]

DEAR FRIEND, — Thank you for permission to write Mrs Higginson. I hope I have not fatigued her — also for thinking of my brother, who is slowly better, and rides for an hour, kind days.

I am glad if I did as you would like. The degradation to displease you, I hope I may never incur.

Often, when troubled by entreaty, that paragraph of yours has saved me — 'Such being the majesty of the art you presume to practise, you can at least take time before dishonoring it,' and Enobarbus said, 'Leave that which leaves itself.'

I shall look with joy for the ʼlittle book' because

it is yours, though I seek you in vain in the magazines where you once wrote. I recently found two
papers of yours that were unknown to me, and wondered anew at your withdrawing thought so sought
by others.

When flowers annually died and I was a child, I
used to read Dr Hitchcock's book on the *Flowers
of North America*. This comforted their absence,
assuring me they lived.

YOUR SCHOLAR.

[1877.]

Thank you, dear friend, for my 'New Year,' but
did you not confer it? Had your scholar permission to fashion yours, it were perhaps too fair. I
always ran home to awe when a child, if anything
befell me. He was an awful mother, but I liked
him better than none.

There remained this shelter after you left me the
other day.

Of your flitting coming it is fair to think, like the
bee's coupé, vanishing in music.

> Would you with the bee return,
> What a firm of noon!
> Death obtains the rose,
> But the news of dying goes
> No further than the breeze.

The ear is the last face. We hear after we see,
which to tell you first is still my destiny.

Meeting a bird this morning, I began to flee.
He saw it and sung.

> Presuming on that lone result,
> His infinite disdain,
> But vanquished him with my defeat —
> 'T was victory was slain.

I shall read the book.
Thank you for telling me.

[After Colonel Higginson had met with a bereavement, in
1877.]

DEAR FRIEND, — We must be less than Death to
be lessened by it, for nothing is irrevocable but
ourselves.

I am glad you are better. I had feared to follow
you, lest you would rather be lonely, which is the
will of sorrow; but the papers had spoken of you
with affectionate deference, and to know you were
deeply remembered might not too intrude.

To be human is more than to be divine, for when
Christ was divine he was uncontented till he had
been human.

I remember nothing so strong as to see you. . . .

[1877.]

DEAR FRIEND, — I think of you so wholly that I
cannot resist to write again, to ask if you are safe?
Danger is not at first, for then we are unconscious,
but in the after, slower days.

Do not try to be saved, but let redemption find
you, as it certainly will.   Love is its own rescue, for
we, at our supremest, are but its trembling emblems.

YOUR SCHOLAR.

After an interval of silence came this letter,
in the same year: —

Must I lose the friend that saved my life without
inquiring why? Affection gropes through drifts of
awe for his tropic door.

That every bliss we know or guess hourly befall
him, is his scholar's prayer.

[January, 1878.]

DEAR FRIEND, — I felt it shelter to speak to you.

My brother and sister are with Mr Bowles, who is
buried this afternoon.

The last song that I heard — that was, since the
birds — was, 'He leadeth me, he leadeth me ; yea,
though I walk' — then the voices stooped, the arch
was so low.

[Summer, 1878.]

DEAR FRIEND, — When you wrote you would come
in November, it would please me it were November
then — but the time has moved.   You went with
the coming of the birds — they will go with your
coming, but to see you is so much sweeter than
birds, I could excuse the spring.

With the bloom of the flower your friend loved, I have wished for her, but God cannot discontinue Himself.

Mr Bowles was not willing to die.

When you have lost a friend, Master, you remember you could not begin again, because there was no world. I have thought of you often since the darkness, though we cannot assist another's night.

I have hoped you were saved.

That those have immortality with whom we talked about it, makes it no more mighty but perhaps more sudden. . . .

> How brittle are the piers
> On which our faith doth tread —
> No bridge below doth totter so,
> Yet none hath such a crowd.
>
> It is as old as God —
> Indeed, 't was built by Him —
> He sent His son to test the plank,
> And he pronounced it firm.

I hope you have been well. I hope your rambles have been sweet, and your reveries spacious.

To have seen Stratford on Avon, and the Dresden Madonna, must be almost peace.

And perhaps you have spoken with George Eliot. Will you 'tell me about it'? Will you come in November, and will November come, or is this the hope that opens and shuts, like the eye of the wax doll?

YOUR SCHOLAR.

[In acknowledgment of his *Short Studies of American Authors,*
1879.]

DEAR FRIEND, — Brabantio's gift was not more
fair than yours, though I trust without his pathetic
inscription, 'Which but thou hast already, with all
my heart I would keep from thee.'

Of Poe, I know too little to think — Hawthorne
appalls — entices.

Mrs Jackson soars to your estimate lawfully as a
bird, but of Howells and James, one hesitates. Your
relentless music dooms as it redeems.

Remorse for the brevity of a book is a rare emotion, though fair as Lowell's 'sweet despair' in the
'slipper hymn.'

> One thing of it we borrow
> And promise to return,
> The booty and the sorrow
> Its sweetness to have known.
> One thing of it we covet —
> The power to forget,
> The anguish of the avarice
> Defrays the dross of it.

Had I tried before reading your gift to thank you,
it had perhaps been possible, but I waited, and now
it disables my lips.

Magic, as it electrifies, also makes decrepit. Thank
you for thinking of me.

YOUR SCHOLAR.

[1880.]

DEAR FRIEND, — You were once so kind as to say you would advise me.   Could I ask it now?

I have promised three hymns to a charity, but without your approval could not give them.

They are short, and I could write them quite plainly, and if you felt it convenient to tell me if they were faithful, I should be very grateful, though if public cares too far fatigue you, please deny

YOUR SCHOLAR.

[1880.]

DEAR FRIEND, — Thank you for the advice.   I shall implicitly follow it.

The one who asked me for the lines I had never seen.

He spoke of 'a charity.'   I refused, but did not inquire.   He again earnestly urged, on the ground that in that way I might 'aid unfortunate children.' The name of 'child' was a snare to me, and I hesitated, choosing my most rudimentary, and without criterion.

I.inquired of you.   You can scarcely estimate the opinion to one utterly guideless.   Again thank you.

YOUR SCHOLAR.

[Early Summer, 1880.]

DEAR FRIEND, — I was touchingly reminded of [a child who had died] this morning by an Indian

woman with gay baskets and a dazzling baby, at the
kitchen door. Her little boy 'once died,' she said,
death to her dispelling him. I asked her what the
baby liked, and she said 'to step.' The prairie
before the door was gay with flowers of hay, and I
led her in. She argued with the birds, she leaned
on clover walls and they fell, and dropped her..
With jargon sweeter than a bell, she grappled
buttercups, and they sank together, the buttercups
the heaviest. What sweetest use of days ! 'T was
noting some such scene made Vaughan humbly
say, —

    'My days that are at best but dim and hoary.'

I think it was Vaughan. . . .

[1884.]

DEAR FRIEND, — May I ask the delight in ad-
vance, of sending you the *Life of Mrs Cross* by her
husband, which the papers promise for publication?

I feared some other pupil might usurp my
privilege.

Emblem is immeasurable — that is why it is better than fulfilment, which can be drained.

CHAPTER VIII

To Mr Perez D. Cowan, Miss Maria Whitney,
Mr Bowles, Mr J. D. Clark, and Mr C. H.
Clark

M R COWAN graduated at Amherst College in 1866, and 'Peter' was Emily
Dickinson's especial appellation for this favorite cousin. The first letter was written upon
the occasion of his marriage to Miss Margaret
Elizabeth Rhea.

To the Rev. Perez D. Cowan

[October 26, 1870.]

DEAR PETER, — It is indeed sweet news. I am
proud of your happiness. To Peter, and Peter's,
let me give both hands. Delight has no competi-
tor, so it is always most.

'Maggie' is a warm name.

I shall like to take it.

Home is the definition of God.

EMILY.

To the Same

It is long since I knew of you, Peter, and much may have happened to both; but that is the rarest book, which, opened at whatever page, equally enchants us.

I hope that you have power, and as much of peace as in our deep existence may be possible.

To multiply the harbors does not reduce the sea.

We learn, through cousin Montague, that you have lost your sister through that sweeter loss which we call gain.

I am glad she is glad.

Her early pain had seemed to me peculiarly cruel.

Tell her how tenderly we are pleased.

Recall me too to your other sisters, who though they may have mislaid me, I can always find; and include me to your sweet wife. We are daily reminded of you by the clergyman, Mr Jenkins, whom you strongly resemble.

Thank you for the paper. It is homelike to know where you are.

We can almost hear you announce the text, when the air is clear; and how social if you should preach us a note some Sunday in recess!

EMILY.

To the Same

[After the death of Mr Cowan's little daughter Margié.]

[November 8, 1879.]

Will it comfort my grieved cousin to know that Emily and Vinnie are among the ones this moment thinking of him with peculiar tenderness, and is his sweet wife too faint to remember to Whom her loved one is consigned?

'Come unto me' could not alarm those minute feet — how sweet to remember.

If you feel able, write a few words; if you do not — remember forgetting is a guile unknown to your faithful cousin

EMILY.

To the Same

[Upon receiving an account of little Margie's life and death.]

[October, 1880.]

DEAR COUSIN, — The sweet book found me on my pillow, where I was detained, or I should have thanked you immediately.

The little creature must have been priceless — yours and not yours — how hallowed !

It may have been she came to show you Immortality. Her startling little flight would imply she did.

May I remind you what Paul said, or do you think of nothing else, these October nights, without her crib to visit? ·

The little furniture of loss has lips of dirks to stab us. I hope Heaven is warm, there are so many barefoot ones. I hope it is near — the little tourist was so small. I hope it is not so unlike earth that we shall miss the peculiar form — the mould of the bird. 'And with what body do they come?' Then they *do* come! Rejoice! What door? What hour? Run, run, my soul! Illuminate the house!

'Body!' then real, — a face and eyes, — to know that it is them! Paul knew the Man that knew the news, He passed through Bethlehem.

With love for you, and your sweet wife, 'whom seeing not, we' trust.

COUSIN EMILY.

To Miss Maria Whitney

> How well I know her not
> Whom not to know has been
> A bounty in prospective, now
> Next door to mine the pain.
>
> EMILY.

The handwriting of this first little stanza sent to Miss Whitney is that of the early middle period, and is too indefinite to be safely dated; but before the next letter, a long interval seems to have elapsed.

To the Same

[1877.]

Vinnie and her sister thank Miss Whitney for the delicate kindness, and remember her with peculiar love these acuter days. . . .

I fear we think too lightly of the gift of mortality, which, too gigantic to comprehend, certainly cannot be estimated.

E. DICKINSON.

To the Same

[1878.]

DEAR FRIEND, — I have thought of you often since the darkness, — though we cannot assist another's night. I have hoped you were saved. That he has received Immortality who so often conferred it, invests it with a more sudden charm. . . .

I hope you have the power of hope, and that every bliss we know or guess hourly befalls you.

E. DICKINSON.

To the Same

. . . To relieve the irreparable degrades it.

Brabantio's resignation is the only one — ' I here do give thee that with all my heart, which but thou hast already, with all my heart I would keep from thee.'

EMILY.

To the Same

[1878.]

DEAR FRIEND, — I am constantly more astonished that the body contains the spirit — except for over-mastering work it could not be borne.

I shall miss saying to Vinnie when we hear the Northampton bell — as in subtle states of the west we do — 'Miss Whitney is going to church,' though must not everywhere be church to hearts that have, or have had, a friend?

> Could that sweet darkness where they dwell
>   Be once disclosed to us,
> The clamor for their loveliness
>   Would burst the loneliness.

I trust you may have the dearest summer possible to loss. One sweet, sweet more, one liquid more, of that Arabian presence !

You spoke very sweetly to both of us, and your sewing and recollecting is a haunting picture, a sweet, spectral protection. Your name is taken as tenderly as the names of our birds, or the flower, for some mysterious cause, sundered from its dew. . . .

In a brief memoir of Parepa, in which she was likened to a rose, — 'thornless until she died,' some bereaved one added. To miss him is his only stab, but that he never gave !

A word from you would be sacred.   EMILY.

. . . The crucifix requires no glove.

To the Same

Intrusiveness of flowers is brooked by even troubled hearts.

They enter and then knock — then chide their ruthless sweetness, and then remain forgiven.

May these molest as fondly !

EMILY.

To the Same

Than Heaven more remote,
For Heaven is the root,
But these the flitted seed,
More flown indeed
Than ones that never were,
Or those that hide, and are.

What madness, by their side,
A vision to provide
Of future days
They cannot praise.

My soul, to find them, come,
They cannot call, they 're dumb,
Nor prove, nor woo,
But that they have abode
Is absolute as God,
And instant, too.

EMILY.

To the Same

The face in evanescence lain
Is more distinct than ours,
And ours, considered for its sake,
As capsules are for flowers.

EMILY.

To the Same

[1879.]

DEAR FRIEND, — Your touching suggestion . . .
is a tender permission. . . .

We cannot believe for each other — thought is
too sacred a despot, but I hope that God, in-what-
ever form, is true to our friend. . . . Consciousness
is the only home of which we *now* know. That
sunny adverb had been enough, were it not fore-
closed.

When not inconvenient to your heart, please
remember us, and let us help you carry it, if you
grow tired. Though we are each unknown to ourself and each other, 't is not what well conferred it,
the dying soldier asks, it is only the water.

We knew not that we were to live,
Nor when we are to die
Our ignorance our cuirass is;
We wear mortality
As lightly as an option gown
Till asked to take it off.
By His intrusion God is known —
It is the same with life.

EMILY.

To the Same

[November, 1882.]

Tuesday.

SWEET FRIEND, — Our mother ceased. While we bear her dear form through the wilderness, I am sure you are with us.

EMILY.

To the Same

[1883.]

DEAR FRIEND, — The guilt of having sent the note had so much oppressed me that I hardly dared to read the reply, and delayed my heart almost to its stifling, sure you would never receive us again. To come unto our own and our own fail to receive us, is a sere response.

I hope you may forgive us.

All is faint indeed without our vanished mother, who achieved in sweetness what she lost in strength, though grief of wonder at her fate made the winter short, and each night I reach finds my lungs more breathless, seeking what it means.

> To the bright east she flies,
> Brothers of Paradise
> Remit her home,
> Without a change of wings,
> Or Love's convenient things,
> Enticed to come.
>
> Fashioning what she is,
> Fathoming what she was,

We deem we dream —
And that dissolves the days
Through which existence strays
Homeless at home.

The sunshine almost speaks, this morning, redoubling the division, and Paul's remark grows graphic, 'the *weight* of glory.'

I am glad you have an hour for books, those enthralling friends, the immortalities, perhaps, each may pre-receive. 'And I saw the Heavens opened.'

I hope that nothing pains you except the pang of life, sweeter to bear than to omit.

With love and wonder,

EMILY.

To the Same

[1883?]

DEAR FRIEND, — Is not an absent friend as mysterious as a bulb in the ground, and is not a bulb the most captivating floral form? Must it not have enthralled the Bible, if we may infer from its selection? 'The lily of the field!'

I never pass one without being chagrined for Solomon, and so in love with 'the lily' anew, that were I sure no one saw me, I might make those advances of which in after life I should repent.

The apple-blossoms were slightly disheartened, yesterday, by a snow-storm, but the birds encouraged them all that they could — and how fortunate that the little ones had come to cheer their damask brethren !

You spoke of coming ' with the apple-blossoms '
— which occasioned our solicitude.

The ravenousness of fondness is best disclosed by
children. . . .

Is there not a sweet wolf within us that demands
its food?

I can easily imagine your fondness for the little
life so mysteriously committed to your care. The
bird that asks our crumb has a plaintive distinction.
I rejoice that it was possible for you to be with it, for
I think the early spiritual influences about a child
are more hallowing than we know. The angel begins
in the morning in every human life. How small the
furniture of bliss ! How scant the heavenly fabric !

> No ladder needs the bird but skies
> To situate its wings,
> Nor any leader's grim baton
> Arraigns it as it sings.
> The implements of bliss are few —
> As Jesus says of *Him*,
> ' Come unto me ' the moiety
> That wafts the cherubim.

EMILY.

To the Same

DEAR FRIEND, — You are like God. We pray to
Him, and he answers ' No.' Then we pray to Him
to rescind the ' no,' and He don't answer at all, yet
' Seek and ye shall find ' is the boon of faith.

You failed to keep your appointment with the
apple-blossoms — the japonica, even, bore an apple

to elicit you, but that must be a silver bell which calls the human heart.

I still hope that you live, and in lands of consciousness.

It is Commencement now.   Pathos is very busy.

The past is not a package one can lay away.   I see my father's eyes, and those of Mr Bowles — those isolated comets.   If the future is mighty as the past, what may vista be?

With my foot in a sling from a vicious sprain, and reminded of you almost to tears by the week and its witness, I send this sombre word.

The vane defines the wind.

Where we thought you were, Austin says you are not.   How strange to change one's sky, unless one's star go with it, but yours has left an astral wake.

Vinnie gives her hand.

Always with love,

EMILY.

To the Same

[1883?]

DEAR FRIEND, — Your sweet self-reprehension makes us look within, which is so wild a place we are soon dismayed, but the seed sown in the lake bears the liquid flower, and so of all your words. ·

I am glad you accept rest.

Too many disdain it.   I am glad you go to the Adirondacks.

To me the name is homelike, for one of my lost went every year with an Indian guide, before the

woods were broken.   Had you been here it would
l.: sw--+. but '' .:, like the peach, is later.   With a
to-morrow in its cupboard, who would be ' an
hungered ' ?

Thank you for thinking of Dick.   He is now the
horse of association.

Men are picking the grass from father's meadow
to lay it away for winter, and it takes them a long
time.   They bring three horses of their own, but
Dick, ever gallant, offers to help, and bears a little
machine like a top, which spins the grass away.

It seems very much like a gentleman getting his
own supper — for what is his supper winter nights
but tumblers of clover?

You speak of ' disillusion.'   That is one of the
few subjects on which I am an infidel.   Life is so
strong a vision, not one of it shall fail.

Not what the stars have done, but what they are
to do, is what detains the sky.

We shall watch for the promised words from the
Adirondacks, and hope the recess will all be joy.
To have been made alive is so chief a thing, all else
inevitably adds.   Were it not riddled by partings, it
were too divine.

I was never certain that mother had died, except
while the students were singing.   The voices came
from another life. . . .

Good-night, dear.   Excuse me for staying so long.
I love to come to you.   To one who creates, or con-
soles, thought, what an obligation !

EMILY.

To the Same

[1883?]

DEAR FRIEND, — Has the journey ceased, or is it still progressing, and has Nature won you away from us, as we feared she would?

Othello is uneasy, but then Othellos always are, they hold such mighty stakes.

Austin brought me the picture of Salvini when he was last in Boston.

The brow is that of Deity — the eyes, those of the lost, but the power lies in the *throat*— pleading, sovereign, savage — the panther and the dove !

Each, how innocent !

I hope you found the mountains cordial — followed your meeting with the lakes with affecting sympathy.

Changelessness is Nature's change.

The plants went into camp last night, their tender armor insufficient for the crafty nights.

That is one of the parting acts of the year, and has an emerald pathos — and Austin hangs bouquets of corn in the piazza's ceiling, also an omen, for Austin believes.

The 'golden bowl' breaks soundlessly, but it will not be whole again till another year.

Did you read Emily Brontë's marvellous verse?

> ' Though earth and man were gone,
> And suns and universes ceased to be,
> And Thou wert left alone,
> Every existence would exist in Thee.'

We are pining to khow of you, and Vinnie thinks
to see you would be the opening of the burr. . . .

EMILY, with love.

To the Same

[Probably 1884.]

DEAR FRIEND, — The little package of Ceylon
arrived in fragrant safety, and Caliban's 'clust'ring
filberds' were not so luscious nor so brown.

Honey in March is blissful as inopportune, and to
caress the bee a severe temptation, but was not
temptation the first zest?

We shall seek to be frugal with our sweet possessions, though their enticingness quite leads us
astray, and shall endow Austin, as we often do, after
a parched day.

For how much we thank you.

Dear arrears of tenderness we can never repay
till the will's great ores are finally sifted; but bullion
is better than minted things, for it has no alloy.

Thinking of you with fresher love, as the Bible
boyishly says, 'New every morning and fresh every
evening,'

EMILY.

To the Same

[Probably 1884.]

DEAR FRIEND, — I cannot depict a friend to my
mind till I know what he is doing, and three of us

want to depict you. I inquire your avocation of Austin, and he says you are 'engaged in a great work'! That is momentous but not defining. The thought of you in the great city has a halo of wilderness.

Console us by dispelling it. . . .

Vinnie is happy with her duties, her pussies, and her posies, for the little garden within, though tiny, is triumphant.

There are scarlet carnations, with a witching suggestion, and hyacinths covered with promises which I know they will keep.

How precious to hear you ring at the door, and Vinnie ushering you to those melodious moments of which friends are composed.

This also is fiction.

I fear we shall care very little for the technical resurrection, when to behold the one face that to us comprised it is too much for us, and I dare not think of the voraciousness of that only gaze and its only return.

Remembrance is the great tempter.

EMILY.

Emily Dickinson's first letter to the son of her old friend, Mr Bowles, was written four years after his father's death, and contained a spray of pressed jasmine.

To Mr Samuel Bowles

[1882.]

DEAR FRIEND, — A tree your father gave me bore this priceless flower.

Would you accept it because of him —

> Who abdicated ambush
> And went the way of dusk,
> And now, against his subtle name,
> There stands an asterisk
> As confident of him as we ;
> Impregnable we are —
> The whole of Immortality
> Secreted in a star.

E. DICKINSON.

To the Same

[1882.]

DEAR FRIEND, — My mother and sister hoped to see you, and I, to have heard the voice in the house that recalls the strange music of your father's. A little bin of blossoms I designed for your breakfast also went astray.

I hope you are in strength, and that the passengers of peace exalt, not rend, your memory. Heaven may give them rank, it could not give them grandeur, for that they carried with themselves.

With fresh remembrance,
E. DICKINSON.

To the Same

[August 2, 1882.]

DEAR FRIEND, — Our friend your father was so beautifully and intimately recalled to-day that it seemed impossible he had experienced the secret of death.

A servant who had been with us a long time, and had often opened the door for him, asked me how to spell 'genius' yesterday. I told her and she said no more. To-day she asked me what 'genius' meant. I told her none had known.

She said she read in a Catholic paper that Mr Bowles was 'the genius of Hampshire,' and thought it might be that past gentleman. His look could not be extinguished to any who had seen him, for 'because I live, ye shall live also,' was his physiognomy.

I congratulate you upon his immortality, which is a constant stimulus to my household, and upon your noble perpetuation of his cherished *Republican.*

Please remember me tenderly to your mother.

With honor,

EMILY DICKINSON.

This is the only letter I have found, written since early girlhood, in which Emily Dickinson signed her name in this way.

About 1882 she wrote of the elder Mr Bowles to another friend, 'I dreamed Saturday night of precious Mr Bowles.   One glance of his would light a world.'   Upon learning of his son's engagement, Emily sent her unique congratulation : —

[October, 1883.]

DEAR FRIEND, —

The clock strikes one that just struck two —
Some schism in the sum ;
A sorcerer from Genesis
Has wrecked the pendulum.
With warmest congratulation,
E. DICKINSON.

After the birth of Samuel Bowles the Fifth :

To the Same

[August, 1885.]

DEAR FRIEND, — I did not know.

God bless you indeed !

Extend to that small hand my own ' right hand of fellowship,' and guide the woman of your heart softly to my own.

I give ' his angels charge ' — well-remembered angels, whose absence only dims our eyes.   The magnanimity I asked, you how freely gave !

If ever of any act of mine you should be in need, let me reply with the laureate, ' Speak that I live to hear.'

Vitally,
E. DICKINSON.

To the Same

[August 19, 1885.]

DEAR FRIEND, — May I ask a service so sacred as that you will address and mail a note to the friend of my friend Mrs Jackson? I do not know Mr Jackson's address, and desire to write him.

That your loved confederate and yourself are in ceaseless peace is my happy faith.

The sweet-peas you hallowed stand in carmine sheaves. Would that you could plunder them.

Gratefully,

E. DICKINSON.

To the Same

[On receiving some flowers.]

DEAR FRIENDS, — Had I not known I was not asleep, I should have feared I dreamed, so blissful was their beauty, but day and they demurred. . . .

With joyous thanks,

E. DICKINSON.

In the dim and early dawn of a fragrant summer morning soon after, Emily caused a large cluster of sweet-peas to be gathered from her dewy, old-fashioned garden, that they might be put on the very first train to Springfield, taking the freshness of summer itself to her friends. This note accompanied them : —

Dawn and dew my bearers be.

Ever,

BUTTERFLY.

And the old garden still overflows with annual fragrance and color. Its armies of many-hued hyacinths run riot in the spring sunshine, while crocuses and daffodils peer above the fresh grass under the apple-trees; a large magnolia holds its pink cups toward the blue sky, and scarlet hawthorn lights a greenly dusky corner.

And then the roses, and the hedges of sweet-peas; the masses of nasturtiums, and the stately procession of hollyhocks, in happy association with huge bushes of lemon verbena! Still later comes the autumn glory, with salvia and brilliant zinnias and marigolds and clustering chrysanthemums, until 'ranks of seeds their witness bear,' and November folds her brown mantle over sleeping flowers.

This sweet garden, with its whiffs of long ago, needs only borders of box and a sun-dial to be the ideally imagined pleasure-spot of vanished generations. And Emily seems its presiding genius; it is instinct with her presence still, though even before her death years had passed since her footsteps pressed its paths, or her fingers gathered its riches.

In different mood from the cheerful letters to Mr Bowles are these more sombre ones to Mr Clark. Begun by association through the

death of a mutual friend, they continued to
be tinged with the sadness of other and following deaths, until his own, when letters to
his brother took their place until almost her
own flitting.

To Mr J. D. Clark

[1882.]

. . . He never spoke of himself, and encroach-
ment I know would have slain him. . . . He was a
dusk gem, born of troubled waters, astray in any
crest below. Heaven might give him peace, it could
not give him grandeur, for that he carried with himself to whatever scene. . . .

> Obtaining but his own extent
> In whatsoever realm,
> 'T was Christ's own personal expanse
> That bore him from the tomb.

To the Same

[Late Autumn, 1882.]

DEAR FRIEND, — It pains us very much that you
have been more ill. We hope you may not be suffering now. Thank you for speaking so earnestly
when our mother died. We have spoken daily of
writing you, but have felt unable. The great attempt to save her life had it been successful would
have been fatigueless, but failing, strength forsook us.

No verse in the Bible has frightened me so much
from a child as 'from him that hath not, shall be

taken even that he hath.' Was it because its dark menace deepened our own door? You speak as if you still missed your mother. I wish we might speak with you. As we bore her dear form through the wilderness, light seemed to have stopped.

Her dying feels to me like many kinds of cold — at times electric, at times benumbing, — then a trackless waste love has never trod. . . .

The letter from the skies, which accompanied yours, was indeed a boon. A letter always seemed to me like Immortality, for is it not the mind alone, without corporeal friend?

I hope you may tell us that you are better.

Thank you for much kindness. The friend anguish reveals is the slowest forgot.

E. DICKINSON.

To the Same

[March, 1883.]

DEAR FRIEND, — In these few weeks of ignorance of you, we trust that you are growing stronger, and drawing near that sweet physician, an approaching spring, for the ear of the heart hears bluebirds already, those enthralling signals. . . . The great confidences of life are first disclosed by their departure, and I feel that I ceaselessly ought to thank you. . . . Our household is scarcely larger than yours — Vinnie and I and two servants composing our simple realm, though my brother is with us often each day. I wish I could show you the hyacinths

A Letter always
seemed to me like
Immortality, for is
it not the Mind
alone, without cor-
poreal friend?
I trust you may
you as ~~that~~ you
are better -
Thank you for
meek kindness.
The friend
Anguish reveals
is the dearest
forgot.
E. Dickinson..

that embarrass us by their loveliness, though to
cower before a flower is perhaps unwise, but beauty
is often timidity — perhaps oftener pain.

A soft 'Where is she?' is all that is left of our
loved mother, and thank you for all you told us
of yours. . . .

Faithfully,

E. DICKINSON.

To the Same

[1883.]

DEAR FRIEND, — To thank you is impossible, because your gifts are from the sky, more precious
than the birds, because more disembodied. I can
only express my rejoiced surprise by the phrase in
the Scripture, ' And I saw the Heavens opened.' . . .

Fathoms are sudden neighbors:

Ignorant till your note that our President's dying
had defrauded you, we are grieved anew, and hasten to offer you our sorrow.

We shall make Mrs Chadbourne's acquaintance
in flowers after a few days. ' Displeasure ' would be
a morose word toward a friend so earnest, and we
only fear when you delay, that you feel more ill.
Allow us to hear the birds for you, should they
indeed come.

E. D.

This is the last letter to Mr Clark, and upon
hearing of his farther illness, she wrote his
brother: —

To Mr C. H. Clark
[April 18, 1883.]

DEAR FRIEND, — Would it be possible you would
excuse me if I once more inquire for the health of
the brother whom association has made sacred?

With the trust that your own is impairless, and
that fear for your brother has not too much de-
pressed you, please accept the solicitude of myself
and my sister.

E. DICKINSON.

To the Same
[April 22, 1883.]

DEAR FRIEND, — The sorrowful tidings of your
note almost dissuade reply, lest I for one moment
take you from your brother's bedside. I have delayed to tell my sister till I hear again, fearing to
newly grieve her, and hoping an encouraging word
by another mail.

Please be sure we are with you in sorrowing
thought, and take your brother's hand for me, if it
is still with you. Perhaps the one has called him of
whom we have so often talked during this grieved
year.

With sympathy,
E. DICKINSON.

To the Same
[May 1, 1883.]

DEAR FRIEND, — The temptation to inquire every
morning for your sufferer is almost irresistible, but

our own invalid taught us that a sick room is at times too sacred a place for a friend's knock, timid as that is.

I trust this sweet May morning is not without its peace to your brother and you, though the richest peace is of sorrow.

With constant and fervent anxiousness, and the hope of an early word, please be sure we share your suspense.

E. DICKINSON.

To the Same

[May 21, 1883.]

DEAR FRIEND, — We have much fear, both for your own strength and the health of your brother, having heard nothing since we last asked, many days ago. Will you not, when possible, give us but a syllable, even a cheering accent, if no more be true? We think of you and your sufferer with intense anxiety, wishing some act or word of ours might be hope or help. The humming-birds and orioles fly by me as I write, and I long to guide their enchanted feet to your brother's chamber.

Excuse me for knocking. Please also excuse me for staying so long. Spring is a strange land when our friends are ill.

With my sister's tenderest alarm, as also my own,

E. DICKINSON.

To the Same

[June 7, 1883.]

I had, dear friend, the deep hope that I might see your brother before he passed from life, or rather life we know, and can scarcely express the pang I feel at its last denial.

His rare and hallowed kindness had strangely endeared him, and I cannot be comforted not to thank him before he went so far.

I never had met your brother but once. An unforgotten once — to have seen him but once more would have been almost like an interview with my 'Heavenly Father' whom he loved and knew. I hope he was able to speak with you in his closing moment. One accent of courage as he took his flight would assist your heart. I am eager to know all you may tell me of those final days. We asked for him every morning, in heart, but feared to disturb you by inquiry aloud. I hope you are not too far exhausted from your 'loved employ.'

To know of you when possible would console us much, and every circumstance of him we had hoped to see. . . .

E. D.

To the Same

[June 16, 1883.]

DEAR FRIEND, — Thank you for the paper. I felt it almost a bliss of sorrow that the name so long in Heaven on earth, should be on earth in Heaven.

Do you know if either of his sons have his mysterious face or his momentous nature?

The stars are not hereditary. I hope your brother and himself resumed the tie above, so dear to each below. Your bond to your brother reminds me of mine to my sister — early, earnest, indissoluble. Without her life were fear, and Paradise a cowardice, except for her inciting voice.

Should you have any picture of your brother, I should rejoice to see it at some convenient hour — and though we cannot know the last, would you sometime tell me as near the last as your grieved voice is able? . . .

Are you certain there is another life? When overwhelmed to know, I fear that few are sure.

My sister gives her grief with mine. Had we known in time, your brother would have borne our flowers in his mute hand. With tears,

                                        E. DICKINSON.

To the Same

[July 9, 1883.]

DEAR FRIEND, — While I thank you immediately for the invaluable gift, I cannot express the bereavement that I am no more to behold it. Believing that we are to have no face in a farther life, makes the look of a friend a boon almost too precious.

The resemblance is faithful — the scholarly gentleness — the noble modesty — the absence of every

dross, quite there. What a consoling prize to you,
his mate through years of anguish so much sharper
to see because endured so willingly.

Chastening would seem unneeded by so supreme
a spirit.

I feel great grief for you — I hope his memory may help you, so recently a life. I wish I might
say one liquid word to make your sorrow less. Is
not the devotion that you gave him an acute balm?
Had you not been with him how solitary the will
of God!

Thank you for every word of his pure career. I
hope it is nearer us than we are aware. Will you
not still tell us of yourself and your home — from
which this patient guest has flown? I am glad he
lies near us — and thank you for the tidings of our
other fugitive, whom to know was life. I can
scarcely tell you how deeply I cherish your thoughtfulness. To still know of the dead is a great permission, and you have almost enabled that. With the
ceaseless sympathy of myself and my sister, and the
trust that our sufferer rests,

                                        E. DICKINSON.

To the Same

[January 4, 1884.]

DEAR FRIEND, — I have been very ill since early
October, and unable to thank you for the sacred
kindness, but treasured it each day, and hasten with
my first steps, and my fullest gratitude. . . . I

never can thank you as I feel. That would be impossible. The effort ends in tears. You seem, by some deep accident, to be the only tie between the Heaven that evanesced, and the Heaven that stays. I hope the winged days that bear you to your brother are not too destitute of song, and wish that we might speak with you of him and of yourself, and of the third member of that sundered trio.   Perhaps another spring would call you to Northampton, and memory might invite you here. . . .

With a deep New Year,

Your friend,

E. DICKINSON.

[Enclosing pressed flowers, February 22, 1884.]

DEAR FRIEND, — I hoped it might gratify you to meet the little flower which was my final ministry to your brother, and which even in that faint hour, I trust he recognized, though the thronged spirit had not access to words.

These are my first out, and their golden trifles are too full of association to remain unshared.

With faithful thought of yourself and your brother, brothers in bereavement even as myself,

E. DICKINSON.

To the Same

[April 21, 1884.]

Never unmindful of your anxiety for your father, dear friend, I refrained from asking, lest even the moment engrossed by reply, might take you from him.

The peril of a parent is a peculiar pang, and one which my sister and myself so long experienced, — oh, would it were longer, for even fear for them were dearer than their absence, — that we cannot resist to offer you our earnest sympathy. I most sincerely trust that the sight is redeemed, so precious to you both, more than vicariously to you — even filially — and that· the added fear has not exhausted you beyond the art of spring to cheer.

I have lost, since writing you, another cherished friend, a word of whom I enclose — and how to repair my shattered ranks is a besetting pain. Be sure that my sister and myself never forget your brother, nor his bereaved comrade.

To be certain we were to meet our lost would be a vista of reunion who òf us could bear? . . .

Faithfully,

E. DICKINSON.

To the Same

[April 22, 1884.]

DEAR FRIEND, — These thoughts disquiet me, and the great friend is gone who could solace them. Do they disturb you?

> The spirit lasts, but in what mode —
> Below, the body speaks,
> But as the spirit furnishes —
> Apart it never talks.

The music in the violin
Does not emerge alone
But arm in arm with touch, yet touch
Alone is not a tune.
The spirit lurks within the flesh
Like tides within the sea
That make the water live; estranged
What would the either be?
Does that know now, or does it cease,
That which to this is done,
Resuming at a mutual date
With every future one?
Instinct pursues the adamant
Exacting this reply —
Adversity, if it may be,
Or wild prosperity,
The rumor's gate was shut so tight
Before my mind was sown,
Not even a prognostic's push
Could make a dent thereon.

With the trust you live,

E. DICKINSON.

To the Same

[January 18, 1885.]

DEAR FRIEND, — Though no New Year be old, to
wish yourself and your honored father a new and
happy one is involuntary, and I am sure we are both
reminded of that sacred past which has forever hallowed us.

I trust the years which they behold are also new
and happy, or is it a joyous expanse of year, without bisecting months — untiring Anno Domini? Had

we but one assuring word, but a letter is a joy of
earth — it is denied the gods.   Vivid in our immortal group we still behold your brother, and never
hear Northampton bells without saluting him. . . .

Have you blossoms and books, those solaces of
sorrow?   That, I would also love to know, and receive for yourself and your father the forgetless
sympathy of

Your friend,

E. DICKINSON.

To the Same

[April 21, 1885.]

DEAR FRIEND, — The flower for which your brother
cared resumes its siren circuit, and choosing a few
for his name's sake, I enclose them to you.   Perhaps
from some far site he overlooks their transit, and
smiles at the beatitudes so recently his own.
Ephemeral, eternal heart!

I hope you are in health, and that the fragile
father has every peace that years possess. . . .

We think of your small mansion with unabated
warmth, though is not any mansion vast that contains
a father?

That this beloved spring inspirit both yourself and
him, is our exceeding wish.

E. DICKINSON.

The final letter to Mr Clark was written a
year later, and will be found in the last chapter.

CHAPTER IX

*To Mr and Mrs J. L. Jenkins, Mrs Hanson
Read, Mrs W. A. Stearns, Mrs Edward
Tuckerman, Mrs J. S. Cooper, Mrs A. B. H.
Davis, Mrs H. F. Hills, Mrs Jameson, Mr
F. F. Emerson, Maggie Maher, Mr and
Mrs George Montague, Mrs W. F. Stearns,
Mr J. K. Chickering, Mrs Joseph Sweetser,
Mr Thomas Niles, Mrs Carmichael, Dr and
Mrs Thomas P. Field, Mr Theodore Holland,
'H. H.,' Miss Eugenia Hall, Mrs E. P.
Crowell, and Mrs J. C. Greenough*

THE characteristic notes in this chapter
were, with few exceptions, written to
friends in Amherst, accompanying flowers or
other dainties, or acknowledging those sent to
herself, — not infrequently a sentence of consolation for some pain, or a few words of cheering
appreciation for a new happiness.

The first may be dated as early as 1872; but
the largest number are, undoubtedly, to be
assigned to the last six or seven years of
Emily Dickinson's life.

After her father's death, her retirement from ordinary forms of human intercourse became almost complete; and these notes were the sole link still binding her to the world, — and to only such part of the world as might be represented by those for whom she cared.

Emily's prose style had developed its incisiveness, — like her own thought, it went straight to the essence of things; and while still dressed in language sufficiently to pass in conventional places, it had gradually become divested of everything superfluous.

While the meaning of certain phrases has sometimes puzzled those who received the notes, there is invariably an original, sparkling interpretation for every sentence, clear to any soul possessing even slight accord with hers. Because frequently couched in the form of apparently mysterious oracles, the meaning is sometimes looked for too deeply, — often it is singularly obvious. The remarkable character of these notes seems to have increased as she lived farther and farther away from the years when she had seen and conversed with her friends; and her life was full of thought and occupation during these introspective days. It is impossible to conceive that any sense of personal isolation, or real loneliness of spirit, because of the absence of humanity from her daily life, could have oppressed a nature so richly endowed.

Most of us would require some sudden blow, some fierce crisis, to produce such a result, — a hidden and unusual life like hers. And we love to believe striking and theatrical things of our neighbors; it panders to that romantic element latent in the plainest. But Emily Dickinson's method of living was so simple and natural an outcome of her increasingly shy nature, a development so perfectly in the line of her whole constitution that no far-away and dramatic explanation of her quiet life is necessary to those who are capable of apprehending her.

That sentence alone would reveal the key wherein she wrote with regret for her long-time maid Margaret: ' I winced at her loss, for I am in the habit of her, and even a new rolling-pin has an embarrassing element.'

Emerson somewhere says, 'Now and then a man exquisitely made can live alone ; ' and Lord Bacon puts the thought with even greater force and directness, — ' Whosoever is delighted in Solitude is either a Wilde Beast or a God.'

To some natures, introspection is a necessity for expression. ' Why should I feel lonely?' exclaimed Thoreau, in his temporary isolation

at Walden, 'Is not our planet in the Milky
Way?' He was, indeed, 'no more lonely than
the North Star,' nor, I believe, was Emily
Dickinson, although congenial companionship
had, in a sense, been very dear to her.

She has herself written: —

> Never for society
> He shall seek in vain
> Who his own acquaintance
> Cultivates; of men
> Wiser men may weary,
> But the man within
> Never knew satiety, —
> Better entertain
> Than could Border Ballad,
> Or Biscayan Hymn;
> Neither introduction
> Need you — unto him.

Georg Ebers once wrote: 'Sheep and geese
become restless when separated from the flock;
the eagle and lion seek isolation,' — a picturesque and perhaps not less strong presentation
of a nearly identical thought.

But although invisible for years, even to
life-long friends, Emily never denied herself to
children. To them she was always accessible,
always delightful, and in their eyes a sort of
fairy guardian. Stories are yet told of her
roguishly lowering baskets of 'goodies' out
of her window by a string to little ones wait-

ing below. Mr MacGregor Jenkins, in a sketch of his recollections of Emily Dickinson,[1] has shown this gracious and womanly side of her nature in a very charming way, quoting a number of her notes to himself and his sister, two members of a quartette of children admitted to her intimacy. Many of Emily Dickinson's daintiest verses are for children, — among them *The Sleeping Flowers*[2] and *Out of the Morning*.[3]

The notes written during their childhood to Mr Jenkins and his sister follow, with others to their father and mother : —

[1872 ?]

HAPPY 'DID' AND MAC, — We can offer you nothing so charming as your own hearts, which we would seek to possess, had we the requisite wiles.

DEAR BOYS, — Please never grow up, which is 'far better.' Please never 'improve' — you are perfect now.

EMILY.

LITTLE WOMEN, — Which shall it be, geraniums or tulips?

The butterfly upon the sky, who does n't know its name,
And has n't any tax to pay, and has n't any home,
Is just as high as you and I, and higher, I believe —
So soar away and never sigh, for that 's the way to grieve.

[1] *The Christian Union*, October 24, 1891.
[2] *Poems*, Second Series, page 122.   [3] Ibid., page 113.

Katie ' Did ' from Katie ' Did n't.'

Will the sweet child who sent me the butterflies, herself a member of the same ethereal nation, accept a rustic kiss, flavored, we trust, with clover?

AMHERST.

[Christmas, 1874.]

. . . Atmospherically it was the most beautiful Christmas on record. The hens came to the door with Santa Claus, the pussies washed themselves in the open air without chilling their tongues, and Santa Claus — sweet old gentleman — was even gallanter than usual. Visitors from the chimney were a new dismay, but all of them brought their hands so full and behaved so sweetly, only a churl could have turned them away. And then the ones at the barn were so happy! Maggie gave the hens a check for potatoes, each of the cats had a gilt-edged bone, and the horse had new blankets from Boston.

Do you remember dark-eyed Mr Dickinson who used to shake your hand when it was so little it had hardly a stem? He, too, had a beautiful gift of roses from a friend away. It was a lovely Christmas. But what made you remember me? Tell me with a kiss — or is it a secret?

EMILY.

To a niece of her father's, who had sent for his grave the roses alluded to, she wrote : —

[December, 1874.]

I am sure you must have remembered that father had 'become as little children,' or you would never have dared send him a Christmas gift, for you know how 'he frowned upon Santa Claus, and all such prowling gentlemen.

To the Rev. J. L. Jenkins and Mrs Jenkins, enclosing some sprays of rowen tied with white ribbon

[Autumn, 187-.]

DEAR MR AND MRS PASTOR, — Mrs Holland pleased us and grieved us, by telling us your triumphs.

We want you to conquer, but we want you to conquer here.

'Marathon' is me. Is there nothing but glow in the new horizon?

You see we keep a jealous heart. That is Love's alloy.

Vinnie is full of wrath, and vicious as Saul toward the Holy Ghost, in whatever form. I heard her declaiming the other night, to a foe that called — and sent Maggie to part them.

Vinnie lives on the hope that you will return. Is it quite fictitious? You are gone too long.

The red leaves take the green leaves' place, and the landscape yields. We go to sleep with the peach in our hands and wake with the stone, but the stone is the pledge of summers to come.

Love for each of you, always, and if there are lands longer than 'always,' love also for those.

These are sticks of rowen for your stove. It was chopped by bees, and butterflies piled it, Saturday afternoons.

EMILY.

To the Same

[1875?]

. . . There would have been no smile on Amherst's face, had she believed her clergyman's sweet wife to be suffering, but the paper spoke so obligingly, we thought it an accident that endeared, rather than endangered. That sorrow dare to touch the loved is a mournful insult — we are all avenging it all the time, though as Lowell quotes from the stranger 'Live — live even to be unkind.'

It is hard to think of our 'little friend' as a sufferer — we, peculiarly, know how hard, through our suffering mother — but the tiniest ones are the mightiest — the wren will prevail . . .

'Bruised for our iniquities' I had almost feared. Amherst, tell her, suggests her — each of you, my shepherd, and will, while will remains.

EMILY.

To the Same

Would you feel more at home with a flower from home in your hand, dear?

To the Same

May the love that occasioned the first Easter shelter a few, this bereaved day.

To the Same

[1877 ?]

DEAR FRIEND, — It was pathetic to see your voice, instead of hearing it, for it had grown sweetly familiar in the house, as a bird's.

Father left us in June — you leave us in May. I am glad there will be no April till another year. . . .

Sorrow is unsafe, when it is real sorrow — I am glad so many are counterfeits — guileless because they believe themselves.

Kiss 'Diddie' and Mac for us — precious refugees, with love for our brother, whom with yourself, we follow the peculiar distance, 'even unto the end.'

Perhaps it is 'the end' now — I think the *bell* thought so, because it bade us all good-by when you stood in the door.

You concealed that you heard it.   Thank you.

EMILY.

[June, 1878.]

You deserved a tiding before, dear.

Your little punctualities are generous and precious. . . .

There is a circus here, and farmers' Commencement, and boys and girls from Tripoli, and Governors and swords parade the summer streets. They lean upon the fence that guards the quiet church ground, and jar the grass, now warm and soft as a tropic nest.

Many people call, and wish for you with tears, and Vinnie beats her wings like a maddened bird, whose home has been invaded.

So much has been sorrow, that to fall asleep in Tennyson's verse, seems almost a pillow. 'To where beyond these voices there is Peace.'

I hope you are each safe. It is homeless without you, and we think of others possessing you with the throe of Othello.

Mother gives her love — Maggie pleads her own. Austin smiles when you mention him. . . .

Daisies and ferns are with us, and he whose meadow they magnify, is always linked with you.

EMILY.

To Mrs Hanson Read, accompanying flowers for the funeral of her two little boys

[December 27, 1873.]

Vinnie says your martyrs were fond of flowers. Would these profane their vase?

EMILY.

To the Same

[Upon a subsequent anniversary.]

My DEAR MRS READ, — We have often thought of you to-day, and almost spoken with you, but thought you might like to be alone — if one can be alone with so thronged a Heaven.

E. DICKINSON.

To Mrs W. A. Stearns

[Autumn, 1874.]

Will the dear ones who eased the grieved days spurn the fading orchard?

EMILY.

To the Same

[Upon receiving an Easter card, probably 1875.]

It is possible, dear friend, that the rising of the one we lost would have engrossed me to the exclusion of Christ's — but for your lovely admonition.

Sabbath morning was peculiarly dear to my father, and his unsuspecting last earthly day with his family was that heavenly one.

Vinnie and I were talking of you as we went to sleep Saturday night, which makes your beautiful gift of to-day almost apparitional.

Please believe how sweetly I thank you.

EMILY.

To the Same

[1875.]

What tenements of clover
Are fitting for the bee,
What edifices azure
For butterflies and me —

What residences nimble
Arise and evanesce
Without a rhythmic rumor
Or an assaulting guess.
                    With love,
                              E. DICKINSON.

To the Same

[1875.]

DEAR FRIEND, — That a pansy is transitive, is its only pang.

This, precluding that, is indeed divine.

Bringing you handfuls in prospective, thank you for the love.   Many an angel, with its needle, toils beneath the snow.

With tenderness for your mate,
                              EMILY.

[Spring, 1876.]

DEAR FRIENDS, — Might these be among the fabrics which the Bible designates as beyond rubies?

Certainly they are more accessible to the fingers of your thief
                              EMILY.

When President Stearns died, this stanza came to Mrs Stearns: —

[June 8, 1876.]
Love's stricken ' why '
Is all that love can speak —
Built of but just a syllable
The hugest hearts that break.
                              EMILY.

At the death of Professor Snell, September 18, 1876, Emily sent to his family a beautiful mass of flowers, purple and white; and with them, this single line: —

I had a father once.

To Mrs Stearns, in response to a box of strawberries received early in March

[1877 ?]

DEAR FRIEND, — The little package of nectar mother opened herself, though her hands are frail as a child's.

She could not believe them real till I had hidden one in her mouth, which somewhat convinced her. She asks me to thank you tenderly. The love of her friends is the only remnant of her grieved life, and she clings to it timidly.

I hope you are quite well, and am sure we sometimes think of each other, endeared by that most hallowed thorn, a mutual loss.

With sweet remembrance for your niece, of whom my sister speaks,

EMILY.

To the Same

[1878.]

DEAR FRIENDS, — The seraphic shame generosity causes is perhaps its most heavenly result.

To make even Heaven more heavenly, is within the aim of us all.

I was much touched by the little fence dividing the devotions, though devotion should always wear a fence, to pre-empt its claim.

Why the full heart is speechless, is one of the great wherefores.

EMILY, with love.

To the Same

[1879?]

DEAR FRIENDS, — I hope no bolder lover brought you the first pond lilies. The water is deeper than the land. The swimmer never stagnates.

I shall bring you a handful of lotus next, but do not tell the Nile.

He is a jealous brook.

EMILY.

To the Same

'A little flower, a faded flower, the gift of one who cared for me.'

Please usurp the pronoun.

EMILY.

The first of the following notes, accompanied with a box of flowers, was an apology for tardy congratulations upon Mrs Tuckerman's safe return from a long visit in Europe:

To Mrs Edward Tuckerman

[January, 1874.]

DEAR FRIEND, — I fear my congratulation, like repentance according to Calvin, is too late to be plausible, but might there not be an exception, were the delight or the penitence found to be durable?

EMILY.

To the Same

[March, 1875.]

DEAR FRIEND, — It was so long my custom to seek you with the birds, they would scarcely feel at home should I do otherwise, though as home itself is far from home since my father died, why should custom tire?

EMILY.

To the Same, sent with yellow flowers when the country was drenched in rain

[May, 1875.]

I send you inland buttercups as out-door flowers are still at sea.

EMILY.

To the Same

[Accompanying a box of the delicious chocolate caramels she sent her friends at New Year's, with the recipe.]

Vinnie says the dear friend would like the rule. We have no statutes here, but each does as it will, which is the sweetest jurisprudence.

With it, I enclose Love's 'remainder biscuit,' somewhat scorched perhaps in baking, but 'Love's oven is warm.' Forgive the base proportions.

The fairer ones were borne away. The canna

was a privilege, the little box a bliss, and the blossoms so real that a fly waylaid them, but I lured him away.

Again receive the love which comes without aspect, and without herald goes.

EMILY.

To the Same

[About 1877.]

DEAR FRIEND, — Accept my timid happiness.

No joy can be in vain, but adds to some bright total, whose dwelling is unknown.

The immortality of flowers must enrich our own, and we certainly should resent a redemption that excluded them.

Was not the 'breath of fragrance' designed for your cheek solely?

The fear that it was crimsons my own, though to divide its Heaven is Heaven's highest half.

E. DICKINSON.

To the Same

[June, 1878.]

Is it that words are suddenly small, or that we are suddenly large, that they cease to suffice us to thank a friend?

Perhaps it is chiefly both.

To the Same

[July, 1878.]

Would it be prudent to subject an apparitional
interview to a grosser test?

The Bible portentously says ' that which is spirit
is spirit.'

> Go not too near a house of rose,
> The depredation of a breeze
> Or inundation of a dew
> Alarm its walls away;
> Nor try to tie the butterfly,
> Nor climb the bars of ecstasy.
> In insecurity to lie
> Is joy's insuring quality.

E. Dickinson.

To the Same

[August, 1878.]

To see is perhaps never quite the sorcery that it
is to surmise, though the obligation to enchantment
is always binding.

It is sweet to recall that we need not retrench, as
magic is our most frugal meal.

I fear you have much happiness, because you
spend so much.

Would adding to it take it away, or is that a
penurious question?

To cherish you is intuitive.

As we take Nature, without permission, let us
covet you.

To the Same
[January, 1879.]

Your coming is a symptom of summer.
The symptom excels the malady.

To the Same
[September, 1879.]

Should dear Mrs Tuckerman have no pears like mine, I should never cease to be harrowed.
Should she, that also would be dismay.
I incur the peril.

EMILY.

To the Same
[January 5, 1880.]

DEAR FRIEND, — Your sweetness intimidates.

Had it been a mastiff that guarded Eden, we should have feared him less than we do the angel.

I read your little letter. It had, like bliss, the minute length.

It were dearer had you protracted it; but the sparrow must not propound his crumb.

> We shall find the cube of the rainbow,
> Of that there is no doubt;
> But the arc of a lover's conjecture
> Eludes the finding out.

Confidingly,

EMILY.

To the Same

[March, 1880.]

The robin is a Gabriel
In humble circumstances,
His dress denotes him socially
Of transport's working classes.
He has the punctuality
Of the New England farmer —
The same oblique integrity,
A vista vastly warmer.
A small but sturdy residence,
A self-denying household,
The guests of perspicacity
Are all that cross his threshold.
As covert as a fugitive,
Cajoling consternation
By ditties to the enemy,
And sylvan punctuation.

EMILY.

To the Same

[1880.]

Will the little hands that have brought me so
much tenderness, the sweet hands in which a bird
would love to lie, the fingers that knew no estrange-
ment except the gulf of down, — will such enfold
a daphne?

Almost I trust they will, yet trust is such a shelv-
ing word ; part of our treasures are denied us, part

of them provisoed, like bequests available far hence, part of them we partake.

Which, dear, are divinest?

EMILY.

To the Same

[November, 1880.]

Thank you, sweet friend, I am quite better.

Were I not, your dainty redemption would save me.

With love and a happy flower,

EMILY.

To the Same

[1880.]

Love is done when love 's begun,
Sages say.
But have sages known?
Truth adjourn your boon
Without day.

EMILY.

To the Same

[After Professor Root's death, December, 1880.]

DEAR FRIEND, — I thought of you, although I never saw your friend.

Brother of Ophir,
Bright adieu,
Honor the shortest
Route to you.

EMILY.

To the Same

[New Year's Day, 1881.]

Saturday.

My bird, who is 'to-day'?
'Yesterday' was a year ago, and yet

> The stem of a departed flower
> Has still a silent rank,
> The bearer from an emerald court
> Of a despatch of pink.

Thank you for the lovely love.

EMILY.

To the Same

[1881.]

To find my sweet friend is more difficult than to bless her, though I trust both are slightly possible this dearest afternoon.

EMILY.

The following little poem-note contained a pressed dandelion tied with scarlet ribbon.

To the Same

[November 8, 1881.]

> The dandelion's pallid tube
> Astonishes the grass,
> And winter instantly becomes
> An infinite *Alas.*
> The tube uplifts a signal bud,
> And then a shouting flower;
> The proclamation of the suns
> That sepulture is o'er.

Vinnie told me, dear friend, you were speaking of Mr Root.

EMILY.

To the Same

[December, 1881.]

DEAR FRIEND, — Vinnie asked me if I had any message for you, and while I was picking it, you ran away.

> Not seeing, still we know,
> Not knowing, guess ;
> Not guessing, smile and hide
> And half caress,
> And quake and turn away ;
> Seraphic fear !
> Is Eden's innuendo
> ' If you dare ' ?

EMILY.

To the Same

[January, 1882.]

DEAR FRIEND, — The gray afternoon — the sweet knock, and the ebbing voice of the boys are a pictorial memory ; and then the little bins and the purple kernels — 't was like the larder of a doll.

To the inditing heart we wish no sigh had come.

> Sweet pirate of the heart,
> Not pirate of the sea,
> What wrecketh thee ?
> Some spice's mutiny —
> Some attar's perfidy ?
> Confide in me.

EMILY.

To the Same

[January, 1883.]

The presence in life of so sweet an one is of itself fortune — a covert wealth of spirit I shall not disclose.

I have taken all the naughty boys, and Vinnie the navy.

What lovely conceits !

Then the little Smyrna in the dish — how tiny, how affecting — though the heart in the rear *not* tiny.   Oh, no, vast as the sea.

To caress its billows is our liquid aim.

EMILY, with love.

To the Same

[June, 1883.]

Sweet foot, that comes when we call it !   I can go but a step a century, now.

How slow the wind, how slow the sea,
How late their feathers be !
Lovingly,

EMILY.

To the Same

[August, 1883.]

We wear our sober dresses when we die,
But summer, frilled as for a holiday,
Adjourns her sigh.

To the Same

[January, 1884.]

DEAR FRIEND : —

To try to speak, and miss the way,
And ask it of the tears,
Is gratitude's sweet poverty,
The tatters that he wears.

A better coat, if he possessed,
Would help him to conceal,
Not subjugate, the mutineer
Whose title is ' the soul.'

EMILY, with love.

To the Same

[February, 1884.]

Do 'men gather grapes of thorns'?

No, but they do of *roses,* and even the classic fox hushed his innuendo, as we unclasped the little box.

Sherbets untold, and recollection more sparkling than sherbets !

How wondrous is a friend, the gift of neither Heaven nor earth, yet coveted of both !

If the 'archangels veil their faces,' is not the sacred diffidence on this sweet behalf?

EMILY.

To the Same

[April, 1884.]

Be encouraged, sweet friend ! How cruel we did not know ! But the battles of those we love are often unseen.

'If Thou hadst been here,' Mary said, 'our brother had not died.' Hanging my head and my heart with it, that you sorrowed alone,

Late, but lovingly,

EMILY.

To the Same

[April, 1885.]

DEAR FRIEND, — We want you to wake — Easter has come and gone.

Morning without you is a dwindled dawn.

Quickened toward all celestial things by crows I heard this morning, accept a loving caw from a

Nameless friend.

'SELAH.'

To the Same

[May, 1885.]

We trust the repairs of the little friend are progressing swiftly, though shall we love her as well, revamped?

Anatomical dishabille is sweet to those who prize us.

A chastened grace is twice a grace. Nay, 't is a holiness.

With a sweet May day,

EMILY.

To the Same

[October, 1885.]

DEAR FRIEND, — I thought of you on your lonely journey, certain the hallowed heroine was gratified, though mute. I trust you return in safety and with closer clutch for that which remains, for dying whets the grasp.

October is a mighty month, for in it little Gilbert died. 'Open the door,' was his last cry, 'the boys are waiting for me.' Quite used to his commandment, his little aunt obeyed, and still two years and many days, and he does not return.

Where makes my lark his nest?

But Corinthians' bugle obliterates the birds', so covering your loved heart to keep it from another shot,   Tenderly,

EMILY.

To Mrs J. S. Cooper

[June, 1874.]

Though a stranger, I am unwilling not to thank you personally for the delicate attention to my family.

For the comprehension of suffering, one must one's self have suffered.

E. DICKINSON.

To the Same

[Later Summer, 1874.]

DEAR FRIEND, — It was my first impulse to take them to my father, whom I cannot resist the grief to expect.

Thank you.

VINNIE'S SISTER.

And to another friend, about the same time, she wrote: —

Should it be possible for me to speak of my father before I behold him, I shall try to do so to you, whom he always remembered.

EMILY.

To Mrs J. S. Cooper

[January, 1875.]

Is it too late to express my sorrow for my grieved friend?

Though the first moment of loss is eternity, other eternities remain.

> Though the great waters sleep
> That they are still the deep
> We cannot doubt.
> No vacillating God
> Ignited this abode
> To put it out.

To the Same

[On the anniversary of her father's death, June 16, 1875.]

DEAR FRIEND, — You thought of it.
How dear, how delicate !
With peculiar love,

YOUR STRANGER.

To the Same

[1875.]

How can one be fatherless who has a father's friend within confiding reach?

To the Same

'My country, 't is of thee,'

has always meant the woods to me.

'Sweet land of liberty,'

I trust is your own.

To the Same

[After a fire, in 1876.]

DEAR FRIEND, — I congratulate you.
Disaster endears beyond fortune.

E. DICKINSON.

To the Same

The keeper of golden flowers need have no fear
of the 'Silver Bill.'

An Indies in the hand, at all times fortifying, is
peculiarly so, perhaps, to-day.

Midas was a rogue.

To the Same

[1876.]

DEAR FRIEND, — Mother thanks you through me,
as she does not use her hand for writing. I hope the
vicariousness may not impair the fervor.

Mother is very fond of flowers and of recollection,
that sweetest flower.

Please accept her happiness, and ours for causing
hers.

E. DICKINSON.

To the Same

Trusting an April flower may not curtail your February, that month of fleetest sweetness.

E. DICKINSON.

To the Same

DEAR FRIEND, — Maggie was taking you a flower as you were going out.

Please accept the design, and bewail the flower, that sank of chagrin last evening.

E. DICKINSON.

To the Same

The founders of honey have no names.

To the Same

My family of apparitions is select, though dim.

To the Same

Vinnie suggests these little friends.

Would they be too grovelling? And I add a face from my garden.

Though you met it before, it might not be charmless.

E. DICKINSON.

To the Same

[1880]

Is sickness pathos or infamy?

While you forget to decide, please confirm this trifle.

To the Same

DEAR FRIEND, — I shall deem the little tumblers forever consecrated by the 'unseemliness.'

With affection,

E. DICKINSON.

To the Same

Please accept the progeny of the pinks you so kindly brought mother in winter, with the hope that ' wisdom is justified of her children.'

To the Same

How strange that Nature does not knock, and yet does not intrude !

To the Same

' Give me thine heart ' is too peremptory a courtship for earth, however irresistible in Heaven.

To the Same

DEAR FRIEND, — So valiant is the intimacy between Nature and her children, she addresses them as ' comrades in arms.'

E. DICKINSON.

To the Same

DEAR FRIEND, — Nothing inclusive of a human heart could be ' trivial.' That appalling boon makes all things paltry but itself.

To thank you would profane you — there are moments when even gratitude is a desecration.

> Go thy great way!
> The stars thou meetest
> Are even as thyself.
> For what are stars but asterisks
> To point a human life?
>
> E. DICKINSON, with love.

To the Same

DEAR FRIEND, — In a world too full of beauty for peace, I have met nothing more beautiful.

E. DICKINSON.

To the Same

[1883?]

DEAR FRIEND, — The thoughtfulness was picturesque and the glimpse delightful. The residence of Vinnie's friends could but be fair to me.

And will you, in exchange, accept a view of *my* house, which Nature painted white without consulting me? But Nature is 'old-fashioned,' perhaps a Puritan.

E. DICKINSON.

To the Same

DEAR FRIEND, — It distressed us that you were pained.

Are you easier now?

You have sheltered our tears too often that yours should fall unsolaced.

Give us half the thorn — then it will tear you less. To divulge itself is sorrow's right, never its presumption.

Faithfully,

E. DICKINSON.

To the Same
[1885 ?]

DEAR FRIEND, — Is not the sweet resentment of friends that we are not strong, more inspiriting even than the strength itself?

E. DICKINSON.

[On sending flowers and apples to Mrs A. B. H. Davis and her daughter.]

DEAR FRIENDS, — We are snatching our jewels from the frost, and ask you to help us wear them, as also the trinkets more rotund, which serve a baser need.

EMILY.

To Mrs Henry Hills
[Christmas, 1878 ?]

With sweet Christmas for the ' little brethren and sisters of the mystic tie.'

EMILY.

To the Same
[January, 1879 ?]

Our gentle neighbor must have known that we did not know she was ill, or we should immediately have inquired for her.

EMILY.

To the Same

[February, 1879.]

We are much grieved for the sufferings of the little one, which are so artlessly undeserved, and beg her mama to assure her of our tender sympathy.

The odor of the flower might please her, as these little beings are only 'on a furlough' from Paradise.

With love for the mama, and sorrow for her weariness,

EMILY.

To the Same

[February 23, 1879.]

'Come unto me.'

Beloved commandment! The darling obeyed it.

To the Same

[February, 1879.]

The power to console is not within corporeal reach — though its attempt is precious.

To die before it feared to die, may have been a boon.

To the Same

[March, 1879.]

DEAR FRIEND, — The only balmless wound is the departed human life we had learned to need.

For that, even Immortality is a slow solace. All other peace has many roots and will spring again.

With cheer from one who knows.

To the Same

DEAR FRIEND, — The gift was sadly exquisite — were the actual 'cross' so divinely adorned, we should covet it.

Thank you for the sacred 'flowers' — typical, both of them.

Gethsemane and Cana are still a travelled route.

EMILY.

To the Same

[Christmas, 1879.]

DEAR FRIEND, — I think Heaven will not be as good as earth, unless it bring with it that sweet power to remember, which is the staple of Heaven here.

How can we thank each other when omnipotent?

You, who endear our mortal Christmas, will perhaps assure us.   E.

To the Same

[1880.]

We are ignorant of the dear friends, and eager to know how they are, and assure them that we are near them in these grieved hours.

EMILY.

To the Same

DEAR FRIEND, — The heavenly flowers were brought to my room.

I had lain awake with the gale and overslept this morning.

That you may wake in Eden, as you enabled me
to do, is my happy wish.

Emily.

To the Same

Without the hope of requiting the Sabbath morning blossoms, still sweetly remembered, please allow
me to try.   E.

To the Same

With untold thanks, and the little dish, founded
while she was here, too late to overtake her, too
small for her to sip, but her large heart will excuse.

Emily, with love.

To the Same

Vocal is but one form of remembrance, dear
friend — the cherishing that is speechless is equally
warm.

To the Same

[With Christmas delicacies, 1880.]

The little annual creatures solicit your regard.

Mrs Hills often sent dainties from New York,
perhaps Florida oranges, confectionery, or hot-
house flowers. Upon one of these occasions
the reply came: —

[1881.]

Tropics, and dairies, and fairies! Thank the
Arabian Nights.

Emily.

To the Same

[1881.]

With a kiss and a flower, one of which will endure,
I am whom you infer.

To the Same

[1882.]

Only a pond lily that I tilled myself.

To the Same

DEAR FRIENDS, — Even the simplest solace, with a
loved aim, has a heavenly quality.

EMILY.

To the Same

[January, 1883.]

DEAR FRIEND, — We often say 'how beautiful!'
But when we mean it, we can mean no more.
A dream personified.   E.

To the Same

[With red lilies, Spring, 1883.]

Persian hues for my dark-eyed neighbor.

To Mrs Jameson

Many and sweet birthdays to our thoughtful
neighbor, whom we have learned to cherish, though
ourself unknown.

E. DICKINSON.

To the Same

How dare a tear intrude on so sweet a cheek?

Gentlest of _ ghbors, recall the 'sparrows' and the great Logician.

Tenderly,

E. DICKINSON.

To the Same

Arthur forgot to set a trap for Santa Claus, but that industrious mouse will excuse him, if he will steal the cakes instead. And Annie.

E. DICKINSON.

To ——

[1880.]

DEAR FRIEND, — No 'sonnet' had George Eliot. The sweet acclamation of Death is forever bounded.

> There is no trumpet like the tomb —
> The Immortality she gave
> We borrowed at her grave.
> For just one plaudit famishing,
> The might of human love.

Beautiful as it is, its criminal shortness maims it.

To Maggie Maher, ill with Typhoid Fever at her own Home

[Autumn, 1880.]

The missing Maggie is much mourned, and I am going out for 'black' to the nearest store.

All are very naughty, and I am naughtiest of all.

The pussies dine on sherry now, and humming-bird cutlets.

The invalid hen took dinn. ⸻ith me, but a hen like Dr T——'s horse soon drove her away. I am very busy picking up stems and stamens as the hollyhocks leave their clothes around.

What shall I send my weary Maggie? Pillows or fresh brooks?

HER GRIEVED MISTRESS.

To the Rev. F. F. Emerson

[1880 ?]

A blossom, perhaps, is an introduction, to whom, none can infer.

To the Same

Though tendered by a stranger, the fruit will be forgiven.

Valor in the dark is my Maker's code.

E. DICKINSON.

To the Same

Mother congratulates Mr Emerson on the discovery of the 'philosopher's stone.' She will never divulge it. It lay just where she thought it did — in making others happy.

E. DICKINSON.

To the Same

Any gift but spring seems a counterfeit, but the birds are such sweet neighbors they rebuke us all.

E. DICKINSON.

To the Same

Mother was much touched by dear Mrs Emerson's thoughtfulness, and thanks her exceedingly sweetly. She also asks a remembrance to Mr Emerson, whom she trusts is well.

Earnestly,

E. DICKINSON.

To the Same

[1881 ?]

Should Mr Emerson ever become ill and idle, mother hopes his clergyman will be as delicately thoughtful of him as he has been of her.

Gratefully,

E. DICKINSON.

To the Same

DEAR FRIEND, — I step from my pillow to your hand to thank its sacred contents, to hoard, not to partake, for I am still weak.

The little package has lain by my side, not daring to venture, or Vinnie daring to have me — a hallowed denial I shall not forget.

I fear you may need the papers, and ask you to claim them immediately, would you desire them.

I trust you are sharing this most sweet climate with Mrs Emerson and yourself, than which remembrance only is more Arabian.

Vinnie brings her love, and her sister what gratitude.

EMILY.

To ——

DEAR FRIEND, — The little book will be subtly cherished. All we secure of beauty is its evanescence. Thank you for recalling us.

Earnestly,

EMILY.

To Mr and Mrs George Montague

[1881 ?]

DEAR COUSIN, — Thank you for the delightful cake, and the heart adjacent.

EMILY.

To the Same

Delicate as bread of flowers. How sweetly we thank you !

To the Same

We trust the dear friend is convalescing.

These loveliest of days are certainly with that design.

EMILY.

DEAR COUSIN, — The 'Golden Rule' is so lovely, it needs no police to enforce it.

COUSIN.

To the Same

To have 'been faithful in a few things' was the delicate compliment paid one by God. Could I not commend a rarer candidate for his approval in my loyal Cousin?

To the Same

[1881 ?]

Which will I thank — the perpetrator, the propagator, or the almoner of the delightful bread — or may I compromise and thank them all?

I for the first time appreciate the exultation of the robin toward a crumb, though he must be a seductive robin, with whom I would share my own.

With the hope to requite the loveliness in a future way,

Gratefully,

EMILY.

To Mrs W. F. Stearns

[May, 1881.]

DEAR FRIEND, — I hope you may know with what unspeakable tenderness we think of you and of your dear child.

Were it any kingdom but the 'Kingdom of Heaven,' how distant!

But my heart breaks — I can say no more.

E. D.

To the Same

[October, 1882.]

DEAR FRIEND, — Affection wants you to know it is here. Demand it to the utmost.

Tenderly,

E. DICKINSON.

One friend writes from New York of her regret that many of Emily's notes to herself have been destroyed. But she adds: 'One little welcome of Emily's to me became a household word; and I can quote it for you, though it should have the setting of her wide, pure margins, and her most dainty penmanship. Here it is: —

'Sweet Mrs Nellie comes with the robins. Robins have wings. Mrs Nellie has wings. A society for the prevention of wings would be a benefit to us all.

'It tells its own story, you see, of a flitting visit to the Grove in the spring, and of her interest in her neighbors and her information as to their interests, though so invisible herself.'

To Mrs Joseph Sweetser

[Autumn, 1879?]

Aunt Katie and the sultans have left the garden now, and parting with my own recalls their sweet companionship.

Mine were not, I think, as exuberant as in other years, — perhaps the Pelham water shocked their stately tastes, — but cherished avariciously because less numerous. I trust your garden was willing to die. I do not think that mine was — it perished with beautiful reluctance, like an evening star.

I hope you were well since we knew of you, and as happy as sorrow would allow.

There are sweets of pathos, when sweets of mirth have passed away.

Mother has had a weary cold, and suffers much from neuralgia since the changing airs, though I trust is no feebler than when you were here. She has her little pleasures as the patient have — the voices of friends, and devotion of home.

The ravens must 'cry,' to be ministered to; she need only sigh. . . . Perhaps it is quite the home it was when you last beheld it. I hope your few are safe, and your flowers encouraging.

News of your sultans and yourself would be equally lovely, when you feel inclined. Blossoms have their leisures.

Lovingly,

EMILY.

To the Same

[December, 1881.]

It was the unanimous opinion of the household that Aunt Katie never wrote so lovely a letter, and that it should be immediately replied to by each

member of the family, from the geraniums down to
the pussies, but unforeseen malignities prevented.
Vinnie lost her sultans too — it was 'Guiteau' year
— Presidents and Sultans were alike doomed.

One might possibly come up, having sown itself
— if it should, you shall share — it is an Eastern
creature, and does not like this soil.   I think its
first exuberance was purely accidental.   Last was a
fatal season.   An 'envious worm' attacked them;
then in early autumn we had midwinter frost.
'When God is with us, who shall be against us,'
but when He is against us, other allies are useless.

We were much amused at your 'gardener.'   You
portrayed his treason so wittily it was more effective
than loyalty.   He knew that flowers had no tongues.

We trust you are safe this Norwegian weather,
and 'desire your prayers' for another snow-storm,
just over our heads, the snows already repealing the
fences.

With love for your health, and the promise of
sultans, and viziers too, if the monarchs come,

Emily.

To the Same

[1884.]

Dear Aunt, — Thank you for 'considering the
lilies.'

The Bible must have had us in mind, when it gave
that liquid commandment.   Were all its advice so
enchanting as that, we should probably heed it.

Thank you for promptness, explicitness, sweetness. Your account of the lilies was so fresh I could almost pick them, and the hope to meet them in person, in autumn, through your loving hand, is a fragrant future.

I hope you are well as you deserve, which is a blest circumference, and give my love to each.

Aunt L—— just looked in on us, and I go to make her dish of homestead Charlotte Russe.

Always,

EMILY.

To the Same

[November, 1884.]

SWEET AND GRACIOUS AUNT KATIE, — The beloved lilies have come, and my heart is so high it overflows, as this was mother's week, Easter in November.

Father rose in June, and a little more than a year since, those fair words were fulfilled, 'and a little child shall lead them' — but boundlessness forbids me. . . .

It is very wrong that you were ill, and whom shall I accuse? The enemy, 'eternal, invisible, and full of glory' — but He declares himself a friend ! It is sweet you are better.

More beating that brave heart has to do before the emerald recess.

With sorrow for Emma's accident, and love for all who cherish you, including the roses, your velvet allies,

Tenderly,

EMILY.

To the Same

Cousin T—— and Cousin O—— little thought when they were paying their antiquated respects to Aunt Katie that they were defrauding Emily of that last moment — but they needed it most — new moments will grow.

When I found it beyond my power to see you, I designed to write you, immediately, but the Lords came as you went, and Judge Lord was my father's closest friend, so I shared my moments with them till they left us last Monday; then seeing directly after, the death of your loved Dr A——, I felt you might like to be alone — though Death is perhaps an intimate friend, not an enemy. Beloved Shakespeare says, 'He that is robbed and smiles, steals something from the thief.' . . .

Maggie said you asked should you 'eat the flower.' Please consult the bees — they are the only authority on Etruscan matters. Vinnie said the sherry I sent you was brandy — a vital misapprehension. Please also forgive it. I did not intend to be so base to the aunt who showed me the first mignonette, and listened with me to the great wheel, from Uncle Underwood's 'study,' and won me in 'divers other ways' too lovely to mention. Of all this we will talk when you come again.

Meanwhile accept your

TRIFLING NIECE.

To the Same

[1885.]

Aunt Katie's rose had many thorns, but it is still a rose, and has borne the extremities of a flower with ethereal patience — and every deference to her is so sweetly deserved, we do not call it courtesy, but only recognition.   It is sweeter that noon should be fair, than that morning should, because noon is the latest, and yet your morning had its dew you would not exchange.   Thank you for telling us of your triumphs.

' Peace hath her victories, no less than War.'

Thank you for speaking so tenderly of our latest lost.   We had hoped the persuasions of the spring, added to our own, might delay his going, but they came too late.   ' I met,' said he in his last note, ' a crocus and a snowdrop in my yesterday's walk,' but the sweet beings outlived him.   I thought the church-yard Tarrytown, when I was a child, but now I trust 't is Trans —

In this place of shafts, I hope you may remain unharmed.

I congratulate you upon your children, and them-selves upon you.

To have had such daughters is sanctity — to have had such a mother, divine.   To still have her — but tears forbid me.   My own is in the grave.   ' So loved her that he died for her,' says the explaining Jesus.

.   With love,   YOUR EMILY.

To the Same

Aunt Katie never forgets to be lovely, and the sweet clusters of yesterday only perpetuate a heart warm so many years.

Tropic, indeed, a memory that adheres so long. They were still vivid and fragrant when they reached my fingers, and were the wrist that bears them bolder, it would give reply. As it is, only a kiss and a gratitude, and every grace of being, from your loving niece. ' I give his angels charge ! '

Should I say his flowers, for qualified as saints they are.

Vinnie's and my transport.

To the Same

DEAR AUNT, — I have found and give it in love, but reluctant to entrust anything so sacred to my father as my grandfather's Bible to a public messenger, will wait till Mr Howard comes, whom Mrs Nellie tells us is due this week. Thank you for loving my father and mother. I hope they are with the Source of love. You did not tell me of your health — I trust because confirmed. Thank you too for sorrow, the one you truly knew.

With Vinnie's affection, in haste and fondness,

EMILY.

To Professor J. K. Chickering

[Autumn, 1882.]

DEAR FRIEND, — I do not know the depth of my indebtedness. Sorrow, benighted with fathoms, cannot find its mind.

Thank you for assisting us.

We were timidly grateful.

E. DICKINSON.

To the Same

DEAR FRIEND, — Thank you for being willing to see me, but may I defer so rare a pleasure till you come again? Grief is a sable introduction, but a vital one, and I deem that I knew you long since through your shielding thought.

I hope you may have an electrical absence, as life never loses its startlingness, however assailed. 'Seen of angels' only, an enthralling aim.

Thank you for the kindness, the fervor of a stranger the latest forgot.

E. DICKINSON.

To the Same

DEAR FRIEND, — I had hoped to see you, but have no grace to talk, and my own words so chill and burn me that the temperature of other minds is too new an awe.

> We shun it ere it comes,
>   Afraid of joy,
> Then sue it to delay,
>   And lest it fly

Beguile it more and more.
May not this be,
Old suitor Heaven,
Like our dismay at thee?

Earnestly,

E. DICKINSON.

To the Same

[1885.]

DEAR FRIEND, — The Amherst heart is plain and whole and permanent and warm.

In childhood I never sowed a seed unless it was perennial — and that is why my garden lasts.

We dare not trust ourselves to know that you indeed have left us.

The fiction is sufficient pain. To know you better as you flee, may be our recompense.

I hope that you are well, and nothing mars your peace but its divinity — for ecstasy is peril.

With earnest recollection,

E. DICKINSON.

To the Same

How charming the magnanimity which conferring a favor on others, by some mirage of valor considers itself receiving one!

Of such is the kingdom of knights!

E. DICKINSON.

It is hard for many persons to believe, even now, that Emily Dickinson had nothing to do with the Saxe Holm stories, and certainly some of their incidental poetry bears strong evidence of her unique touch. The little mystery of those remarkable tales was so carefully guarded that after a time people lost interest in surmising, and are now content to accept them as they are. The *No Name* series of Roberts Brothers was not so long a secret, and in the volume of its verse, *A Masque of Poets*, appeared, probably through the efforts of her old friend 'H. H.,' Emily Dickinson's *Success*, afterward the opening poem in the first of her published volumes. However obtained, it formed the beginning of an occasional and pleasant correspondence between herself and Mr Niles, always the genial, helpful, and generous friend of writers. She often sent him poems, which, contrary to her usual custom, she had named herself.

To Mr Thomas Niles

[1880?]

DEAR FRIEND, — I bring you a chill gift — *My Cricket*[1] and *The Snow*.[2] A base return, indeed, for the delightful book which I infer from you, but an earnest one.

---

[1] *Poems*, Second Series, page 167.
[2] *Poems*, Second Series, page 174.

To the Same

[1883 ?]

Thank you, Mr Niles.

I am very grateful for the mistake. I should think it irreparable deprivation to know no farther of her here, with the impregnable chances.

The kind but incredible opinion of ' H. H.' and yourself I would like to deserve.

Would you accept a pebble I think I gave to her, though I am not sure.

With thanks,

E. DICKINSON.

The ' pebble ' was that wonderful stanza,

How happy is the little stone
That rambles in the road alone,
And does n't care about careers,
And exigencies never fears ;
Whose coat of elemental brown
A passing universe put on ;
And independent as the sun,
Associates, or glows alone,
Fulfilling absolute decree
In casual simplicity.

To the Same

[1885]

DEAR FRIEND, — Thank you for the kindness. I am glad if the bird seemed true to you.

Please efface the others, and receive these three, which are more like him — *A Thunder Storm,*[1] *A Humming Bird,*[2] and *A Country Burial.*[3]

The life of Marian Evans had much I never knew — a doom of fruit without the bloom, like the Niger fig : —

> Her losses make our gains ashamed —
> She bore life's empty pack
> As gallantly as if the East
> Were swinging at her back.
> Life's empty pack is heaviest,
> As every porter knows —
> In vain to punish honey,
> It only sweeter grows.

To Mrs Carmichael
[1882?]

. . . I fear Vinnie gave my message as John Alden did the one from Miles Standish, which resulted delightfully for John, but not as well for his friend.

Had you seen the delighted crowd that gathered round the box — did you ever see a crowd of three? — you would have felt requited. Your presenting smile was alone wanting.

'Dear Mrs Carmichael,' said one ; 'The one that never forgets,' said another; and a tear or two in the eyes of the third, and the reception was over. Can you guess which the third was?

[1] *Poems*, Second Series, page 158.
[2] Ibid., p. 130.
[3] Ibid., p. 207.

The candy was enchanting, and is closeted in a deep pail, pending Vinnie's division, and the little box, like Heaven and mice, far too high to find.

Failure be my witness that I have sought them faithfully.

We often think of your evening circle — Mr Skeel presiding at the piano, and Mrs Skeel and yourself taking mutual lessons.

I am studying music now with the jays, and find them charming artists.

Vinnie and Gilbert have pretty battles on the pussy question, and you are needed for umpire, oftener than you think.

'Were n't you chasing pussy?' said Vinnie to Gilbert. 'No, she was chasing herself.'

'But was n't she running pretty fast?' said pussy's Nemesis. 'Well, some slow and some fast,' said the beguiling villain.

With the little kiss he gave me last, and a pair of my own, and love for Mr and Mrs Skeel,

Warmly,

EMILY.

To the Same

[1884?]

LOVED MRS CARMICHAEL AND MRS SKEEL, — I heard long since at school that Diogenes went to sea in a tub. Though I did not believe it, it is credible now.

Against the peril of ocean steamers I am sweetly

provided, and am sure you had my safety in mind, in your lovely gifts.

I have taken the passengers from the hold — passengers of honey — and the deck of silk is just promenaded by a bold fly, greedy for its sweets. The little tub with the surcingle I shall keep till the birds, filling it then with nectars, in Mrs Skeel's sweet honor.

Will each of the lovely friends present my thanks to the other, as Vinnie's correspondence with them is too impressive for what dear Dickens calls 'the likes of me' to invade.

Their sweet intercession with Santa Claus in my behalf, I shall long remember.

Always,

EMILY.

To the Same

[1885 ?]

My consoleless Vinnie convinces me of the misfortune of having known dear Mrs Carmichael, whom 'to name is to praise,' for indeed, were we both intelligent mourners, I fear delight would close; but the 'fair uncertainty' aids me, which is denied Vinnie.

Of her noble loss it is needless to speak — that is incalculable.

Of her sweet power to us when we were overwhelmed, that, too, shall be mute. She has 'borne our grief and carried our sorrow,' that is the criterion. . . .

Let me hope she is well to-day, and sheltered by every love she deserves, which were indeed countless.

We congratulate sweet Mrs Skeel on her beloved booty, and ask a remembrance in her prayer for those of· us bereaved.

Lovingly,

EMILY.

To Dr and Mrs Field, who had sent flowers

[1884 ?]

Expulsion from Eden grows indistinct in the presence of flowers so blissful, and with no disrespect to Genesis, Paradise remains.

Beaconsfield says 'the time has now come when it must be decided forever, who possesses the great gates to India.'

I think it must be my neighbor.

With delicate gratitude,

E. DICKINSON.

To the Same

[1885.]

I was much chagrined by the delayed flower — please accept its apology.

E. DICKINSON.

To the Same

[1885.]

Should you not have this flower, the first of spring with me, I should regret not sending it. Your azaleas are still vivid, though the frailer flowers are flitted away.

E. DICKINSON.

To ——

I send a violet, for L——. I should have sent a
stem, but was overtaken by snow-drifts. I regret
deeply not to add a butterfly, but have lost my hat,
which precludes my catching one.

To —— ——, *with flowers*

With the leave of the bluebirds, without whose
approval we do nothing.

E. DICKINSON.

To Mr Theodore Holland

[1885.]

DEAR SIR, — Your request to 'remain sincerely'
mine demands investigation, and if after synopsis of
your career all should seem correct, I am tersely
yours.   I shall try to wear the unmerited honor with
becoming volume.

Commend me to your kindred, for whom, although
a stranger, I entertain esteem.

I approve the paint — a study of the Soudan, I
take it, but the Scripture assures us our hearts are
all Dongola.

E. DICKINSON.

To —— ——

[1885.]

. . . If you saw a bullet hit a bird, and he told
you he was n't shot, you might weep at his courtesy,

but you would certainly doubt his word. Thomas's
faith in anatomy was stronger than his faith in
faith. . . . Vesuvius don't talk — Ætna don't. One
of them said a syllable, a thousand years ago, and
Pompeii heard it and hid forever. She could n't
look the world in the face afterward, I suppose.
Bashful Pompeii ! . . .

To ——

DEAR FRIEND, — I thank you with wonder. Should
you ask me my comprehension of a starlight night,
awe were my only reply, and so of the mighty book.
It stills, incites, infatuates, blesses and blames in one.
Like human affection, we dare not touch it, yet flee,
what else remains ?

But excuse me — I know but little. Please tell
me how it might seem to you.

How vast is the chastisement of beauty, given us
by our Maker ! A word is inundation, when it comes
from the sea.

Peter took the marine walk at the great risk.

E. DICKINSON.

What book may be thus described is, unhappily, not known, as I have been unable to discover even to whom the note was written.

A severe disappointment in the preparation
of these volumes is the fact that Emily's letters
to ' H. H.' cannot be found.

Entertained delightfully during the summer of 1893 at Mr Jackson's lovely home in Colorado Springs, I was very happy to learn that these letters had certainly not been destroyed. During the months before her death Mrs Jackson had herself arranged her mass of papers, letters, and manuscripts, each marked for its fate ; and Emily's letters were especially reserved in a package apart, as unique and too valuable to share the fate of much other correspondence. But though careful search has been most kindly made by her family, the letters still remain in hiding, and the inference is that they must have been accidentally destroyed in flames intended for other things.

Among Emily's own papers I have found this draft of a letter to Mrs Jackson, discarded on account of a number of substituted words; and I give it just as it is, with both erasures and substitutes, as an interesting study of her afterthoughts : —

To 'H. H.'

[March, 1885.]

DEAR FRIEND, — To reproach my own foot in behalf of yours is involuntary, and finding meagre [1] solace in ' whom He loveth He chasteneth,' your valor [2] astounds me. It was only a small wasp, said

---

[1] Myself little.   [2] Prowess.

the French physician, repairing the sting, but the
strength to perish is sometimes withheld — though
who but you can [1] tell a foot.

> Take all away from me
> But leave me ecstasy,
> And I am richer then
> Than all my fellow-men.
> Is it becoming me
> To dwell so wealthily,
> When at my very door
> Are those possessing more,
> In abject [2] poverty ?

That you glance at [3] Japan as [4] you breakfast,
not in the least surprises me, thronged [5] only with
music, like the decks [6] of birds.

Thank you for hoping I am well. Who could be
ill in March, that month of proclamation? Sleigh-
bells and jays contend in my matinée, and the
north surrenders instead of the south, a reverse of
bugles.

Pity me, however, I have finished *Ramona.* Would
that like Shakespeare it were just published !

Knew I how to pray, to intercede for your foot
were intuitive, but I am but a pagan.

Of God we ask one favor, that we may be forgiven. For what, He is presumed to know. The
crime, from us, is hidden.

[1] Could.   [3] Compass.   [5] Clogged.
[2] Boundless.   [4] Before.   [6] Wheels.

Immured the whole of life
Within a magic prison,
We reprimand the happiness
That too competes with Heaven.

May I once more know, and that you are saved?
Yours,
E. DICKINSON.

After Mrs Jackson's death, August 12, 1885, Emily wrote of her: —

Helen of Troy will die, but Helen of Colorado, never. Dear friend, can you walk, were the last words that I wrote her.

Dear friend, I can fly —
Her immortal reply.

To ——

SWEET FRIENDS, — I send a message by a mouth that cannot speak.

The ecstasy to guess
Were a receipted bliss
If grace could talk.

With love.

To ——

. . . What a hazard an accent is! When I think of the hearts it has scuttled or sunk, I almost fear to lift my hand to so much as a punctuation.

*To Mrs E. P. Crowell, when about to sail for
Europe*

[March 2, 1885.]

Is it too late to touch you, dear ?
We this moment knew.
Love marine and love terrene,
Love celestial too.

I give his angels charge.

EMILY.

To Miss Eugenia Hall

[1885?]

Let me thank the little cousin in flowers, which,
without lips, have language.

Somewhat cousin,

EMILY.

To the Same

DEAR 'GENIE,' — The lovely flower you sent me
is like a little vase of spice, and fills the hall with
cinnamon.

You must have skilful hands to make such sweet
carnations. Perhaps your doll taught you. I know
that dolls are sometimes wise. Robins are my dolls.
I am glad you love the blossoms so well. I hope
you love birds, too. It is economical. It saves
going to Heaven.

Lovingly,

EMILY.

To the Same, with a Wedding Gift, October 20,
1885

Will the sweet cousin who is about to make the
Etruscan experiment, accept a smile which will last
a life, if ripened in the sun?

COUSIN EMILY.

Three notes were sent at different times, with
flowers, to Mrs J. C. Greenough: —

Lest any bee should boast.

Trusting the happy flower will meet you at the
door where spring will soon be knocking, we chal-
lenge your 'come in.'

EMILY.

The flower keeps its appointment — should the
heart be tardy?

When Memory rings her bell, let all the thoughts
run in.

EMILY.

To Mrs Greenough, after her Mother's Death,
October, 1885

DEAR FRIEND, — I had the luxury of a mother a
month longer than you, for my own mother died in
November, but the anguish also was granted me to
see the first snow upon her grave the following day,
which, dear friend, you were spared.

But Remembrance engulfs me, and I must cease.

I wish I could speak a word of courage, though that love has already done.   Who could be mother-less who has a mother's grave within confiding reach?

Let me enclose the tenderness born of bereavement.

To have had a mother — how mighty !

EMILY.

CHAPTER X

To Mrs Todd, Mrs Tuckerman, the Misses ——, Mr Clark, and Mrs Currier

FROM the many notes sent me by Emily Dickinson during the last four years of her life, it was a difficult matter to select those best fitted for publication. But the first one available was probably this response to a small panel which I had painted for her, — a group of Indian pipes, those weird white flowers of shade and silence: —

To Mrs Todd

[Winter, 1882.]

DEAR FRIEND, — That without suspecting it you should send me the preferred flower of life, seems almost supernatural, and the sweet glee that I felt at meeting it I could confide to none. I still cherish the clutch with which I bore it from the ground when a wondering child, an unearthly booty, and maturity only enhances mystery, never decreases it. To duplicate the vision is even more amazing, for God's unique capacity is too surprising to surprise. I know not how to thank you. We do not thank the rainbow, although its trophy is a snare.

To give delight is hallowed — perhaps the toil of angels, whose avocations are concealed.

I trust that you are well, and the quaint little girl with the deep eyes, every day more fathomless.

With joy,

E. DICKINSON.

A few days later came another, enclosing that brilliant, meteoric flash in words, her 'humming-bird,' printed at page 130 in the second volume of the *Poems* : —

To the Same

DEAR FRIEND, — I cannot make an Indian pipe, but please accept a humming-bird, —

> A route of evanescence
> With a revolving wheel;
> A resonance of emerald,
> A rush of cochineal;
> And every blossom on the bush
> Adjusts its tumbled head, —
> The mail from Tunis, probably,
> An easy morning's ride.

When, after her death, the great mass of Emily Dickinson's verses had been collated and an appropriate drawing for the cover was desired, there seemed a peculiar fitness in this ethereal flower; and the design was cut from the little panel which stood so long in her room.

Many of her most beautiful verses came to me, in the following years; and one autumn day this: —

[1884.]

How martial the apology of nature ! We die, said the deathless of Thermopylæ, in obedience to law.

> Not sickness stains the brave,
> Nor any dart,
> Nor doubt of scenes to come,
> But an adjourning heart.

After I had sent her a painting of the gorgeous blossoms of the trumpet vine, which, on first seeing, she had called 'the Soudan,' she wrote: —

[March 21, 1885.]

DEAR FRIEND, — Nature forgot. The circus reminded her.

Thanks for the Ethiopian face.

The Orient is in the west.

'You knew, oh Egypt,' said the entangled Antony.

And later, —

[September, 1885.]

Why should we censure Othello, when the criterion Lover says, 'Thou shalt have no other gods before me'?

Music had always charm for Emily Dickinson. Frequently, when I had been singing, or playing upon the piano at her request, a dainty note would come in to me, with a glass of wine, or a rare rose; in one instance a cream whip, with the single line, 'Whom He loveth He chasteneth,'—of which the application might have been taken in various ways.

I can never forget the twilight seclusion of the old drawing-room, the square piano in its corner, the ancient mahogany furniture, and Emily just outside the door, her dress a spot of white in the dim hall. With the waning afternoon, I would play one thing and another, or sing melodies which often sounded too light and modern and sunshiny for surroundings so like a dreamy corner of the past. At first it seemed to me as if a visitor from another world had alighted for a time, wishing, for some inscrutable reason, to be entertained on a foreign planet. Later, it became not only entirely natural, but so much a habit that I should have missed my solitary recitals quite as much as my often invisible auditor.

Other notes to me, having especial reference to particular persons or occasions, are not of sufficient general interest to be given here.

As her unique life drew toward its close, she became, for the last two years, a semi-invalid, — she who had always rejoiced in strength and bravery enough for her own aeed, and that of all her friends.

Only a handful of notes remains, written during the final weeks while Emily brightened the old house with her airy, yet forceful and brilliant personality, for, even ill, she was a pervasive presence.

Upon the death of Professor Tuckerman, March 15, 1886, she wrote : —

To Mrs Tuckerman

DEAR ONE, — ' Eye hath not seen nor ear heard.' What a recompense ! The enthusiasm of God at the reception of His sons ! How ecstatic ! How infinite ! Says the blissful voice, not yet a voice, but a vision, ' I will not let thee go, except I bless thee.'

EMILY.

Sometime during this month, also, she wrote her cousins : —

To the Misses ——

[March, 1886.]

I scarcely know where to begin, but love is always a safe place. I have twice been very sick, dears, with a little recess of convalescence, then to be more sick, and have lain in my bed since November, many years, for me, stirring as the arbutus does, a pink and russet hope ; but that we will leave with our pillow. When your dear hearts are quite convenient, tell us of their contents, the fabric cared for most, not a fondness wanting.

Do you keep musk, as you used to, like Mrs Morene of Mexico? Or cassia carnations so big they split their fringes of berry? Was your winter a tender shelter — perhaps like Keats's bird, 'and hops and hops in little journeys '?

Are you reading and well, and the W ——s near and warm? When you see Mrs French and Dan give them a tear from us.

Vinnie would have written, but could not leave my side. Maggie gives her love. Mine more sweetly still.

EMILY.

To Mr C. H. Clark

[April 5, 1886.]

DEAR FRIEND, — Are you living and well, and your father in peace, and the home in —— Street without effacing change? I received your very kind

message, I think in November, since which I have
been very ill, and begin to roam in my room a little,
an hour at a time.

Do you, as time steals on, know anything of the
W —— whom Mr —— so loved, and of whom he
said with a smile, 'Should he find a gold watch in
the street he would not pick it up, so unsullied was
he'? . . .

My sister gives her faithful remembrance to
yourself and your father, the brother so cherished
never once forgot.

You will recall the flower sacred to your brother.

No sloth has memory.

E. DICKINSON.

To Mrs Currier

[April 10, 1886.]

. . . Mr Hunt was tinning a post this morning,
and told us L—— did n't feel quite as well as usual,
and I have n't felt quite as well as usual since the
chestnuts were ripe, though it was n't the chestnuts'
fault, but the crocuses are so martial and the daffodils to the second joint, let us join hands and
recover.

'I do remember an apothecary,' said that sweeter
robin than Shakespeare, was a loved paragraph
which has lain on my pillow all winter, but perhaps
Shakespeare has been 'up street' oftener than I
have, this winter.

Would father's youngest sister believe that in the

'Shire town' where he and Blackstone went to school, a man was hung yesterday, for the murder of a man by the name of Dickinson, and that Miss M—— was poisoned by a strolling juggler to be tried in the Supreme Court next week?

Don't you think fumigation ceased when father died?

Poor, romantic Miss M—— ! But perhaps a *Police Gazette* was better for you than an essay.

I hope you are both stronger, and ask a word of gain with these ecstatic days. I give my anxious love, and Vinnie's faithfulness with mine.

Your EMILY.

To Mr C. H. Clark

[April 15, 1886.]

Thank you, dear friend, I am better. The velocity of the ill, however, is like that of the snail. I am glad of your father's tranquillity, and of your own courage. Fear makes us all martial.

I could hardly have thought it possible that the scholarly stranger to whom my father introduced me, could have mentioned my friend, almost itself a vision, or have still left a legend to relate his name. With the exception of —— . . . your name alone remains.

'Going home,' was he not an aborigine of the sky?

The last time he came in life I was with my lilies

and heliotropes. Said my sister to me, 'The gentleman with the deep voice wants to see you, Emily' —
hearing him ask of the servant.

'Where did you come from?' I said, for he spoke
like an apparition. 'I stepped from my pulpit to
the train,' was his simple reply; and, when I asked,
'how long?' — 'twenty years,' said he, with inscrutable roguery.

But the loved voice has ceased; and to some
one who heard him 'going home ' it was sweet to
speak. . . . Thank you for each circumstance, and
tell me all you love to say. . . .

Excuse me for the voice, this moment immortal.

E. DICKINSON.

This letter, in her bold, clear, detached hand
(to an accustomed eye slightly less firm than
usual), is the last one, so far as known, which
Emily Dickinson wrote. Afterward, she continued to be delicate, though hardly alarmingly
so; but just before the fifteenth of May, 1886,
she sent two words to her cousins, freighted
with startling import, —

LITTLE COUSINS, — Called back.

EMILY.

Almost immediately she fell asleep, and
never woke again to earthly sunshine.

In the quiet of leafy Amherst, in the old
brick mansion behind its hedges and pines,
she lived and wrote, and there she

> ' Ascended, from our vision
> To countenances new.'

We can be only grateful that she was moved
to crystallize in words her thronging visions of
blossom, and bird, and 'blue, beloved air,' —
of ' life, death, and that vast forever ' which was
her nearest companion.

This is hardly the place to speak in detail of
Emily Dickinson's verses, their electrical quality, or their impressive effect upon the public,
four years after her death.   They are pervaded
by a singular cadence of hidden rhythmical
music, which becomes sympathetically familiar
upon intimate acquaintance.

Dr Holmes somewhere says that rhymes
' are iron fetters : it is dragging a chain and
a ball to march under their encumbrance;'
and if in Emily Dickinson's work there is frequently no rhyme where rhyme should be,
a subtle something, welcome and satisfying,
takes its place.   An orchid among every-day,
sweet-smelling flowers, strangeness and irregu-
larity seem but to enhance her fascination.

A striking characteristic of her verse is
its epigrammatic quality; terseness and vigor

predominate, rather than feminine grace and smoothness.   Homely experiences which all recognize, but few record, were to her texts for profound generalization.   When the unmeaning mass of much modern poetry is compared with Emily Dickinson's swift revelations, the operation suggests comparing distilled water with richest Burgundy.   And as such water is no less insipid if served in cut-glass flagons, so we cannot care in what kind of bottle has been stored for years the condensed sweetness of tropic suns.

The eighteenth of May, 1886, Emily Dickinson was carried lovingly over the threshold she had not passed beyond in years.

> ' She went as softly as the dew
> From a familiar flower.
> Not like the dew did she return
> At the accustomed hour.'

To the few who gathered, that sunny afternoon, her friend, fellow-poet, and ' master' read Emily Brontë's noble *Last Lines*, with their lofty voicing of an unchangeable belief in the soul's immortality, — ' a favorite,' as Colonel Higginson so fitly said, ' with our friend, who has now put on that Immortality which she seemed never to have laid off.'

She had lived in voluntary retirement from outside eyes; and now, in the sweet May sunshine, tender hands bore her through meadows starry with daisies into a silence and seclusion but little deeper.

INDEX

Ingram Content Group UK Ltd.
Milton Keynes UK
UKHW022002140423
420212UK00005B/54